Learning Java by Building Android Games

Get ready for a fun-filled experience of learning Java by developing games for the Android platform

John Horton

PUBLISHING

BIRMINGHAM - MUMBAI

Learning Java by Building Android Games

First published: January 2015

Production reference: 1230115

Published by Packt Publishing Ltd.
Livery Place
35 Livery Street
Birmingham B3 2PB, UK.

ISBN 978-1-78439-885-9

www.packtpub.com

Credits

Author
John Horton

Reviewers
Tony Atkins
Thorsten Harbig
Boon Hian Tek

Commissioning Editor
Pramila Balan

Acquisition Editor
Harsha Bharwani

Content Development Editor
Pooja Nair

Technical Editor
Shruti Rawool

Copy Editor
Vikrant Phadke

Project Coordinator
Leena Purkait

Proofreaders
Ting Baker
Simran Bhogal
Maria Gould
Ameesha Green
Paul Hindle

Indexer
Monica Ajmera Mehta

Production Coordinator
Arvindkumar Gupta

Cover Work
Arvindkumar Gupta

About the Author

John Horton is a technology enthusiast based in UK. When he is not writing apps, books, or blog articles for www.gamecodeschool.com, he can usually be found playing computer games or indulging in a Nerf war.

A very big thanks to all the reviewers. I would also like to express my gratitude to the people at Packt Publishing who made this book possible, including Priyanka Budkuley for getting the project started, Pooja, Harsha, Shruti, Vikrant, Leena, Ting, Simran, Maria, Ameesha, Paul, Monica, and Arvindkumar.

To Jo, Jack, James, Ray, Rita, and Skipper, I dedicate this book to you.

About the Reviewers

Tony Atkins is a developer and entrepreneur focused on building assistive apps with Android. He lives and works in Amsterdam.

He has reviewed the book, *Sakai CLE Courseware Management: The Official Guide*, *Packt Publishing*.

> I would like to thank my wife, Elaine, and son, Phillip, for bringing joy to my life each day.

Thorsten Harbig was born on August 30, 1977. He grew up at Lake Constance in southern Germany. He studied computer science, spent 7 months in Belgium working on his diploma thesis, and finished his master's degree in energy savings on mobile phones from Aalborg University in Denmark. Since then, he has worked as a software consultant for companies in the finance and automotive sectors and as a trainer for Java EE courses.

Since the last 3 years, Thorsten has shifted his focus to project management, beginning with small software projects using agile methods, and lately working on software and hardware projects, covering the entire process as follows: starting with an idea, working on requirements, performing the design and realization, and planning the manufacturing and packaging at the end.

Thorsten always looks for new, interesting topics to work on, and wants to share new achievements with colleagues and others who are interested.

Boon Hian Tek is a Java developer who follows the "learn two languages a year" advice. He is a polyglot of both spoken languages and programming languages. He works with a group of talented (but demented) developers who together produce and maintain some highly transactional web systems.

www.PacktPub.com

Support files, eBooks, discount offers, and more

For support files and downloads related to your book, please visit www.PacktPub.com.

Did you know that Packt offers eBook versions of every book published, with PDF and ePub files available? You can upgrade to the eBook version at www.PacktPub.com and as a print book customer, you are entitled to a discount on the eBook copy. Get in touch with us at service@packtpub.com for more details.

At www.PacktPub.com, you can also read a collection of free technical articles, sign up for a range of free newsletters and receive exclusive discounts and offers on Packt books and eBooks.

https://www2.packtpub.com/books/subscription/packtlib

Do you need instant solutions to your IT questions? PacktLib is Packt's online digital book library. Here, you can search, access, and read Packt's entire library of books.

Why subscribe?

- Fully searchable across every book published by Packt
- Copy and paste, print, and bookmark content
- On demand and accessible via a web browser

Free access for Packt account holders

If you have an account with Packt at www.PacktPub.com, you can use this to access PacktLib today and view 9 entirely free books. Simply use your login credentials for immediate access.

Table of Contents

Preface

If you are completely new to any one of Java, Android, or game programming, and are aiming at publishing Android games for fun or for a business purpose, but you have no clue as to where to start, then this book is for you. This book also acts as a refresher for those who already have experience in Java on other platforms.

Android is the fastest growing operating system, and Android devices can empower, entertain, and educate the planet. Android uses one of the most popular programming languages—Java, which is a high-performance, secure, and object-oriented language.

In each chapter, we will build on what you learned from the previous chapter, steadily gaining an understanding of more advanced Java concepts and putting them to work by building Android games.

What this book covers

Chapter 1, *Why Java, Android, and Games?*, tells us why we might choose Java, Android, and games over other languages, platforms, and types of apps. Then we quickly prepare our Android and Java development environment by installing the Java Development Kit and Android Studio.

Chapter 2, *Getting Started with Android*, shows us how to design, build, and run a game menu UI on a real Android device. This is the first part of our math game project.

Chapter 3, *Speaking Java – Your First Game*, covers the Java fundamentals and their use in an Android environment to make a simple math quiz game.

Chapter 4, *Discovering Loops and Methods*, contains more Java fundamentals such as decision-making and looping. Then we use them to add features to our math game. This chapter also covers some basic Android game essentials such as locking and handling screen rotation, and introduces the device sensors.

Chapter 5, Gaming and Java Essentials, takes us on a quick ride through some vital essentials for any game. We also make the UI more exciting with animation and by storing player scores. Demonstrated with a Simon-style memory game, storing the sequence with Java arrays and a for loop.

Chapter 6, OOP – Using Other People's Hard Work, is the chapter where everything you have learned so far is tied up with a pretty ribbon. You should find yourself muttering phrases like, "Oh, I see" and "So that's how it works." We explore object-oriented programming (OOP) in this chapter.

Chapter 7, Retro Squash Game, teaches us how to draw graphics pixel by pixel with the Android Canvas class. We can then combine these new skills with what we already know and make a retro, pong-style squash game.

Chapter 8, The Snake Game, covers the beginning of our most advanced game project—an animated *Snake*-style arcade game. We will also be able to practice more of the important Java fundamentals that you learned in the previous chapters.

Chapter 9, Making Your Game the Next Big Thing, puts the icing on the cake by teaching you how to publish your game and add online leaderboards and achievements. This will also let you examine the concept of Java libraries.

Appendix, Self-test Questions and Answers, contains all the answers to the questions to test your understanding of the topic.

What you need for this book

You will need a modest version of Windows (XP, Vista, 7, or 8), and a Mac, Linux PC, or laptop. Both 32-bit and 64-bit systems are compatible. All of the software needed in excess of this is free and acquiring it is fully explained in the book.

Who this book is for

This book is for you if you are completely new to any one of Java, Android, or game programming. As the book assumes no previous knowledge, it is also for you if you are new to all three (Java, Android, and game programming).

If you want to publish Android games for fun or for business and are not sure where to start, then this book will show you what to do, step by step from the start.

If you have experience in Java on another platform (perhaps PC or Mac), then this book will be a good Java refresher, and will also show you how to apply your existing skills in an Android context.

If you have previously programmed in another language but want to learn Java for any platform from the start, then you will be able to learn from this book and move through the practical examples more quickly.

The book does assume that you are fairly confident in using your operating system of choice. The step-by-step tutorials are in Windows, but if you have a decent understanding of Mac or Linux, you can probably follow along quite easily with them too.

Conventions

In this book, you will find a number of text styles that distinguish between different kinds of information. Here are some examples of these styles and explanations of their meanings.

Code words in text, database table names, folder names, filenames, file extensions, pathnames, dummy URLs, user input, and Twitter handles are shown as follows: "In the Android Studio Project Explorer, double-click on the layout folder to reveal the activity_main.xml file within it."

A block of code is set as follows:

```
import android.support.v7.app.ActionBarActivity;
import android.os.Bundle;
import android.view.Menu;
import android.view.MenuItem;
```

When we wish to draw your attention to a particular part of a code block, the relevant lines or items are set in bold:

```
int partA = 9;
int partB = 9;
correctAnswer = partA * partB;
int wrongAnswer1 = correctAnswer - 1;
int wrongAnswer2 = correctAnswer + 1;
```

Any command-line input or output is written as follows:

```
info: a = 10
info: b = Alan Turing
info: c = true
```

New terms and **important words** are shown in bold. Words that you see on the screen, for example, in menus or dialog boxes, appear in the text like this: "When prompted to import another class, click on **OK**."

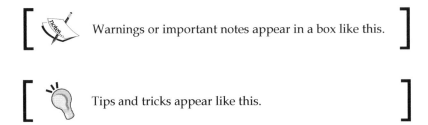

Warnings or important notes appear in a box like this.

Tips and tricks appear like this.

Reader feedback

Feedback from our readers is always welcome. Let us know what you think about this book—what you liked or disliked. Reader feedback is important for us as it helps us develop titles that you will really get the most out of.

To send us general feedback, simply e-mail feedback@packtpub.com, and mention the book's title in the subject of your message.

If there is a topic that you have expertise in and you are interested in either writing or contributing to a book, see our author guide at www.packtpub.com/authors.

Customer support

Now that you are the proud owner of a Packt book, we have a number of things to help you to get the most from your purchase.

Downloading the example code

You can download the example code files from your account at http://www.packtpub.com for all the Packt Publishing books you have purchased. If you purchased this book elsewhere, you can visit http://www.packtpub.com/support and register to have the files e-mailed directly to you.

Downloading the color images of this book

We also provide you with a PDF file that has color images of the screenshots/diagrams used in this book. The color images will help you better understand the changes in the output. You can download this file from: http://www.packtpub.com/sites/default/files/downloads/8859OS_ColoredImages.pdf.

Errata

Although we have taken every care to ensure the accuracy of our content, mistakes do happen. If you find a mistake in one of our books—maybe a mistake in the text or the code—we would be grateful if you could report this to us. By doing so, you can save other readers from frustration and help us improve subsequent versions of this book. If you find any errata, please report them by visiting http://www.packtpub.com/submit-errata, selecting your book, clicking on the **Errata Submission Form** link, and entering the details of your errata. Once your errata are verified, your submission will be accepted and the errata will be uploaded to our website or added to any list of existing errata under the Errata section of that title.

To view the previously submitted errata, go to https://www.packtpub.com/books/content/support and enter the name of the book in the search field. The required information will appear under the **Errata** section.

Piracy

Piracy of copyrighted material on the Internet is an ongoing problem across all media. At Packt, we take the protection of our copyright and licenses very seriously. If you come across any illegal copies of our works in any form on the Internet, please provide us with the location address or website name immediately so that we can pursue a remedy.

Please contact us at copyright@packtpub.com with a link to the suspected pirated material.

We appreciate your help in protecting our authors and our ability to bring you valuable content.

Questions

If you have a problem with any aspect of this book, you can contact us at questions@packtpub.com, and we will do our best to address the problem.

1
Why Java, Android, and Games?

Welcome to *Learning Java by Building Android Games*, which I hope is just the beginning of your exciting journey into designing and writing games. By the end of this book, we will have made four complete games: a math quiz with dynamically increasing difficulty, a memory game in the style of the classic Simon toy, a pong-style squash game, and a clone of the classic *Snake* game.

Besides these games, we will build more than a dozen working apps to practice and demonstrate individual concepts to aid our learning of Java, Android, and games. Our games and apps will feature sound FX, graphics, and animations. We will learn everything from using the standard Android **User Interface** (**UI**) designer to creating smooth animations by plotting individual pixels.

Although I will encourage you to work with me and implement the specific projects that are detailed step by step throughout the book, I fully expect that once you grasp the different concepts, you will want to use them in your own unique creations without delay. This is exactly what I hope you will be inspired to do.

The game projects themselves are not the objective of the book but the means to a much loftier goal. By the end of the book, you will be able to design and implement your own 2D Android games, to sell or just to give away, on Google Play.

 There is a bit of ground work to cover first, but I promise it won't take long and it won't be complicated either. Anyone can learn to program.

However, there are so many differing opinions among experts, which breeds confusion among beginners concerning the best ways of learning to program. So it is a good idea to look at why learning Java, Android, and games is an ideal pathway for beginners. This will be the first thing we will discuss in this book.

Here is what we will learn in this chapter:

- Is this book for me?
- Why should I use games to learn to program?
- Why should I learn Java and Android?
- Setting up our development environment

Is this book for me?

If you have already decided that Java, Android, or games are what you want to learn, then the next question might be, "Is this specific book for me?".

There are plenty of Java books for beginners and books by much more accomplished authors and programmers than myself. I have read many of them and admire the authors. However, when these books drift away—which they all do—to topics such as Java-native interfaces, web browser applets, or server-side remote communication, I sometimes find myself questioning their immediate relevance to me.

At this point, at least subconsciously, my commitment would wane and the learning process would slow or stop.

If you just want to learn pure Java

If you just want to learn Java on its own, this book will be a solid start. Although the Android stuff might be considered overhead to your pure Java learning, this is much less than the multitude of potentially unnecessary topics that would be introduced in any other Java book. The only caveat with this book is that the necessary overhead is all at the beginning. But once this minimal overhead is cleared, we can focus quite intently on Java.

With regard to the amount of overhead:

- It will take about six pages to set up our programming environment in this chapter
- It will take *Chapter 2, Getting Started with Android*, to get familiar with the Android tools, create your first working project, and glimpse your first real Java code
- From then on, it will be nearly pure Java and building games

You will soon see that the tiny amount of overhead is not excessive and is well worthwhile.

If Android is your focus

If it was Android itself that made you look at this book, then I am proud to say this is the first book that will teach you Android without assuming you have any prior Java or programming knowledge whatsoever.

Where this book will take you

By the end of this book, you will be able to easily take one of many paths including these:

- Learning Java at a higher level for any platform
- Intermediate level Android learning including pure game frameworks (which will be covered in more detail in *Chapter 9, Making Your Game the Next Big Thing*)
- A higher level of games development
- Much easier tackling of any modern object-oriented language for things such as iOS, Windows, or web development

So if you know you want to learn Android or Java, hopefully, I have gone some way to make you commit to the way this book will help you. But why games, Android, or Java at all?

Why build games to learn to program?

Fun, of course! But there are other reasons too. Successfully running any program we have written is immensely satisfying, even more so when it involves using some code that we previously didn't understand.

But making our own games, as you will soon realize, creates a feeling of pleasure that is not easy to describe—it has to be experienced. Then there are added bonuses of sharing our creations with friends on a phone or tablet or even sharing them publicly on the Google Play Store, and you might realize that once you start making games, you can't stop.

As we create more complex games steadily, you'll realize that all techniques and pieces of code can be rehashed to create other games, and you can then start planning your very own unique masterpieces. This is exhilarating to say the least.

And as with many subjects, the more we practice the better we get. So games are a perfect way to start learning to program Java. However, most beginners' books for Android games require a fairly high level of Java knowledge. But as we will see, it is perfectly possible to keep the practical examples as fun game projects and still start with the very basics of Java.

There is a slight trade-off in doing things this way. We will not always approach the working game examples in a "by-the-book" manner. This is to avoid the problem of doing cartwheels before mastering the forward roll.

The learning outcome priority will always be the Java programming concept, followed by understanding the Android environment and game design principles. Having said that, we will closely examine and practice plenty of Android and game programming fundamentals.

Of course, from what we have just discussed, you can probably surmise that it would have been possible to teach a bit more Java in the same number of pages if we hadn't been making games.

This is true, but then we lose all the benefits that come with using games as the subject matter. Making games really can be a joy, and when our brains are open and eager for information, we will learn much faster. The minimal overhead of learning this way is negated a hundred times over. If games don't interest you in the slightest, then there are plenty of Java beginners' guides out there that take the traditional approach. Just don't expect quite the same thrill as when you publish your first game with online leaderboards and achievements.

Why Android and Java?

A part of successful learning is the commitment by the student, not just to do the work, but in their belief that they are doing the right thing in the right way. So many technology-based courses and books don't get that commitment from the reader, not subconsciously anyway.

The problem is the students' belief that they might be, partly at least, wasting their time with something that is or will soon become outdated or perhaps is not quite right for them. This can be true to a large extent with programming. So why should you spend your finite time learning Java, on Android?

Android is the fastest evolving and growing OS ever

At one time, Android updates emerged almost every two months. Even now, they emerge about once in six months. By comparison, Windows takes years between versions and even iOS updates come only yearly and usually change relatively little between versions. Android is obviously evolving and improving at an unprecedented rate.

 Look at the history of Android versions since Version 1 at `http://www.cnet.com/news/history-of-android/`.

The first humble version of Android was released in 2008, around the same time when consumers were already quite excited about the then much flashier iPhone. News stories were also reporting that developers were getting rich by selling apps in the iTunes app store.

But in the last full year before this book was written, Samsung alone shipped more Android units than Apple sold all iOS devices combined. I am not joining the war on whose devices are best. I enjoy aspects of both Android and Apple, but purely in terms of picking a platform to learn on, you are probably in the right place at the right time with Android.

Android developers have great prospects

Now you might have picked up this book just for the fun and satisfaction that comes with learning to program games. But if you decide to develop your learning further, you will find that the demand for Android programmers is enormous and therefore very lucrative too.

 Some data suggests salaries in excess of 100,000 US dollars. For more information, go to `http://www.indeed.com/salary?q1=Android+Developer&l1=United+States`.

Android is open source

What open source means is that although Google develops all the flavors of Android that are used on the newest devices, once the code is released, anybody can do whatever they like with it. Google only exerts control for a limited amount of time.

In practice, most Android users have the pure Google OS or the modified versions turned out by big manufacturers such as Samsung and HTC, but there is nothing to stop anybody taking the OS and changing, adapting, or converting it into whatever they like. In short, Android could never be taken away from the programming community.

Java is here to stay

Okay, so we see Android isn't likely to disappear but could Java become redundant? And will your significant time investment be wasted? On Android, as with most platforms, you can use many languages and tools. Android, however, was designed from the ground up to facilitate Java development. All other languages and tools are not invalid but tend to serve a fairly specific purpose, rather than be a real alternative to Java. In fact, as far as games are concerned, many of the alternatives to a pure Java development environment are also Java-based and require a good level of skill in Java to use. For example, the popular LibGDX game development library, which allows you to simultaneously make games for Android, iOS, Windows, Linux, Mac and even the Web, still uses Java! We will talk more about this in *Chapter 9, Making Your Game the Next Big Thing*. The point is that Java and Android are tied together and will likely thrive together.

Java is not just for Android

Java has been around a lot longer than Android, since the beginning of the 1990s in fact. Although what Java has been used for has evolved and diversified over more than two decades, the originally implemented strengths of the language itself remain the same today.

Java was designed to be platform- or computer-independent. This is achieved by the use of a **virtual machine** (**VM**). This is a program written in another language that decodes the Java program that we write and interacts with the computer platform it is running on. So as long as there is a VM for the computer you want to run your Java program on, with a few caveats, your Java program will work. So if you learn Java, you are learning a language that is used everywhere from the smart fridge to the Web and most places in between.

It is true, however, that the VM on each platform can and usually does implement features to specifically suit the uses it is likely to be put to. A clear example of this would be mobile-device-specific features such as sensors, GPS, or the built-in camera on many Android devices. Using Java with Android, you can take photos, detect the air pressure, and work out exactly where in the world you are. Most fridge VMs probably will not do this. So you can't always just run a Java program designed for device x on device y, but the language and syntax is the same. Learning Java on Android prepares you in a large part for Java in any situation. So rest assured that Java isn't going away any time soon.

Java is fast and easy to use

There is a decades-long debate over which language is the best overall or which language is the best to learn programming. Critics of Java will likely say things about Java's speed. It is true that the Java memory management along with the VM interpretation process does have some speed cost. However, these things have benefits; they significantly improve our productivity and the way that the Android VM interacts with a device largely negates the minor speed penalty. And since Android 4.4, it does so completely with **Android Run Time** (**ART**), which installs apps written in Java as fully native applications. Now Java programmers can build games in a friendly, interpreted language and have them run as if they were written in a more challenging natively compiled language.

A summary of Java and Android

In a rapidly changing world, if you are worried about where to invest your precious learning time, it is hard to have more confidence. Here we have a language (Java) whose fundamentals have remained almost the same for nearly a quarter of a century, and a platform (Android) that is backed by the biggest names in hardware, software, and retail, and though it's admittedly hugely influenced, it's not actually owned by anyone.

I am not an evangelist of any technology over another although it is true that I love doing stuff on Android. But you can be sure in your mind that if you are considering the best path to begin learning programming, there is a very strong argument that Java and Android are the best choice.

If you want to learn Java for any of its numerous uses, then this is a very good place to start. If you want to develop for Android or get into Android development of any sort, then Java is the absolute fundamental way to start, and making games has the enormous benefits we have already discussed.

By the end of the book, you will be able to write Java code for almost any Java-supported platform. You will be able use almost everything you learn in this book, away from the Android environment.

If you are planning to pursue a career or business by making Android games or any Android apps, then this book is possibly the only place to start for beginners.

If you are completely new to Java and want the easiest possible path to mastering it—the fastest growing platform on the planet—then *Learning Java by Building Android Games* will probably be just right for you.

So hopefully you are assured that the path this book will take to learn Java is as easy, fun, and thorough as learning Java can be. Let's get set up so we can start building games.

Setting up our development environment

The first thing we need to do is prepare our PC to develop for Android using Java. Fortunately, this is made quite simple for us.

 If you are learning on Mac or Linux, everything in this book will still work. The next two tutorials have Windows-specific instructions and screenshots. However, it shouldn't be too difficult to vary the steps slightly to suit Mac or Linux.

All we need to do is:

1. Install a software package called the **Java Development Kit (JDK)**, which allows us to develop in Java.
2. Install Android Studio, a program designed to make Android development fast and easy. Android Studio uses the JDK and some other Android-specific tools that automatically get installed when we install Android Studio.

Installing the JDK

The first thing we need to do is get the latest version of the JDK. To complete this guide, perform the following steps:

1. You need to be on the Java website, so visit `http://www.oracle.com/technetwork/java/javase/downloads/index.html`.

2. Find the three buttons shown in the following screenshot and click on the one that says **JDK** (highlighted). They are on the right-hand side of the web page. Click on the **DOWNLOAD** button under the **JDK** option:

3. You will be taken to a page that has multiple options to download the JDK. In the **Product/File description** column, you need to click on the option that matches your operating system. Windows, Mac, Linux and some other less common options are all listed.

4. A common question here is, "do I have 32- or 64-bit windows?". To find out, right-click on your **My Computer** (This PC on Windows 8) icon, click on the **Properties** option, and look under the **System** heading in the **System type** entry, as shown in the following screenshot:

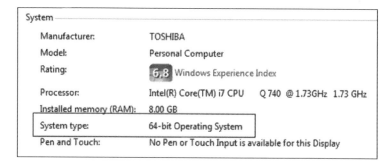

5. Click on the somewhat hidden **Accept License Agreement** checkbox:

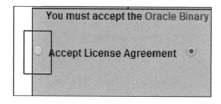

6. Now click on the download option for your OS and system type as previously determined. Wait for the download to finish.

7. In your Downloads folder, double-click on the file you just downloaded. The latest version at time of writing this for a 64-bit Windows PC was jdk-8u5-windows-x64. If you are using Mac/Linux or have a 32-bit OS, your filename will vary accordingly.

8. In the first of several install dialogs, click on the **Next** button and you will see the next dialog box:

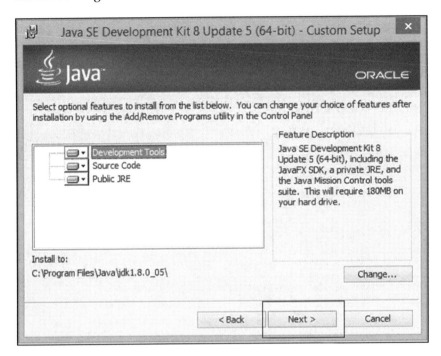

9. Accept the defaults shown in the previous screenshot by clicking on **Next**. In the next dialog box, you can accept the default install location by clicking on **Next**.

10. Next is the last dialog of the Java installer. Click on **Close**.

    The JDK is now installed. Next we will make sure that Android Studio is able to use the JDK.

11. Right-click on your **My Computer** (This PC on Windows 8) icon and navigate to **Properties | Advanced system settings | Environment variables | New** (under **System variables,** not under **User variables**). Now you can see the **New System Variable** dialog, as shown in the following screenshot:

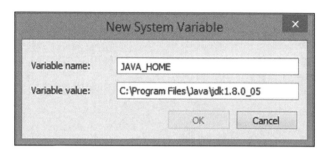

12. Type JAVA_HOME for **Variable name** and enter C:\Program Files\ Java\jdk1.8.0_05 for the **Variable value** field. If you installed the JDK somewhere else, then the file path you enter in the **Variable value:** field will need to point to wherever you put it. Your exact file path will likely have a different ending to match the latest version of Java at the time you downloaded it.

13. Click on **OK** to save your new settings. Now click on **OK** again to clear the **Advanced system settings** dialog.

Now we have the JDK installed on our PC. We are about half way towards starting to learn Java programming, but we need a friendly way to interact with the JDK and to help us make Android games in Java.

Android Studio

We learned that Android Studio is a tool that simplifies Android development and uses the JDK to allow us to write and build Java programs. There are other tools you can use instead of Android Studio. There are pros and cons in them all. For example, another extremely popular option is Eclipse. And as with so many things in programming, a strong argument can be made as to why you should use Eclipse instead of Android Studio. I use both, but what I hope you will love about Android Studio are the following elements:

- It is a very neat and, despite still being under development, a very refined and clean interface.

- It is much easier to get started compared to Eclipse because several Android tools that would otherwise need to be installed separately are already included in the package.

- Android Studio is being developed by Google, based on another product called IntelliJ IDEA. There is a chance it will be the standard way to develop Android in the not-too-distant future.

 If you want to use Eclipse, that's fine; all of the code in this book will work. However, some the keyboard shortcuts and user interface buttons will obviously be different. If you do not have Eclipse installed already and have no prior experience with Eclipse, then I even more strongly recommend you to go ahead with Android Studio.

Installing Android Studio

So without any delay, let's get Android Studio installed and then we can begin our first game project. To do this, let's visit `https://developer.android.com/sdk/installing/studio.html`.

1. Click on the button labeled **Download Android Studio** to start the Android studio download. This will take you to another web page with a very similar-looking button to the one you just clicked on.

2. Accept the license by checking in the checkbox, commence the download by clicking on the button labeled **Download Android Studio for Windows**, and wait for the download to complete. The exact text on the button will probably vary depending on the current latest version.

3. In the folder in which you just downloaded Android Studio, right-click on the `android-studio-bundle-135.12465-windows.exe` file and click on **Run as administrator**. The end of your filename will vary depending upon the version of Android Studio and your operating system.

4. When asked if you want to **Allow the following program from an unknown publisher to make changes to your computer**, click on **Yes**. On the next screen, click on **Next**.

5. On the screen shown in the following screenshot, you can choose which users of your PC can use Android Studio. Choose whatever is right for you as all options will work, and then click on **Next**:

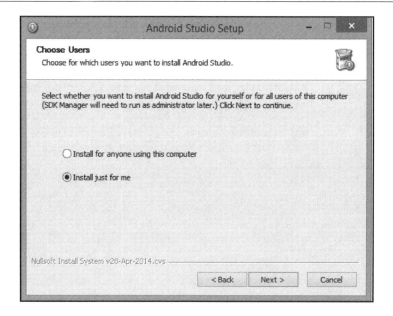

6. In the next dialog, leave the default settings and then click on **Next**.

7. Then on the **Choose start menu folder** dialog box, leave the defaults and click on **Install**.

8. On the **Installation complete** dialog, click on **Finish** to run Android Studio for the first time.

9. The next dialog is for users who have already used Android Studio, so assuming you are a first time user, select the **I do not have a previous version of Android Studio or I do not want to import my settings** checkbox, and then click on **OK**:

That was the last piece of software we needed. The simple nine-step process we just went through has actually set up a whole range of Android tools that we will begin to use in the next chapter.

Summary

We discussed why games, Java, and Android are not only extremely exciting but also arguably the best way to learn to program. This is because games can be an extremely motivating subject matter and Java and Android have enormous strengths with regards to popularity and longevity, and are open to all of us to use for free.

We also set up the Java development kit and installed Android Studio, getting ready for the next chapter where we will actually create a part of a working game and take our first look at some Java code.

2

Getting Started with Android

In this chapter, we will take a roller coaster ride through all the Android topics that you need to learn in order to get started with Java. It won't just be theoretical though. We will be designing a **user interface (UI)** of a game menu and we will see and edit our first Java code as well.

In addition, we will see how we can run our apps in either an Android emulator on our PC/Mac or on a real Android device if we have one.

Some of what we will cover in this chapter will be the tip of the iceberg. That is, there is a lot more below the surface to some of the topics we discuss than would be appropriate for the second chapter of a learning Java book. Sometimes, we might need to take a bit of information on faith.

This will then enable us to actually design and run our very own Android app by the end of this chapter. Then we can start learning Java for real at the beginning of the next chapter.

If this chapter seems a little tough, then don't worry; keep going because each subsequent chapter lifts the lid a bit more from some of the less clear topics.

For this chapter and the next two, we will be building a math game. We will start simply and by the end of *Chapter 4*, *Discovering Loops and Methods*, we will scale to game features that use significant Java skills.

In this chapter, we will:

- Start our first game project
- Explore Android Studio
- Use the Android Studio visual designer to make our game UI
- Learn about structuring our code for Android
- Take our first look at some Java code
- Build and install our game on an emulator and a real device

Our first game project

Now we will get straight down to actually doing something with Android Studio. Run Android Studio by double-clicking on the Android Studio icon either on your desktop's start menu or in the folder where you installed it.

If you get any errors in a dialog box mentioning **Privilege elevation**, then try running Android Studio with administrator privileges. To do this, find the Android Studio icon by clicking on the Windows **Start** button and searching for **Android Studio**. Now right-click on the icon and click on **Run as administrator**. Do this every time you run Android Studio.

Preparing Android Studio

So with Android Studio and Java installed, we just need to add the latest versions of the Android API that we will use to make our first game. Here is what to do to install the API:

1. From the menu bar at the top of the Android Studio UI, navigate to **Tools | Android | SDK Manager**. Scroll down in the **Android SDK Manager** window and select the checkbox for **Android 4.4.2 (API 19)**.

Note that because Android is evolving so quickly, by the time you read this chapter, there might be APIs newer than 19—20, 21, and so on. If this is the case for you, select the newer (higher numbered) API instead.

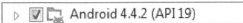

2. Click on **Install Packages**.

3. On the next screen, click on the **Accept license** checkbox and then click on the **Install** button. Android Studio will download and install the appropriate packages.

What we just did was setting up Android Studio to make available the latest, prewritten code called an API that we will interact with throughout the book.

Building the project

1. Click on **New Project...** as indicated in the following screenshot:

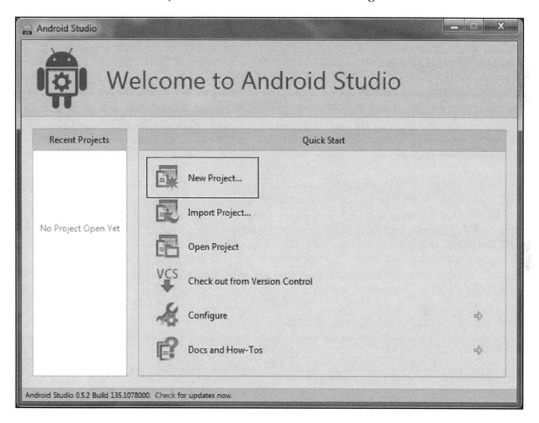

2. The **Create New Project** configuration window will appear. Fill in the **Application name** field with `Math Game Chapter 2` and **Company Domain** with `packtpub.com` (or you could use your own company website name here), as shown in the following screenshot:

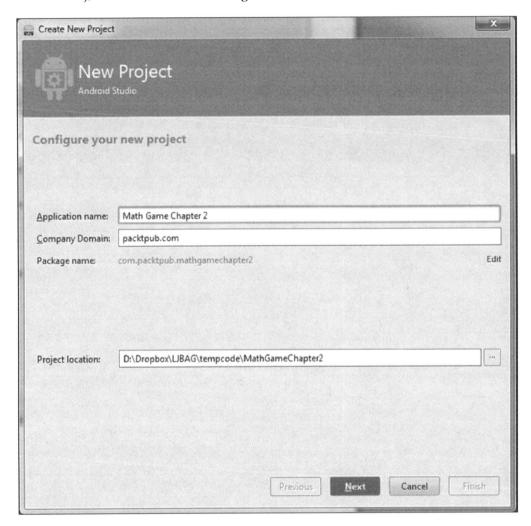

3. Now click on the **Next** button. On the next screen, check that the **Phone and Tablet** checkbox has a tick in it. Now we have to choose the earliest version of Android we want to build our app for. Go ahead and play with a few options in the drop-down selector. You will see that the earlier the version we select, the greater is the percentage of devices our app can support. However, the trade-off here is that the earlier the version we select, the fewer are the cutting-edge Android features available in our apps. A good balance is to select **API 8: Android 2.2 (Froyo)**. Go ahead and do that now as shown in the next screenshot:

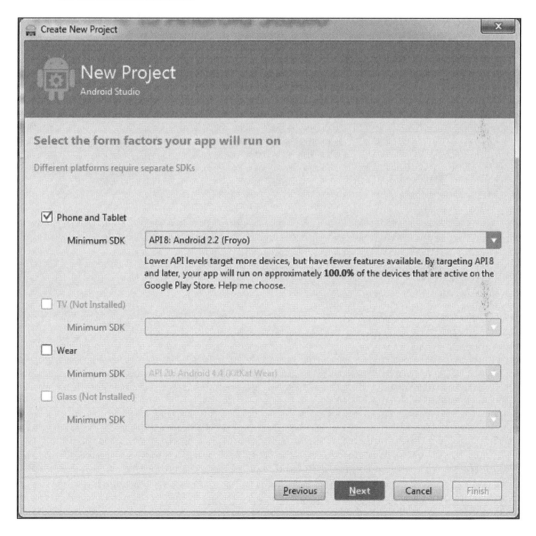

4. Click on **Next**. Now select **Blank Activity** as shown in the next screenshot and click on **Next** again:

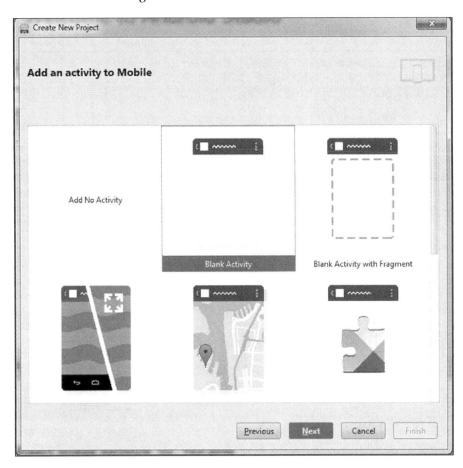

5. On the next screen, simply change **Activity Name** to `MainActivity` and click on **Finish**.

By default, Android Studio shows a **Tip of the day** dialog every time it starts. Some of the tips might not make sense while you are still learning Java but many of them are really useful and reveal great shortcuts and other time savers. It is well worth taking a few seconds to read them when they show up. As already discussed, Android Studio is built from IntelliJ IDEA, and you can find a complete list of keyboard shortcuts at `http://www.jetbrains.com/idea/webhelp/keyboard-shortcuts-you-cannot-miss.html`.

6. Clear **Tip of the day** by clicking on **Close**.

If you are completely new to programming, then the code, options, and files might seem a bit daunting. Don't worry; stick to them as we don't need to concern ourselves with most of them in order to learn Java. When the time does come to interact with the finer details, we will do things one step at a time.

It might be hard to believe that at this stage, but we have just created our first working app. We could build and run it on an Android device, and soon we will.

Let's take a deeper look at Android Studio before we progress with our game.

Exploring Android Studio

Android Studio is a very deep tool, but it is only necessary to learn one part at a time in order to get started. What might be useful for us is naming a few parts of the UI so that we can refer to them easily as we progress through the book.

Take a look at this numbered diagram and a quick explanation of some of the key parts of Android Studio. If you can, try and memorize the parts to make future discussions of them easier for you.

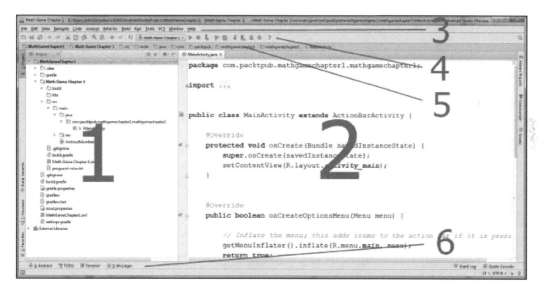

Here is a handy table that you can quickly refer to and remember which part of Android Studio we are referring to. What follows is a more detailed explanation of each area.

Number	Name
1	Project Explorer
2	The editor
3	Menu bar
4	Toolbar
5	Navigation bar
6	Important tool windows

- **Project Explorer (1)**: This is shown as **1** in the screenshot and is a bit like Windows Explorer. It shows us all the files and folders that have been generated for our project. We will do a number of things from here as the book continues. Actually, if you delve into the files and folders that Android Studio creates, the Project Explorer is not an exact mapping. It is slightly simplified and highlighted to make managing and exploring our project easier.

- **The Editor (2)**: As the name suggests, we will edit our Java code files here in the editor. However, as we will soon see, the **Editor** window changes depending on the type of file we are editing. We will also be viewing and editing UI designs here.

- **Menu bar (3)**: Like most programs, the **Menu** bar gives us access to the full functionality of Android Studio.

- **Tool bar (4)**: This contains lots of really useful one-click options to do things such as deploying and debugging our games. Hover the mouse cursor over an icon to get a pop-up tip and gain greater insight into each toolbar icon.

- **Navigation bar (5)**: Like a file path, this shows exactly where the file that is currently in the editor is located within the project.

- **Important tool windows (6)**: These are a number of tabs that can be popped up and popped down again by clicking on them. If you like, try some of them now to see how they work.

Let's talk a bit more about the parts of the Android Studio UI and how the editor window can transform itself into a visual UI designer. After that, when we are familiar enough, we will look at building a simple menu screen for our math game.

Using the Android Studio visual designer

The Android Studio editor window is a very dynamic area. It presents different file types in the most useful way possible. A little earlier, when we created our project, it also made a basic UI for us. UIs in Android can be built-in Java code or, as we will see, in a visual designer without the need for a single line of Java. However, as we will investigate after we have built the UI of our game menu, to get the UI to do anything useful, we need to interact with it. This interaction is always done with Java code. The visual designer also generates the UI code for us. We will take a very quick look at that too.

As the book progresses, we will mainly shy away from Android UI development, as that is a staple of more non-game apps. We will instead spend more time looking at directly drawing pixels and images to make our games. Nonetheless, the regular Android UI has its uses, and the Android Studio visual designer is the quickest way to get started.

Let's have a look at that now:

1. In the Android Studio Project Explorer, double-click on the `layout` folder to reveal the `activity_main.xml` file within it. This should be easy to see unless you have collapsed the directories. If you can't see the `layout` folder, navigate to it using the Project Explorer. It can be found at `Math Game Chapter2/src/main/res/layout` via the Android Studio Project Explorer, as shown in the following screenshot:

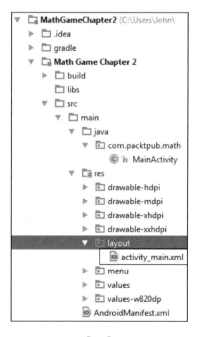

2. Now double-click on **activity_main.xml** to open it in the editor window. After a brief loading time, you will see something very similar to the next screenshot. The following screenshot shows the entire contents of what previously contained just our code. As you can see, what was just a text window now has multiple parts. Let's take a closer look at this screenshot:

In the preceding screenshot labeled (**1**), called **Palette**, you can choose from the available Android UI elements and simply click and drag them onto your UI design. Area (2) is the visual view of the UI you are building, where you will click and drag elements from the palette. To the right of the visual UI view, you will see the **Component Tree** area (3). The component tree allows you to examine the structure of the complex UI and select specific elements more easily. Under this tree is the **Properties** panel (4). Here you can adjust the properties of the currently selected UI element. These can be simple things such as color and size or much more advanced properties.

Note the tabs labelled (**5**). These tabs allow you to switch between the two main views that Android Studio provides for this type of layout file. These views, as you can see, are **Design** and **Text**. The design view is the default view and is shown in the previous screenshot. The text view also shows your under-construction UI, but it shows the code that has been autogenerated for us instead of the **Palette** element and the component tree.

We don't need to worry about this code as it is all handled for us. It can be good to look on this tab from time to time so that we can begin to understand what the design tool generates for us. But it is not necessary to do this to learn Java. This code is called **eXtensible Markup Language (XML)**.

3. Take a quick look at the **Text** tab, click on the **Design** tab when you're done, and we will move on.

Now we have seen an overview of the visual designer and an even briefer glimpse of the automatically generated code that it generates for us. We can take a closer look at some of the actual UI elements that we will be using in our project.

Android UI types

We will now take a whirlwind tour of some really useful Android UI elements, a few key properties, and how to add them together to make a UI. These will introduce us to some of the possibilities as well as how to use them. We will then quickly use what we know to make our menu.

TextView

On the visual UI area, click on the words **Hello world!**. What we have just selected is a widget known as a TextView. TextViews can be small text like this one or large heading type text, which might be useful in our game menu.

3. Notice that after you select it, you have the option to click on **...** to give you more options. Click on **...** and scroll to the bottom of the list of options. These are all the image files that we can display in this ImageView. Just for fun, scroll to the bottom of the list, choose **ic_launcher**, and click on **OK**. We can make any image we like available and this is a simple, powerful way to build an attractive game menu screen.

4. Change the **layout:width** property to 150dp and the **layout:height** property to 150dp. The unit **dp** is a way of sizing elements and widgets that remains relatively constant across devices with screens that have very different numbers of pixels.

5. Delete the ImageView in exactly the same way as you deleted the other views previously.

ButtonView

The use of ButtonView is probably given away by its name. Try to click and drag a few buttons onto our layout. Notice that there are a few types of ButtonView, such as **Small Button**, **Button**, and, if you look further down the **Widget** list, **ImageButton**. We will be using the regular ButtonView, labelled simply as **Button**.

Now we will do something with each of these Android UI elements combined to make our game menu.

 You can download the entire sample from the code download section of the book's companion website.

Using the sample code

All of the code in this book is organized in projects. If a project spans more than one chapter, a project is provided for each chapter in its finished state. This helps you see the progression and not just the end result. All you need to do to open the project in Android Studio is explained as follows:

1. Download the code for this book.

2. In **Android Studio** from the menu bar, navigate to **File | Close project**.

3. Now create a new blank project as we did previously. Browse to where you downloaded the code for this book.

4. Navigate to the Chapter2/MathGameChapter2 folder. Here you will find the code for all the files we create in this chapter.

5. Open the code files using a plain text editor such as the free Notepad++.

6. Copy and paste in your Android Studio project or just compare the code as you see it.

 Although every line of code required in this book is supplied for your convenience, you still need to create each project for yourself through Android Studio. You can then simply copy and paste either the code in its entirety in the file with the matching name, or just the part of the code that you might be struggling with. Keep in mind that if you create a project with a different package name, then you must *omit* the line of code that is the package name from the supplied code files. The reasons for this will be clearer when we talk more about packages later in the chapter.

Let's actually see how to do it all for ourselves.

Making our game menu

For now we will just make our game menu functional. Later in *Chapter 5, Gaming and Java Essentials*, we will see how we can make it look good by adding some cool animation to make the menu more visually interesting and fun.

Here is what we are aiming for in this tutorial:

Before you start coding, you should design your layouts on paper first. However, the Android Studio designer is so friendly there is a strong argument, especially for simple layouts, to refine your design actually in the layout designer. Perform the following steps to create the game menu:

1. Delete all widgets from your designer by clicking on them one at a time and then tapping the *Delete* key on each in turn. Be careful not to delete the **RelativeLayout** layout element as we are going to use it as a base for all the other elements.

2. Click and drag a **Large Text** element from the palette to the top center of the design area and give it the following properties. Remember that you can change properties in the **Properties** panel by clicking to the right of the property to be changed. Change the **text** property to My Math Game and **size** to 30sp.

3. Click and drag an **ImageView** element from the palette to the center of the design, slightly below the previous TextView. Change the **layout:width** property to 150dp and the **layout:height** property to 150dp.

4. Now click and drag three buttons for **Play**, **High Scores** and **Quit**. Center them vertically, below the previous ImageView and one below the other, as per our design shown previously.

5. Click on the top button, configure the **text** property, and enter the value Play.

6. Click on the middle button, configure the **text** property, and enter the value High Scores.

7. Click on the lowest button, configure the **text** property, and enter the value Quit.

8. As the buttons now contain different amounts of text relative to each other, they will be of slightly different sizes. You can even them up to match the intended layout by clicking and dragging the edges of the smaller buttons to match the larger ones. This is done in mostly the same way as you might resize an application window in Windows.

9. Save the project with *Ctrl + S* or by navigating to **File | Save All**.

If you are going to be testing your games on a much larger or much smaller screen than the Nexus 4 shown in the designer, then you might like to adjust the values of the sp and dp units used in this tutorial.

A full discussion of Android UI on multiple devices is beyond the scope of this book and is not necessary to make any of the games in this book. If you want to start designing for different screens right away, take a look at http://developer.android.com/training/multiscreen/index.html.

You can view what your menu looks like on other devices simply by selecting the device from the drop-down menu shown in the following screenshot:

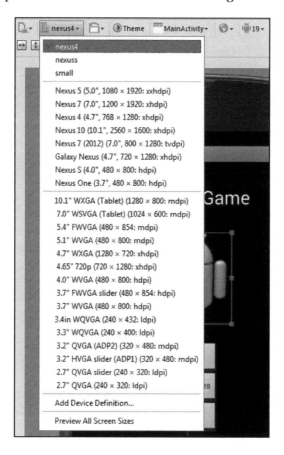

Before we make our menu come to life on an actual device, let's take a look at the structure of an Android app and how we can use that structure when writing our Java code.

Structuring our code for Android

If you have ever used an Android device, you have probably noticed that it works quite differently from many other operating systems. For example, you are using an application—say you're checking what people are doing on Facebook. Then you get an e-mail notification and you tap the e-mail icon to read it. Midway through reading the e-mail, you might get a Twitter notification and because you're waiting on important news from someone you follow, you interrupt your e-mail reading and change the app to Twitter with a touch.

After reading the tweet, you fancy a game of Angry Birds, but midway through the first daring fling, you suddenly remember that Facebook post. So you quit Angry Birds and tap the Facebook icon.

Then you resume Facebook, probably at the same point you left it. You could have resumed reading the e-mail, decided to reply to the tweet, or started an entirely new app. All this backwards and forwards takes quite a lot of management on the part of the operating system, apparently independent from the individual apps themselves.

The difference between a Windows PC and Android in the context we have just discussed is that with Android, although the user decides which app they are using, the Android OS decides if and when to actually close down (destroy) an application. We just need to consider this when coding our games.

Life cycle phases – what we need to know

The Android system has different **phases** that any given app can be in. Depending on the phase, the Android system determines how the app is viewed by the user or whether it is viewed at all. Android has these phases so that it can decide which app is in current use and then allocate the right amount of resources such as memory and processing power. But also allow us as game developers to interact with these phases. What if someone quits our game to answer a phone call? Will they lose their progress?

Android has a fairly complex system that, when simplified a little for the purpose of explanation, ensures that every app on an Android device is in one of the following phases:

- Being created
- Starting
- Resuming
- Running
- Pausing

- Stopping
- Being destroyed

The list of phases will hopefully appear fairly logical. As an example, the user presses the Facebook app icon and the app is **created**. Then it is *started*. All are fairly straightforward so far but next in the list is **resuming**! It is not as illogical as it might first appear if, for a moment, we can just accept that the app resumes after it starts, and then all will become clear as we proceed.

After **resuming,** the app is *running*. This is when the Facebook app has control over the screen and probably the greater share of system memory and processing power. Now what about our example where we switched from the Facebook app to the e-mail app?

As we tap to go to read our e-mail, the Facebook app will probably have entered the **paused** phase, and the e-mail app will enter the **being created** phase followed by **resuming** and then **running**. If we decide to revisit Facebook, as in the scenario earlier, the Facebook app will probably then go straight to the **resume** phase and then **running** again, most likely exactly on the post where we left it.

Note that at any time, Android can decide to *stop* or *destroy* an app, in which case, when we run the app again, it will need to be *created* all over again. So had the Facebook app been inactive long enough or had Angry Birds required so many system resources that Android would have *destroyed* the Facebook app, then our experience of finding the exact post we were previously reading might have been different.

Now, if all this phase stuff is starting to get confusing, then you will be pleased to know that the only reasons to mention are as follows:

- You know it exists
- We occasionally need to interact with it
- We will take things step by step when we do

Life cycle phases – what we need to do

When we are making games, how do we possibly interact with this complexity? The good news is that the Android code that was autogenerated when we created our first project does most of the interaction for us.

All we have to do as game developers is make sure that Android knows what to do with our app in each phase when it happens. Even more good news is that all of these phases are handled by default, unless we override the default handling.

This means we can go ahead with learning Java and making games until we come to one of the few instances where we need to do something in our game, specifically in one of the phases.

Dividing our game into activities

The Java code that we write will be divided into sections or parts called **activities**. We can think of activities as different screens for our game. For example, during the book, we will often create an activity for a home screen, an activity for the game screen and an activity for the high score screen.

Each activity will have its own life cycle and will be further divided into parts that will correspond to (go into) one of the Android phases we just discussed. The parts in Java are known as **methods**. Methods are a significant concept in Java programming.

At this stage, however, all we need to know is that methods are used to compartmentalize the Java code we write and that some methods are provided by the Android system so that we can easily handle the otherwise complex Android life cycle.

The forthcoming list is a quick explanation of the methods provided by Android for our convenience, to manage the phases of the life cycle. To clarify our discussion of life cycle phases methods are listed next to their corresponding phases that we have been discussing. However, as you will see, the method names make it fairly clear on their own where they fit in.

In the list, there is also a brief explanation or suggestion about when we should use a given method and thereby interact during a specific phase. We will meet most of these methods as we progress through the book. We will see the onCreate method later in this chapter. Here is the list:

- onCreate: This method is executed when the activity is being created. Here we get everything ready for the game, including graphics, sound, and perhaps the high scores.
- onStart: This method is executed when the app is in the starting phase.
- onResume: This method runs after onStart but can also be entered, perhaps most logically, after our activity is resumed after being previously paused. We might reload a previously saved game situation when the app had been interrupted, perhaps by a phone call or the user running another app.
- onPause: This occurs when our app is pausing. Here we might want to save the current game. You are probably getting the hang of these methods.
- onStop: This relates to the stopping phase. This is where we might undo everything we did in onCreate. If we reach here, our activity will probably get destroyed sometime soon.

- `onDestroy`: This is when our activity is finally being destroyed—our last chance to dismantle our game. If we reach here, we will definitely be going through the phases of the life cycle from the beginning again.

All the method descriptions and their related phases should appear straightforward. Perhaps, the only real question is about the running phase. As we will see, when we write our code in other methods/phases, the `onCreate`, `onStart`, and `onResume` methods will prepare the game, which persists, forming the running phase. The `onPause`, `onStop`, and `onDestroy` methods will occur afterwards. Now we can actually take a look at one of these methods and some other methods as well.

Our first look at Java

So what about all that code that Android Studio generated when we created our new project earlier? This is the code that will bring our game menu to life. Let's take a closer look. The very first line of code in the editor window is this:

```
package com.packtpub.mathgamechapter2;
```

This line of code defines the package that we named when we first created the project. As the book progresses, we will write more complex code that spans more than one file. All the code files we create will need the package they belong to, clearly defined like the previous line of code, at the top. The code doesn't actually *do* anything in our game. Notice also that the line ends with a semicolon (;). This is a part of the Java syntax and it denotes the end of a line of code. Remove a semicolon and you will get an error because Android Studio tries to make sense of two lines together. Try it if you like.

> Remember that if you are going to be copying and pasting the code from the download bundle, this is the one line of code that might vary depending on how you set up your project. If the package name in the code file is different from the package name you created, always use the package name from when you created the project.

To see the next four lines of code, you might need to click on the small **+** icon to reveal them. Android Studio tries to be helpful by simplifying our view of the code. Notice that there are several little **-** icons as well down the side of the editor window. You can expand and collapse them to suit yourself without affecting the functionality of the program. This is shown in the following screenshot:

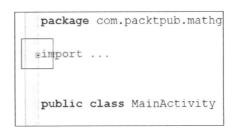

Once you have expanded the code, you will see these four lines:

```
import android.support.v7.app.ActionBarActivity;
import android.os.Bundle;
import android.view.Menu;
import android.view.MenuItem;
```

Notice that all the preceding lines start with the word `import`. This is an instruction to include other packages in our game, not just our own. This is very significant because it makes available to us all of the hard work of other programmers, the Android development team in this case. It is precisely these imports that give us the ability to use the methods we discussed earlier, and allow us to interact with the Android life cycle phases. Notice again that all the lines end with a semicolon (`;`).

The next line introduces a fundamental building block of Java known as a **class**. Classes are something that we will continually expand our knowledge and understanding of throughout the book. For now, take a look at this line of code, then we will discuss it in detail:

```
public class MainActivity extends ActionBarActivity {
```

Word by word, here is what is going on. The preceding line is saying: make me a new `public class` called `MainActivity` and base it upon (`extends`) `ActionBarActivity`.

You might remember that `MainActivity` is the name we chose while creating this project. `ActionBarActivity` is the code (known as a class) written by the Android development team that enables us to put our Java into Android.

If you have a keen eye, you might notice there is no semicolon at the end of this line. There is, however, an opening curly brace ({). This is because `MainActivity` encompasses the rest of the code. In effect, everything is part of our `MainActivity` class, which is built based on the `ActionBarActivity` class/code. If you scroll down to the bottom of the editor window, you will see a closing curly brace (}). This denotes the end of our class called `MainActivity`.

- We do not need to know how a class works yet

- We will use classes to access some methods contained within its code and without doing any more, we are already, by default, taking advantage of the Android life cycle methods we discussed earlier

- We can now pick and choose if, when, and which methods defined in these classes we wish to override or leave as default

So, it is the `ActionBarActivity` class that contains the methods that enable us to interact with the Android life cycle. Actually, there are a number of different classes that enable us to do this and in a moment, we will change from using `ActionBarActivity` to a more appropriate class that also does all the things just mentioned.

> It is not important at this point to properly understand Java classes; just understand that you can import a package and a package can contain one or more classes that you can then use the functionality of or base your own Java programs on.
>
> We will bump into classes regularly in the next few chapters. Think of them as programming black boxes that do stuff. In *Chapter 6, OOP – Using Other People's Hard Work*, we will open the black box and really get to grips with them and we will even start making our own classes.

Moving on with the code, let's look at what the code that is contained within our class actually does.

Here is the code chunk directly after the crucial line we have just been discussing:

```
@Override
    protected void onCreate(Bundle savedInstanceState) {
        super.onCreate(savedInstanceState);
        setContentView(R.layout.activity_main);
    }
```

Hopefully, some of this code will start to make sense now and tie in with what we have already discussed. Although the precise syntax will still feel a little alien, we can continue learning Java as long as we are aware of what is happening.

The first thing we notice in the preceding code is the word `@override`. Remember when we said that all the methods that interact with the Android life cycle were implemented by default and we can pick and choose if and when to override them? This is what we are doing here with the `onCreate` method.

The `@override` word says that the method that follows next is being overridden. The `protected void onCreate(Bundle savedInstanceState)` { line contains the method we are overriding. You might be able to guess that the action starts with the opening { at the end of the line in question and ends with the closing } three lines later.

The somewhat odd-looking `protected void` before the method name `onCreate` and `(Bundle savedInstanceState)` after the method name are unimportant at this time because they are handled for us. It is to do with the data that travels between various parts of our program. We just need to know that what happens here will take place in the creating phase of the Android lifecycle. The rest will become clear in *Chapter 4, Discovering Loops and Methods*. Let's move on to the line:

```
super.onCreate(savedInstanceState);
```

Here, the `super` keyword is referencing the code in the original `onCreate` method, which is still there even though we can't see it. The code is saying: even though I am overriding you, I want you to set things up, just like you normally do first. Then, after `onCreate` has done loads of work that we don't see and don't need to see, the method continues and we actually get to do something ourselves with this line of code:

```
setContentView(R.layout.activity_main);
```

Here we are telling Android to set the main content view (our users screen), which is the cool game menu we created earlier. To be specific, we are stating it is an R or resource in the `layout` folder and the file is called `activity_main`.

Cleaning up our code

The next two blocks of code were created by Android Studio on the assumption that we would want to override another two methods. We don't, because they are methods more often used in non-gaming apps:

1. Delete the entire content shown in the following code. Be careful not to delete the closing curly brace of our `MainActivity` class:

    ```
    @Override
        public boolean onCreateOptionsMenu(Menu menu) {

            // Inflate the menu; this adds items to the action bar if
    it is present.
            getMenuInflater().inflate(R.menu.main, menu);
    ```

```
            return true;
        }

        @Override
        public boolean onOptionsItemSelected(MenuItem item) {
            // Handle action bar item clicks here. The action bar will
            // automatically handle clicks on the Home/Up button, so
long
            // as you specify a parent activity in AndroidManifest.
xml.
            int id = item.getItemId();
            if (id == R.id.action_settings) {
                return true;
            }
            return super.onOptionsItemSelected(item);
        }
```

2. Now we can delete a couple of the @import statements. The reason for this is that we just deleted the overridden methods of classes (imported earlier) we no longer need. Notice that the following lines in the editor window are grey. Note that the program would still work if you leave them in. Delete them both now to make your code as clear as possible:

```
import android.view.Menu;
import android.view.MenuItem;
```

3. Some final amendments before our code is done: at this point, you might be thinking that we have deleted and changed so much of our code that we might as well have started from an empty page and typed it in. This is almost true. But the process of having Android Studio create a new project for us and then making these amendments is more thorough and also avoids quite a few steps. Here are the last code changes. Change the import android. support.v7.app.ActionBarActivity; line to import android.support. app.Activity;.

4. Now you will get several red lines underlining our code and indicating errors. This is because we are attempting to use a class we have not yet imported. Simply amend the public class MainActivity extends ActionBarActivity { line to public class MainActivity extends Activity {.

What we did with those last two changes was using a slightly more appropriate version of the Activity class. To do this, we also had to change what we imported.

When you're done, your editor window should look exactly like this:

```
package com.packtpub.mathgamechapter2.mathgamechapter2;

import android.support.v7.app.ActionBarActivity;
import android.os.Bundle;


public class MainActivity extends ActionBarActivity {

    @Override
    protected void onCreate(Bundle savedInstancePhase) {
        super.onCreate(savedInstancePhase);
        setContentView(R.layout.activity_main);
    }

}
```

Downloading the example code

You can download the example code fies from your account at http://www.packtpub.com for all the Packt Publishing books you have purchased. If you purchased this book elsewhere, you can visit http://www.packtpub.com/support and register to have the fies e-mailed directly to you.

Now that we know what's going on and our code is clean and lean, we can actually take a look at the beginnings of our game in action!

If any of what we have just discussed seemed complicated, there is no need for concern. Android forces us to work within the Activity lifecycle, so the previous steps were unavoidable. Even if you didn't follow all the explanations about classes and methods and so on, you are still perfectly placed to learn Java from here. All the classes and methods will seem much more straightforward as the book progresses.

Building and installing our game

Soon, we will actually see our menu in action. But before we do that, we need to find out how to use the Android emulators and how to build our game. Then we will put these together and put our game into an emulator or real device to see it as our players would.

Emulators and devices

Now we have the first part of our game ready to run. We need to test it to check for any errors, crashes, or anything else unintended. It is also important to ensure that it looks good and runs correctly on the device types/sizes and that you want to target.

We will not go into any details about handling different device types. All our games are fullscreen and we will later lock the orientation and dynamically calculate aspects such as screen resolution. So we can get away with writing for a single device type and focus on learning Java.

It might be useful to know for now that you can create a different layout file for any screen size categorization or pixel density. All you need to do is place the layout file using exactly the same filename in the appropriate folder. The Android device will then *know* the most appropriate layout for it to use. For a detailed discussion, see the Google developers website at `http://developer.android.com/guide/practices/screens_support.html`.

Note that you do not need to understand any of the information at the preceding link to learn Java and publish your first games.

There are a few options to do this and we will look at two. First, we will use Android Studio and the Android Development Tools to make a device emulator so that we can use, test, and debug our games on a wide range of device emulators on the same PC/Mac we are developing on. So we don't need to own a device. This will allow us to get crash reports from our games.

Then we will install the game directly to a real device so that we can see exactly what the owner of that device will see when they download our app.

There are more options. For example, you can connect a real device via USB and debug directly on the device with the errors and syntactical feedback in Android Studio. The process for this might vary for different devices and since we won't be focusing on anything but basic debugging, we will not cover that in this book.

Creating an emulator

Let's get our emulator up and emulating:

1. On the right-hand side of the Android Studio quick launch bar, find the AVD manager icon:

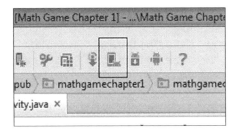

2. Click on the icon to start the Android Virtual Device Manager. Then click on the **Create Virtual Device...** button on the bottom-left side to bring up the **Virtual Device Configuration** window.

3. Now click on the **Nexus 4** option and then click on **Next**.

4. Now we need to choose the version of Android we will use to build and test our games on. The latest version (at time of writing) is **Lollipop - 21 - x86**. It is the only option where we don't need to complete a download to continue. So select it (or whatever the default is at the time you are reading this) and then click on **Next** to continue.

5. On the next screen we can leave all the default settings. So click on **Finish**.

We now have a ready-to-run Android emulator.

Running the emulator

Now we will launch (switch on) our virtual device then actually run our game that we made earlier by performing the following steps:

1. Click on **Nexus 4 API 21** under the **Name** column. Now click on the triangular play icon to the right of the description of our emulator.

> Android emulators take a long time to start. Even on a high-specification PC. Expect to wait at least a few minutes or even 10.

2. Once it has started, unlock the device by clicking and dragging anywhere on the screen of the emulated device. This is analogous to swiping to unlock a real Nexus 4. Here is what our Nexus 4 virtual device looks like when it is running and unlocked:

You can play with this emulator in almost the same way as you can a real Android device. However, you cannot download apps from Google Play. You might notice that the emulator is a bit slow compared to a real device, even compared to an old one. Shortly, we will look at running our apps on a real device.

Running our game on the emulator

Once the emulator is running, it's usually best to leave it running so that each time we want to use it, we don't have to wait for it to start. Let's use the emulator:

1. Launch the emulator if it is not already running and make sure the device is unlocked as described previously.

2. Click on the run icon in the toolbar (shown next) to run your app. You can achieve the same thing by navigating to **Run | Math Game Chapter 2** from the menu bar:

3. After a pause while Android Studio builds our application, a pop-up dialog will ask you which device you want to run the app on. Choose the device with **Nexus 4 API 21** in the description. This is the already running device that we created earlier. Now press **OK**.

4. Notice at this point that the useful Android window appears at the bottom section of Android Studio. In the unlikely event of you having any problems, just check for typos in the code. If things really don't work out, just go back to the *Using the sample code* section to compare with or copy and paste the supplied code.

After another pause, our game menu screen will appear on the emulator. Of course, it doesn't do anything yet, but it is running and the buttons can be pressed.

When you're done, you can press the back or home icons to quit the application, just as you would on a real Android device.

Now we have seen one of the ways we can test our app by running it in the Android emulator. Let's find out how to make our code into an app we can distribute and use on a real device.

Building our game

To run our game on a real Android device, we need to create a .apk file, that is, a file that ends with the extension .apk. A .apk file is a compressed archive of files and folders that the Android system uses to run and install our app. These are the steps to use Android Studio to make a .apk of our game:

1. From the menu bar, navigate to **Build | Generate Signed APK**.

2. A slightly verbose window will pop up and say: **For Gradle-based projects, the signing configuration should be specified in the Gradle build scripts**. You can safely dismiss this window by clicking on **OK**.

3. Next up is the **Generate Signed APK Wizard** dialog. Here, we are creating a key that identifies the key holder as authorized to distribute the APK. At the end of this process, you will have a `.keys` file that you can use each time you build a `.apk` file. So this step can be missed out in future. Click on the **Create new** button.

4. In the **Key Store Path** field, type or go to a location on your hard drive where you would like to store your key. You will then be prompted to choose a filename for the keystore. This is arbitrary. Type `MyKeystore` and click on **OK**.

5. Type a password in the **Password** field and then retype it in the **Confirm** field. This is the password to a store that will help protect your key.

6. Next, in the **Alias** field, type a memorable alias. You can think of this as a kind of username for your key. Again type a password in the **Password** field and then retype it in the **Confirm** field. This is the password to your key.

7. Leave the **Validity Years** dropdown at the default of **25**.

8. You can then fill out your Name and organization details (if any) and click on **OK**.

9. Now our key and keystore are complete, and we can click on **OK** on the **Generate Signed APK wizard** dialog.

10. We are then prompted to select **Run Proguard**. Encrypting and optimizing our `.apk` is unnecessary at this time. So just click on **Finish** to generate our app's `.apk` file.

11. The generated `.apk` file will be put in the same directory that you chose to put the project files. For example, `MathGameChapter2/app`.

We have now built a `.apk` file that can be run on any Android device that was specified when we first created the project.

Installing the setup to a device

So we have our `.apk` file and we know were to find it. Here is how we will run it on our Android device.

We can use one of a number of methods to get the .apk file into the device. The method I find one of the easiest is the use of a cloud storage service such as Dropbox. You can then simply click and drag the .apk file to your Dropbox folder and you're done. Alternatively, your Android device probably came with PC synchronization software that allows you to drag and drop files to and from your device. After you have placed the .apk file on your Android device, continue with the tutorial.

Most Android phones are set not to install apps from anywhere except the Google Play Store. So we need to change this. The exact menus you will navigate to might vary very slightly on your device but the following options tend to be almost the same on most devices, old and new:

1. Find and tap the **Settings** app. Most Android phones also have a **Settings** menu option. Either will do. Now select **Security** and scroll down to the **Unknown sources** option. Tap the **Unknown sources** checkbox to allow apps to be installed from unknown sources.

2. Locate the file on your Android device using the Dropbox app or your devices file browser depending on the method you chose to put the APK on your device. Tap the `MathGameChapter2.apk` file.

3. You can now install the app just like any other. When prompted, press **Install** and then **Open**. The game will now be running on your device.

Hold your device in a portrait orientation as this is how the UI was designed. Congratulations on running your very own Android app on your own device. In a later version of the math game, we will lock the orientation to make this more user friendly.

Future projects

Throughout the book, we will test and run our game projects. It is entirely up to you which of the methods we discussed you prefer. If you are getting crashes or unexplained bugs, then you will need to use an emulator. If all is working well, then the quickest and probably most pleasing way will be to run it on a device you own.

Self-test questions

Q1) What should you do if all this talk of life cycles, classes, and methods is a bit bemusing?

Q2) What exactly is a Java class?

Q3) What is the difference between a method and a class?

Q4) Take a look at the Android developer site and its more technical explanation of the phases of the life cycle at `http://developer.android.com/reference/android/app/Activity.html`. Can you see the phase and its related method that we haven't discussed? When would it be triggered in an app? What is the precise pathway an activity takes from creation to destruction?

Summary

We discussed that so far, it has not been not important to completely understand exactly how the code works. This is because it will act just as a container for the code we write in the rest of the book. However, as we cover in detail topics such as methods in *Chapter 4, Discovering Loops and Methods*, and classes in *Chapter 6, OOP – Using Other People's Hard Work*, we will begin to make sense of all of the code in our games.

We discussed the somewhat complex Android life cycle in detail. We learned that all we need to understand at this stage is that we must write our code within the correct methods that relate to different phases of the life cycle. Then we will have no trouble making good progress with learning Java. As with classes and methods, all will be explained along the way and become clearer with practice.

We also learned the key areas of the Android Studio UI. We built our start menu for our math game using the Android Studio designer. Furthermore, we created the Java code necessary to make the game appear on the player's device. This was achieved mainly by modifying the code that was automatically generated for us.

This was probably the most difficult chapter of the book because it was necessary to introduce a few things such as Java classes, Java methods, and the Android life cycle. We did this because we need to know what is going on around us as we learn Java.

From now on, however, we can take things a step at a time in a very logical manner. If you have reached this point, you will have no problem completing the toughest of the projects in this book.

If this chapter made your brain ache a little, rest assured that the fact that you have made it this far is a very good indication that you are going to be a Java ace someday soon. Starting from the basics, let's learn some Java now.

3
Speaking Java – Your First Game

In this chapter, we will start writing our very own Java code at the same time as we begin understanding Java syntax. We will learn how to store, retrieve, and manipulate different types of values stored in the memory. We will also look at making decisions and branching the flow of our code based on the values of this data.

In this order, we will:

- Learn some Java syntax and see how it is turned into a running app by the compiler
- Store data and use it with variables
- Learn how to express yourself in Java with expressions
- Continue with the math game by asking a question
- Learn about decisions in Java
- Continue with the math game by getting and checking the answer

Acquiring the preceding Java skills will enable us to build the next two phases of our math game. This game will be able to ask the player a question on multiplication, check the answer and give feedback based on the answer given, as shown in the following screenshot:

Java syntax

Throughout this book, we will use plain English to discuss some fairly technical things. You will never be asked to read a technical explanation of a Java or Android concept that has not been previously explained in a non-technical way.

Occasionally, I might ask or imply that you accept a simplified explanation in order to offer a fuller explanation at a more appropriate time, like the Java class as a black box; however, you will never need to scurry to Google in order to get your head around a big word or a jargon-filled sentence.

Having said that, the Java and Android communities are full of people who speak in technical terms and to join in and learn from these communities, you need to understand the terms they use. So the approach this book takes is to learn a concept or appreciate an idea using an entirely plain speaking language, but at the same time, it introduces the jargon as part of the learning.

Then, much of the jargon will begin to reveal its usefulness, usually as a way of clarification or keeping the explanation/discussion from becoming longer than it needs to be.

The very term, "Java syntax," could be considered technical or jargon. So what is it? The Java syntax is the way we put together the language elements of Java in order to produce code that works in the Java/Dalvik virtual machine. Syntax should also be as clear as possible to a human reader, not least ourselves when we revisit our programs in the future. The Java syntax is a combination of the words we use and the formation of those words into sentence like structures.

These Java elements or words are many in number, but when taken in small chunks are almost certainly easier to learn than any human-spoken language. The reason for this is that the Java language and its syntax were specifically designed to be as straightforward as possible. We also have Android Studio on our side, which will often let us know if we make a mistake and will even sometimes think ahead and prompt us.

I am confident that if you can read, you can learn Java; because learning Java is very easy. What then separates someone who has finished an elementary Java course from an expert programmer? The same things that separate a student of language from a master poet. Mastery of the language comes through practice and further study.

In the last chapter, I will show you the right direction if you want to go on to master Java yourself.

The compiler

The compiler is what turns our human-readable Java code into another piece of code that can be run in a virtual machine. This is called **compiling**. The Dalvik virtual machine will run this compiled code when our players tap on our app icon. Besides compiling Java code, the compiler will also check for mistakes. Although we might still have mistakes in our released app, many discovered when our code is compiled.

Making code clear with comments

As you become more advanced in writing Java programs, the solutions you use to create your programs will become longer and more complicated. Furthermore, as we will see in later chapters, Java was designed to manage complexity by having us divide our code into separate chunks, very often across multiple files.

Comments are a part of the Java program that do not have any function in the program itself. The compiler ignores them. They serve to help the programmer to document, explain, and clarify their code to make it more understandable to themselves at a later date or to other programmers who might need to use or modify the code.

So, a good piece of code will be liberally sprinkled with lines like this:

```
//this is a comment explaining what is going on
```

The preceding comment begins with the two forward slash characters, //. The comment ends at the end of the line. It is known as a single-line comment. So anything on that line is for humans only, whereas anything on the next line (unless it's another comment) needs to be syntactically correct Java code:

```
//I can write anything I like here
but this line will cause an error
```

We can use multiple single-line comments:

```
//Below is an important note
//I am an important note
//We can have as many single line comments like this as we like
```

Single-line comments are also useful if we want to temporarily disable a line of code. We can put // in front of the code and it will not be included in the program. Recall this code, which tells Android to load our menu UI:

```
//setContentView(R.layout.activity_main);
```

In the preceding situation, the menu will not be loaded and the app will have a blank screen when run, as the entire line of code is ignored by the compiler. There is another type of comment in Java—the multiline comment. This is useful for longer comments and also to add things such as copyright information at the top of a code file. Also like the single-line comment, it can be used to temporarily disable code, in this case usually multiple lines.

Everything in between the leading /* signs and the ending */ signs is ignored by the compiler. Here are some examples:

```
/*
This program was written by a Java expert
You can tell I am good at this because my
code has so many helpful comments in it.
*/
```

There is no limit to the number of lines in a multiline comment. Which type of comment is best to use will depend upon the situation. In this book, I will always explain every line of code explicitly but you will often find liberally sprinkled comments within the code itself that add further explanation, insight or clarification. So it's always a good idea to read all of the code:

```
/*
The winning lottery numbers for next Saturday are
9,7,12,34,29,22
But you still want to learn Java? Right?
*/
```

 All the best Java programmers liberally sprinkle their code with comments.

Storing data and using it with variables

We can think of a variable as a labeled storage box. They are also like a programmer's window to the memory of the Android device, or whatever device we are programming. Variables can store data in memory (the storage box), ready to be recalled or altered when necessary by using the appropriate label.

Computer memory has a highly complex system of addressing that we, fortunately, do not need to interact with in Java. Java variables allow us to make up convenient names for all the data that we want our program to work with; the JVM will handle all the technicalities that interact with the operating system, which in turn, probably through several layers of buck passing, will interact with the hardware.

So we can think of our Android device's memory as a huge warehouse. When we assign names to our variables, they are stored in the warehouse, ready when we need them. When we use our variable's name, the device knows exactly what we are referring to. We can then tell it to do things such as "get box A and add it to box C, delete box B," and so on.

In a game, we will likely have a variable named as something along the lines of `score`. It would be this `score` variable that we use to manage anything related to the user's score, such as adding to it, subtracting or perhaps just showing it to the player.

Some of the following situations that might arise:

- The player gets a question right, so add 10 to their existing `score`
- The player views their stats screen, so print `score` on the screen
- The player gets the best score ever, so make `hiScore` the same as their current `score`

These are fairly arbitrary examples of names for variables and as long as you don't use any of the characters keywords that Java restricts, you can actually call your variables whatever you like. However, in practice, it is best to adopt a naming convention so that your variable names will be consistent. In this book, we will use a loose convention of variable names starting with a lowercase letter. When there is more than one word in the variable's name, the second word will begin with an uppercase letter. This is called "camel casing."

Here are some examples of camel casing:

- `score`
- `hiScore`
- `playersPersonalBest`

Before we look at some real Java code with some variables, we need to first look at the types of variables we can create and use.

Types of variables

It is not hard to imagine that even a simple game will probably have quite a few variables. In the previous section, we introduced the `hiScore` variable as an example. What if the game has a high score table that remembers the names of the top 10 players? Then we might need variables for each player.

And what about the case when a game needs to know if a playable character is dead or alive, or perhaps has any lives/retries left? We might need code that tests for life and then ends the game with a nice blood spurt animation if the playable character is dead.

Another common requirement in a computer program, including games, is the right or wrong calculation: true or false.

To cover these and many other types of information you might want to keep track of, Java has **types**. There are many types of variables and, as we will see in *Chapter 6, OOP – Using Other People's Hard Work*, we can also invent our own types or use other people's types. But for now, we will look at the built-in Java types. To be fair, they cover just about every situation we are likely to run into for a while. Some examples are the best way to explain this type of stuff.

We have already discussed the hypothetical but highly likely score variable. The variable score is likely to be a number, so we have to convey this (that the score is a number) to the Java compiler by giving the score an appropriate type. The hypothetical but equally likely playerName will, of course, hold the characters that make up the player's name. Jumping ahead a couple of paragraphs, the type that holds a regular number is called int, and the type that holds name-like data is called String. And if we try and store a player name, perhaps "Ada Lovelace" in score, which is meant for numbers, we will certainly run into trouble.

The compiler says no! Actually, the error would say this:

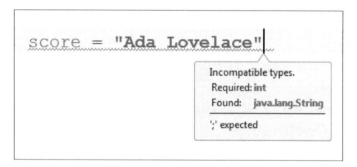

As we can see, Java was designed to make it impossible for such errors to make it to a running program. Did you also spot in the previous screenshot that I had forgotten the semicolon at the end of the line? With this compiler identifying our errors, what could possibly go wrong?

Here are the main types in Java. Later, we will see how to start using them:

- int: This type is used to store integers. It uses 32 pieces (**bits**) of memory and can therefore store values with a magnitude a little in excess of 2 billion, including negative values.

- long: As the name hints at, this data type can be used when even larger numbers are required. A long data type uses 64 bits of memory and 2 to the power of 63 is what we can store in this type. If you want to see what that looks like, try this: 9,223,372,036,854,775,807. Perhaps surprisingly, there are uses for long variables but if a smaller variable will do, we should use it so that our program uses less memory.

You might be wondering when you might use numbers of this magnitude. The obvious examples would be math or science applications that do complex calculations but another use might be for timing. When you time how long something takes, the Java Date class uses the number of milliseconds since January 1, 1970. The long data type could be useful to subtract a start time from an end time to determine an elapsed time. We will use long in *Chapter 5, Gaming and Java Essentials*.

- float: This is for floating-point numbers, that is, numbers where there is precision beyond the decimal point. As the fractional part of a number takes memory space just as the whole number portion, the range of numbers possible in a float is therefore decreased compared to non-floating-point numbers. So, unless our variable will definitely use the extra precision, float would not be our data type of choice.

- double: When the precision in float is not enough we have double.

- short: When even an int data type is overkill, the super-skinny short fits into the tiniest of storage boxes, but we can only store around 64,000 values, from -32,768 to 32,767.

- byte: This is an even smaller storage box than a short type. There is plenty of room for these in memory but a byte can only store values from -128 to 127.

- boolean: We will be using plenty of Booleans throughout the book. A Boolean variable can be either true or false—nothing else. Perhaps Booleans answer questions such as:

  - Is the player alive?

  - Has a new high score been reached?

  - Are two examples for a Boolean variable enough?

- char: This stores a single alphanumeric character. It's not going to change anything on its own but it could be useful if we put lots of them together.

I have kept this discussion of data types to a practical level that is useful in the context of this book. If you are interested in how a data type's value is stored and why the limits are what they are, visit the Oracle Java tutorials site at http://docs.oracle.com/javase/tutorial/java/nutsandbolts/datatypes.html. Note that you do not need any more information than we have already discussed to continue with this book.

As we just learned, each type of data that we might want to store will require a specific amount of memory. So we must let the Java compiler know the type of the variable before we begin to use it.

The preceding variables are known as the **primitive** types. They use predefined amounts of memory and so, using our storage analogy, fit into predefined sizes of the storage box.

As the "primitive" label suggests, they are not as sophisticated as the reference types.

Reference types

You might have noticed that we didn't cover the `String` variable type that we previously used to introduce the concept of variables.

Strings are a special type of variable known as a reference type. They quite simply refer to a place in memory where the storage of the variable begins, but the reference type itself does not define a specific amount of memory. The reason for this is fairly straightforward: we don't always know how much data will need to be stored until the program is actually run.

We can think of strings and other reference types as continually expanding and contracting storage boxes. So won't one of these `String` reference types bump into another variable eventually? If you think about the devices memory as a huge warehouse full of racks of labeled storage boxes, then you can think of the Dalvik virtual machine as a super-efficient forklift truck driver that puts the different types of storage boxes in the most appropriate place.

And if it becomes necessary, the virtual machine will quickly move stuff around in a fraction of a second to avoid collisions. It will even incinerate unwanted storage boxes when appropriate. This happens at the same time as constantly unloading new storage boxes of all types and placing them in the best place, for that type of variable. Dalvik tends to keep reference variables in a part of the warehouse that is different from the part for the primitive variables, and we will learn more details about this in *Chapter 6, OOP – Using Other People's Hard Work*.

So strings can be used to store any keyboard character, like a `char` data type but of almost any length. Anything from a player's name to an entire book can be stored in a single string. We will be using strings regularly including in this chapter.

There are a couple more reference types we will explore. Arrays are a way to store lots of variables of the same type, ready for quick and efficient access. We will look at arrays in *Chapter 5, Gaming and Java Essentials*.

Think of an array as an aisle in our warehouse with all the variables of a certain type lined up in a precise order. Arrays are reference types, so Dalvik keeps these in the same part of the warehouse as strings.

The other reference type is the mysterious object or class that we will look at in *Chapter 6, OOP – Using Other People's Hard Work*.

So we know that each type of data that we might want to store will require an amount of memory. Hence, we must let the Java compiler know the type of the variable before we begin to use it.

Declaration

That's enough of theory. Let's see how we would actually use our variables and types. Remember that each primitive type requires a specific amount of real device memory. This is one of the reasons that the compiler needs to know what type a variable will be of. So we must first **declare** a variable and its type before we attempt to do anything with it.

To declare a variable of type int with the name score, we would type:

```
int score;
```

That's it! Simply state the type, in this case int, then leave a space, and type the name you want to use for this variable. Also note the semicolon on the end of the line as usual to show the compiler that we are done with this line and what follows, if anything, is not part of the declaration.

For almost all the other variable types, declaration would occur in the same way. Here are some examples. The variable names are arbitrary. This is like reserving a labeled storage box in the warehouse:

```
long millisecondsElapsed;
float gravity;
double accurateGravity;
boolean isAlive;
char playerInitial;
String playerName;
```

Initialization

Here, for each type, we initialize a value to the variable. Think about placing a value inside the storage box, as shown in the following code:

```
score = 0;
millisecondsElapsed = 1406879842000;//1st Aug 2014 08:57:22
```

```
gravity = 1.256;
double accurateGravity =1.256098;
isAlive = true;
playerInitial = 'C';
playerName = "Charles Babbage";
```

Notice that the `char` variable uses single quotes (`'`) around the initialized value while the `String` uses double quotes (`"`).

We can also combine the declaration and initialization steps. In the following snippet of code, we declare and initialize the same variables as we did previously, but in one step each:

```
int score = 0;
long millisecondsElapsed = 1406879842000;//1st Aug 2014 08:57:22
float gravity = 1.256;
double accurateGravity =1.256098;
boolean isAlive = true;
char playerInitial = 'C';
String playerName = "Charles Babbage";
```

Whether we declare and initialize separately or together is probably dependent upon the specific situation. The important thing is that we must do both:

```
int a;

//The line below attempts to output a to the console
Log.i("info", "int a = " + a);
```

The preceding code would cause the following result:

```
Compiler Error: Variable a might not have been
initialized
```

There is a significant exception to this rule. Under certain circumstances variables can have **default values**. We will see this in *Chapter 6, OOP – Using Other People's Hard Work*. But it is good practice to both declare and initialize variables.

Changing variables with operators

Of course, in almost any program, we are going to need to do something with these values. Here is a list of perhaps the most common Java operators that allow us to manipulate variables. You do not need to memorize them as we will look at every line of code when we use them for the first time:

- **The assignment operator (=)**: This makes the variable to the left of the operator the same as the value to the right. For example, `hiScore = score;` or `score = 100;`.

- **The addition operator (+)**: This adds the values on either side of the operator. It is usually used in conjunction with the assignment operator, such as `score = aliensShot + wavesCleared;` or `score = score + 100;`. Notice that it is perfectly acceptable to use the same variable simultaneously on both sides of an operator.

- **The subtraction operator (-)**: This subtracts the value on the right side of the operator from the value on the left. It is usually used in conjunction with the assignment operator, such as `lives = lives - 1;` or `balance = income - outgoings;`.

- **The division operator (/)**: This divides the number on the left by the number on the right. Again, it is usually used in conjunction with the assignment operator, as shown in `fairShare = numSweets / numChildren;` or `recycledValueOfBlock = originalValue / .9;`.

- **The multiplication operator (*)**: This multiplies variables and numbers, such as `answer = 10 * 10;` or `biggerAnswer = 10 * 10 * 10;`.

- **The increment operator (++)**: This is a really neat way to add 1 to the value of a variable. The `myVariable = myVariable + 1;` statement is the same as `myVariable++;`.

- **The decrement operator (--)**: You guessed it: a really neat way to subtract 1 from something. The `myVariable = myVariable -1;` statement is the same as `myVariable--;`.

> The formal names for these operators are slightly different from the names used here for explanation. For example, the division operator is actually one of the multiplicative operators. But the preceding names are far more useful for the purpose of learning Java and if you used the term "division operator", while conversing with someone from the Java community, they would know exactly what you mean.

There are actually many more operators than these in Java. We will see a whole bunch later in this chapter when we learn about decisions in Java.

> If you are curious about operators there is a complete list of them on the Java website at http://docs.oracle.com/javase/tutorial/java/nutsandbolts/operators.html. All the operators required to complete the projects in this book will be fully explained in this book. The link is provided for the curious among us.

Expressing yourself in Java

Let's try using some declarations, assignments and operators. When we bundle these elements together into some meaningful syntax, we call it an expression. So let's write a quick app to try some out.

Here we will make a little side project so we can play with everything we have learned so far. We will need to create a new project, just as we did in the previous chapter but we will not need a UI this time.

Instead, we will simply write some Java code and examine its effects by outputting the values of variables to the Android console, called **logcat**. We will see exactly how this works by building the simple project and examining the code and the console output:

> The following is a quick reminder of how to create a new project.

1. Close any currently open projects by navigating to **File | Close Project**.

2. Click on **Start a new Android Studio project**.

3. The **Create New Project** configuration window will appear. Fill in the **Application name** field and **Company Domain** with packtpub.com or you could use your own company website name here instead.

4. Now click on the **Next** button. On the next screen, make sure the **Phone and Tablet** checkbox has a tick in it. Now we have to choose the earliest version of Android we want to build our app for. Go ahead and play with a few options in the drop-down selector. You will see that the earlier the version we select, the greater is the percentage of devices our app can support. However, the trade-off here is that the earlier the version we select fewer cutting-edge Android features will be available in our apps. A good balance is to select **API 8: Android 2.2 (Froyo)**.

5. Click on **Next**. Now select **Blank Activity** and click on **Next** again.

6. On the next screen, simply change **Activity Name** to MainActivity and click on **Finish**.

7. As we did in *Chapter 2, Getting Started with Android*, to keep our code clear and simple, you can delete the two unneeded methods (onCreateOptionsMenu and onOptionsItemSelected) and their associated @override and @import statements. However, this is not necessary for the example to work.

 For a detailed explanation and images of creating a new project, see *Chapter 2, Getting Started with Android*.

As with all the examples and projects in this book, you can copy or review the code from the download bundle. You will find the code for this tutorial in the Chapter3/ExpressionsInJava/MainActivity.java file. Just create the project as described previously and paste the code from MainActivity.java file from the download bundle to the MainActivity.java file that was generated when you created the project in Android Studio. Just ensure that the package name is the same as the one you chose when the project was created. However, I strongly recommend going along with the tutorial so that we can learn how to do everything for ourselves.

 As this app uses the logcat console to show its output, you should run this app on the emulator only and not on a real Android device. The app will not harm a real device, but you just won't be able to see anything happening.

1. Create a new blank project called Expressions In Java.

2. Now, in the onCreate method just after the line where we use the setContentView method, add this code to declare and initialize some variables:

```
//first we declare and initialize a few variables
int a = 10;
String b = "Alan Turing";
boolean c = true;
```

3. Now add the following code. This code simply outputs the value of our variables in a form where we can closely examine them in a minute:

```
//Let's look at how Android 'sees' these variables
//by outputting them, one at a time to the console
Log.i("info", "a = " + a);
Log.i("info", "b = " + b);
Log.i("info", "c = " + c);
```

4. Now let's change our variables using the addition operator and another new operator. See if you can work out the output values for variables a, b, and c before looking at the output and the code explanation:

```
//Now let's make some changes
a++;
a = a + 10;
b = b + " was smarter than the average bear Booboo";
b = b + a;
c = (1 + 1 == 3);//1 + 1 is definitely 2! So false.
```

5. Let's output the values once more in the same way we did in step 3, but this time, the output should be different:

```
//Now to output them all again
Log.i("info", "a = " + a);
Log.i("info", "b = " + b);
Log.i("info", "c = " + c);
```

6. Run the program on an emulator in the usual way. You can see the output by clicking on the **Android** tab from our "useful tabs" area below the Project Explorer.

Here is the output, with some of the unnecessary formatting stripped off:

```
info: a = 10
info: b = Alan Turing
info: c = true
info: a = 21
info: b = Alan Turing was smarter than the average bear Booboo21
info: c = false
```

Now let's discuss what happened. In step 2, we declared and initialized three variables:

- a: This is an int that holds the value 10
- b: This is a string that holds the name of an eminent computer scientist.
- c: This is a Boolean that holds the value false

So when we output the values in step 3, it should be no surprise that we get the following:

```
info: a = 10
info: b = Alan Turing
info: c = true
```

In step 4, all the fun stuff happens. We add 1 to the value of our int a using the increment operator like this: a++;. Remember that a++ is the same as a = a + 1.

We then add 10 to a. Note we are adding 10 to a after having already added 1. So we get this output for a 10 + 1 + 10 operation:

```
info: a = 21
```

Now let's examine our string, b. We appear to be using the addition operator on our eminent scientist. What is happening is what you could probably guess. We are adding together two strings "Alan Turing" and "was smarter than the average bear Booboo." When you add two strings together it is called **concatenating** and the + symbol doubles as the concatenation operator.

Finally, for our string, we appear to be adding int a to it. This is allowed and the value of a is concatenated to the end of b.

```
info: b = Alan Turing was smarter than the average bear Booboo21
```

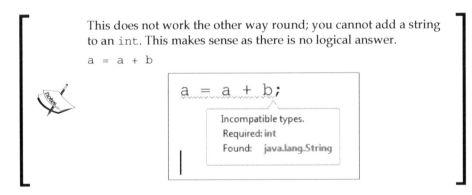

This does not work the other way round; you cannot add a string to an int. This makes sense as there is no logical answer.

```
a = a + b
```

```
a = a + b;
```
Incompatible types.
Required: int
Found: java.lang.String

Finally, let's look at the code that changes our Boolean, c, from true to false: c = (1+1=3) ;. Here, we are assigning to c the value of the expression contained within the brackets. This would be straightforward, but why the double equals (==)? We have jumped ahead of ourselves a little. The double equals sign is another operator called the **comparison** operator.

So we are really asking, *does* 1+1 equal 3? Clearly the answer is false. You might ask, "why use == instead of =?" Simply to make it clear to the compiler when we mean to assign and when we mean to compare.

Inadvertently using = instead of == is a very common error.

The assignment operator (=) assigns the value on the right to the value on the left, while the comparison operator (==) compares the values on either side.

The compiler will warn us with an error when we do this but at first glance you might swear the compiler is wrong. We will learn more on this comparison operator and others later in the chapter and throughout the book.

Now let's use everything we know and a bit more to make our math game project.

Math game – asking a question

Now that we have all that knowledge under our belts, we can use it to improve our math game. First, we will create a new Android activity to be the actual game screen as opposed to the start menu screen. We will then use the UI designer to lay out a simple game screen so that we can use our Java skills with variables, types, declaration, initialization, operators, and expressions to make our math game generate a question for the player. We can then link the start menu and game screens together with a push button.

If you want to save typing and just review the finished project, you can use the code downloaded from the Packt Publishing website. If you have any trouble getting any of the code to work, you can review, compare, or copy and paste the code from the already completed code provided in the download bundle.

The completed code is in the following files that correspond to the filenames we will be using in this tutorial:

- Chapter3/MathGameChapter3a/java/MainActivity.java
- Chapter3/MathGameChapter3a/java/GameActivity.java
- Chapter3/MathGameChapter3a/layout/activity_main.xml
- Chapter3/MathGameChapter3a/layout/activity_game.xml

As usual, I recommend following this tutorial to see how we can create all of the code for ourselves.

Creating the new game activity

We will first need to create a new Java file for the game activity code and a related layout file to hold the game activity UI.

1. Run Android Studio and select your `Math Game Chapter 2` project that we built in *Chapter 2, Getting Started with Android*. It might have been opened by default. Now we will create the new Android activity that will contain the actual game screen, which will run when the player taps the **Play** button on our main menu screen.

2. To create a new activity, we now need another layout file and another Java file. Fortunately Android Studio will help us do this. To get started with creating all the files we need for a new activity, right-click on the `src` folder in the Project Explorer and then go to **New | Activity**. Now click on **Blank Activity** and then on **Next**.

3. We now need to tell Android Studio a little bit about our new activity by entering information in the above dialog box. Change the **Activity Name** field to `GameActivity`. Notice how the **Layout Name** field is automatically changed for us to `activity_game` and the **Title** field is automatically changed to `GameActivity`.

4. Click on **Finish**. Android Studio has created two files for us and has also registered our new activity in a manifest file, so we don't need to concern ourselves with it.

5. If you look at the tabs at the top of the editor window, you will see that `GameActivity.java` has been opened up ready for us to edit, as shown in the following screenshot:

6. Ensure that `GameActivity.java` is active in the editor window by clicking on the **GameActivity.java** tab shown previously.

7. Back in *Chapter 2, Getting Started with Android*, we talked about how Android overrides some methods for us by default, and that most of them were not necessary. Here again, we can see the code that is unnecessary. If we remove it, then it will make our working environment simpler and cleaner. You might also remember from *Chapter 2, Getting Started with Android*, that the process of deleting and amending sections of code, although not complex, is a fairly long process. To avoid this here, we will simply use the code from `MainActivity.java` as a template for `GameActivity.java`. We can then make some minor changes.

8. Click on the **MainActivity.java** tab in the editor window. Highlight all of the code in the editor window using *Ctrl + A* on the keyboard.

9. Now copy all of the code in the editor window using the *Ctrl + C* on the keyboard.

10. Now click on the **GameActivity.java** tab.

11. Highlight all of the code in the editor window using *Ctrl + A* on the keyboard.

12. Now paste the copied code and overwrite the currently highlighted code using *Ctrl + V* on the keyboard.

13. Notice that there is an error in our code denoted by the red underlining as shown in the following screenshot. This is because we pasted the code referring to `MainActivity` in our file that is called `GameActivity`.

```
package com.packtpub.mathgamechapter2a.mathgamechapter2a;

import ...


public class MainActivity extends Activity {

    @Override
    protected void onCreate(Bundle savedInstanceState) {
        super.onCreate(savedInstanceState);
        setContentView(R.layout.activity_main);
    }

}
```

Simply change the text **MainActivity** to **GameActivity** and the error will disappear. Take a moment to see if you can work out what other minor change is necessary, before I tell you.

14. Remember that `setContentView` loads our UI design. Well what we need to do is change `setContentView` to load the new design (that we will build next) instead of the home screen design. Change `setContentView(R.layout.activity_main);` to `setContentView(R.layout.activity_game);`.

15. Save your work and we are ready to move on.

Note the Project Explorer where Android Studio puts the two new files it created for us. I have highlighted two folders in the next screenshot. In future, I will simply refer to them as our `java` code folder or `layout` files folder.

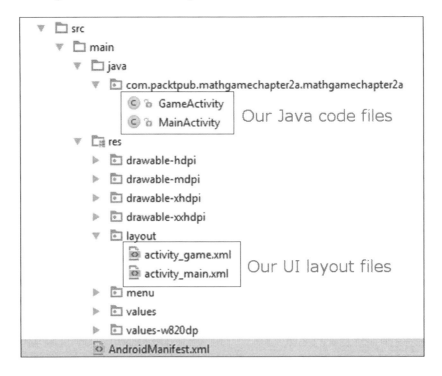

You might wonder why we didn't simply copy and paste the `MainActivity.java` file to begin with and saved going through the process of creating a new activity? The reason is that Android Studio does things behind the scenes. Firstly, it makes the layout template for us. It also registers the new activity for use through a file we will see later, called `AndroidManifest.xml`. This is necessary for the new activity to be able to work in the first place. All things considered, the way we did it is probably the quickest.

The code at this stage is exactly the same as the code for the home menu screen. We state the package name and import some useful classes provided by Android:

```
package com.packtpub.mathgamechapter3a.mathgamechapter3a;
```

```
import android.app.Activity;
import android.os.Bundle;
```

We create a new activity, this time called `GameActivity`:

```
public class GameActivity extends Activity {
```

Then we override the `onCreate` method and use the `setContentView` method to set our UI design as the contents of the player's screen. Currently, however, this UI is empty:

```
super.onCreate(savedInstanceState);
setContentView(R.layout.activity_main);
```

We can now think about the layout of our actual game screen.

Laying out the game screen UI

As we know, our math game will ask questions and offer the player some multiple choices to choose answers from. There are lots of extra features we could add, such as difficulty levels, high scores, and much more. But for now, let's just stick to asking a simple, predefined question and offering a choice of three predefined possible answers.

Keeping the UI design to the bare minimum suggests a layout. Our target UI will look somewhat like this:

The layout is hopefully self-explanatory, but let's ensure that we are really clear; when we come to building this layout in Android Studio, the section in the mock-up that displays **2 x 2** is the question and will be made up of three text views (both numbers, and the = sign is also a separate view). Finally, the three options for the answer are made up of **Button** layout elements. We used all of these UI elements in the previous chapter, but this time, as we are going to be controlling them using our Java code, there are a few extra things we need to do to them. So let's go through it step by step:

1. Open the file that will hold our game UI in the editor window. Do this by double-clicking on `activity_game.xml`. This is located in our UI `layout` folder, which can be found in the project explorer.

2. Delete the **Hello World** TextView, as it is not required.

3. Find the **Large Text** element on the palette. It can be found under the **Widgets** section. Drag three elements onto the UI design area and arrange them near the top of the design as shown in the next screenshot. It does not have to be exact; just ensure that they are in a row and not overlapping, as shown in the following screenshot:

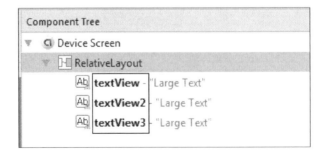

4. Notice in the **Component Tree** window that each of the three TextViews has been assigned a name automatically by Android Studio. They are **textView**, **textView2**, and **textView3**:

5. Android Studio refers to these element names as an **id**. This is an important concept that we will be making use of. So to confirm this, select any one of the textViews by clicking on its name (id), either in the component tree as shown in the preceding screenshot or directly on it in the UI designer shown previously. Now look at the **Properties** window and find the **id** property. You might need to scroll a little to do this:

Notice that the value for the **id** property is **textView**. It is this id that we will use to interact with our UI from our Java code. So we want to change all the IDs of our TextViews to something useful and easy to remember.

6. If you look back at our design, you will see that the UI element with the **textView** id is going to hold the number for the first part of our math question. So change the id to textPartA. Notice the lowercase t in text, the uppercase P in Part, and the uppercase A. You can use any combination of cases and you can actually name the IDs anything you like. But just as with naming conventions with Java variables, sticking to conventions here will make things less error-prone as our program gets more complicated.

7. Now select **textView2** and change **id** to textOperator.

8. Select the element currently with id **textView3** and change it to textPartB. This TextView will hold the later part of our question.

9. Now add another **Large Text** from the palette. Place it after the row of the three TextViews that we have just been editing.

   This **Large Text** will simply hold our equals to sign and there is no plan to ever change it. So we don't need to interact with it in our Java code. We don't even need to concern ourselves with changing the ID or knowing what it is. If this situation changed, we could always come back at a later time and edit its ID.

10. However, this new TextView currently displays **Large Text** and we want it to display an equals to sign. So in the **Properties** window, find the **text** property and enter the value =. We have changed the **text** property before in *Chapter 2, Getting Started with Android*, and you might also like to change the text property for textPartA, textPartB, and textOperator. This is not absolutely essential because we will soon see how we can change it via our Java code; however, if we change the **text** property to something more appropriate, then our UI designer will look more like it will when the game runs on a real device.

11. So change the text property of **textPartA** to 2, **textPartB** to 2, and **textOperator** to x. Your UI design and Component tree should now look like this:

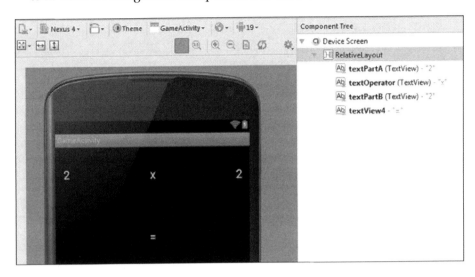

12. For the buttons to contain our multiple choice answers, drag three buttons in a row, below the = sign. Line them up neatly like our target design.

13. Now, just as we did for the TextViews, find the **id** properties of each button, and from left to right, change the **id** properties to buttonChoice1, buttonChoice2, and buttonChoice3.

14. Why not enter some arbitrary numbers for the **text** property of each button so that the designer more accurately reflects what our game will look like, just as we did for our other TextViews? Again, this is not absolutely essential as our Java code will control the button appearance.

15. We are now actually ready to move on. But you probably agree that the UI elements look a little lost. It would look better if the buttons and text were bigger. All we need to do is adjust the textSize property for each TextView and for each Button. Then, we just need to find the textSize property for each element and enter a number with the sp syntax. If you want your design to look just like our target design from earlier, enter 70sp for each of the TextView textSize properties and 40sp for each of the Buttons textSize properties. When you run the game on your real device, you might want to come back and adjust the sizes up or down a bit. But we have a bit more to do before we can actually try out our game.

16. Save the project and then we can move on.

As before, we have built our UI. This time, however, we have given all the important parts of our UI a unique, useful, and easy to identify ID. As we will see we are now able to communicate with our UI through our Java code.

Coding a question in Java

With our current knowledge of Java, we are not yet able to complete our math game but we can make a significant start. We will look at how we can ask the player a question and offer them some multiple choice answers (one correct and two incorrect).

At this stage, we know enough of Java to declare and initialize some variables that will hold the parts of our question. For example, if we want to ask the times tables question *2 x 2*, we could have the following variable initializations to hold the values for each part of the question:

```
int partA = 2;
int partB = 2;
```

The preceding code declares and initializes two variables of the `int` type, each to the value of 2. We use `int` because we will not be dealing with any decimal fractions. Remember that the variable names are arbitrary and were just chosen because they seemed appropriate. Clearly, any math game worth downloading is going to need to ask more varied and advanced questions than *2 x 2*, but it is a start.

Now we know that our math game will offer multiple choices as answers. So, we need a variable for the correct answer and two variables for two incorrect answers. Take a look at these combined declarations and initializations:

```
int correctAnswer = partA * partB;
int wrongAnswer1 = correctAnswer - 1;
int wrongAnswer2 = correctAnswer + 1;
```

Note that the initialization of the variables for the wrong answers depends on the value of the correct answer, and the variables for the wrong answers are initialized after initializing the `correctAnswer` variable.

Now we need to put these values, held in our variables, into the appropriate elements on our UI. The question variables (partA and partB) need to be displayed in our UI elements, textPartA and textPartB, and the answer variables (correctAnswer, wrongAnswer1, and wrongAnswer2) need to be displayed in our UI elements with the following IDs: buttonChoice1, buttonChoice2, and buttonChoice3. We will see how we do this in the next step-by-step tutorial. We will also implement the variable declaration and initialization code that we discussed a moment ago:

1. First, open GameActivity.java in the editor window. Remember that you can do this by double-clicking on **GameActivity** in our java folder or clicking on its tab above the editor window if GameActivity.java is already open.

2. All of our code will go into the onCreate method. It will go after the setContentView(R.layout.activity_game); line but before the closing curly brace } of the onCreate method. Perhaps, it's a good idea to leave a blank line for clarity and a nice explanatory comment as shown in the following code. We can see the entire onCreate method as it stands after the latest amendments. The parts in bold are what you need to add. Feel free to add helpful comments like mine if you wish:

```java
@Override
    protected void onCreate(Bundle savedInstanceState) {
        super.onCreate(savedInstanceState);
        //The next line loads our UI design to the screen
        setContentView(R.layout.activity_game);

        //Here we initialize all our variables
        int partA = 9;
        int partB = 9;
        int correctAnswer = partA * partB;
        int wrongAnswer1 = correctAnswer - 1;
        int wrongAnswer2 = correctAnswer + 1;

    }//onCreate ends here
```

3. Now we need to add the values contained within the variables to the TextView and Button of our UI. But first, we need to get access to the UI elements we created. We do that by creating a variable of the appropriate class and linking it via the ID property of the appropriate UI element. We already know the class of our UI elements: TextView and Button. Here is the code that creates our special class variables for each of the necessary UI elements. Take a close look at the code, but don't worry if you don't understand all of it now. We will dissect the code in detail once everything is working. Enter the code immediately after the code entered in the previous step. You can leave a blank line for clarity if you wish. Just before you proceed, note that at two points while typing in this code, you will be prompted to import another class. Go ahead and do so on both occasions:

```
/*Here we get a working object based on either the button
or TextView class and base as well as link our new objects
directly to the appropriate UI elements that we created
previously*/

TextView textObjectPartA =
   (TextView)findViewById(R.id.textPartA);

TextView textObjectPartB =
   (TextView)findViewById(R.id.textPartB);

Button buttonObjectChoice1 =
   (Button)findViewById(R.id.buttonChoice1);

Button buttonObjectChoice2 =
   (Button)findViewById(R.id.buttonChoice2);

Button buttonObjectChoice3 =
   (Button)findViewById(R.id.buttonChoice3);
```

In the preceding code, if you read the multiline comment, you will see that I used the term **object**. When we create a variable type based on a class, we call it an object. Once we have an object of a class, we can do anything that that class was designed to do. This is very powerful and is explored thoroughly in *Chapter 6, OOP – Using Other People's Hard Work*.

4. Now we have five new objects linked to the elements of our UI that we need to manipulate. What precisely are we going to do with them? We need to display the values of our variables in the text of the UI elements. We can use the objects we just created combined with a method provided by the class, and use our variables as values for that text. As usual, we will dissect this code further at the end of this tutorial. Here is the code to enter directly after the code in the previous step. Try and work out what is going on before we look at it together:

```
//Now we use the setText method of the class on our objects
//to show our variable values on the UI elements.
//Just like when we output to the console in the exercise -
//Expressions in Java, only now we use setText method
//to put the values in our variables onto the actual UI.
textObjectPartA.setText("" + partA);
textObjectPartB.setText("" + partB);

//which button receives which answer, at this stage is arbitrary.

buttonObjectChoice1.setText("" + correctAnswer);
buttonObjectChoice2.setText("" + wrongAnswer1);
buttonObjectChoice3.setText("" + wrongAnswer2);
```

5. Save your work.

If you play with the assignment values for partA and partB, you can make them whatever you like and the game adjusts the answers accordingly. Obviously, we shouldn't need to reprogram our game each time we want a new question and we will solve that problem soon. All we need to do now is link the game section we have just made to the start screen menu. We will do that in the next tutorial.

Now let's explore the trickier and newer parts of our code in more detail.

In step 2, we declared and initialized the variables required so far:

```
//Here we initialize all our variables
int partA = 2;
int partB = 2;
int correctAnswer = partA * partB;
int wrongAnswer1 = correctAnswer - 1;
int wrongAnswer2 = correctAnswer + 1;
```

Then in step 3, we got a reference to our UI design through our Java code. For the TextViews, it was done like this:

```
TextView textObjectPartA = (TextView)findViewById(R.id.textPartA);
```

For each of the buttons, a reference to our UI design was obtained like this:

```
Button buttonObjectChoice1 =
   Button) findViewById(R.id.buttonChoice1);
```

In step 4, we did something new. We used a the `setText` method to show the values of our variables on our UI elements (`TextView` and `Button`) to the player. Let's break down one line completely to see how it works. Here is the code that shows the `correctAnswer` variable being displayed on `buttonObjectChoice1`.

```
buttonObjectChoice1.setText("" + correctAnswer);
```

By typing `buttonObjectChoice1` and adding a period, as shown in the following line of code, we have access to all the preprogrammed methods of that object's class type that are provided by Android:

```
buttonObjectChoice1.
```

The power of Button and the Android API

There are actually lots of methods that we can perform on an object of the Button type. If you are feeling brave, try this to get a feeling of just how much functionality there is in Android.

Type the following code:

```
buttonObjectChoice1.
```

Be sure to type the period on the end. Android Studio will pop up a list of possible methods to use on this object. Scroll through the list and get a feel of the number and variety of options:

```
//to show our var     setBackgroundResource (int resid)        void
                      setBackground (Drawable background)       void
textObjectPartA.se    setText (char[] text, int start, int ... void
textObjectPartB.se    equals (Object o)                        boolean
                      setVisibility (int visibility)           void
//which button re     onInitializeAccessibilityEvent (Acces... void
                      onInitializeAccessibilityNodeInfo (Ac... void
buttonObjectChoice    addChildrenForAccessibility (ArrayLis... void
buttonObjectChoice    addFocusables (ArrayList<View> views,... void
buttonObjectChoice    addFocusables (ArrayList<View> views,... void

buttonObjectChoice1.
}//onCreate ends here
```

If a mere button can do all of this, think of the possibilities for our games once we have mastered all the classes contained in Android. A collection of classes designed to be used by others is collectively known as an **Application Programmers Interface (API)**. Welcome to the Android API!

In this case, we just want to set the button's text. So, we use `setText` and concatenate the value stored in our `correctAnswer` variable to the end of an empty string, like this:

```
setText("" + correctAnswer);
```

We do this for each of the UI elements we require to show our variables.

Playing with autocomplete

If you tried the previous tip, *The power of Button and the Android API*, and explored the methods available for objects of the Button type, you will already have some insight into autocomplete. Note that as you type, Android Studio is constantly making suggestions for what you might like to type next. If you pay attention to this, you can save a lot of time. Simply select the correct code completion statement that is suggested and press *Enter*. You can even see how much time you saved by selecting **Help | Productivity Guide** from the menu bar. Here you will see statistics for every aspect of code completion and more. Here are a few entries from mine:

Finish lookup even when non-focused	Code Completion	1,281 times
Basic code completion	Code Completion	1,847 times
Variable name completion	Code Completion	2,131 times

As you can see, if you get used to using shortcuts early on, you can save a lot of time in the long run.

Linking our game from the main menu

At the moment, if we run the app, we have no way for the player to actually arrive at our new game activity. We want the game activity to run when the player clicks on the **Play** button on the main `MainActivity` UI. Here is what we need to do to make that happen:

1. Open the file `activity_main.xml`, either by double-clicking on it in the Project Explorer or by clicking on its tab in the editor window.

2. Now, just like we did when building the game UI, assign an ID to the **Play** button. As a reminder, click on the **Play** button either on the UI design or in the component tree. Find the **id** property in the **Properties** window. Assign the `buttonPlay` value to it. We can now make this button do stuff by referring to it in our Java code.

3. Open the file `MainActivity.java`, either by double-clicking on it in the Project Explorer or clicking on its tab in the editor window.

4. In our `onCreate` method, just after the line where we `setContentView`, add the following highlighted line of code:

```
setContentView(R.layout.activity_main);
Button buttonPlay = (Button)findViewById(R.id.buttonPlay);
```

5. We will dissect this code in detail once we have got this working. Basically we are making a connection to the **Play** button by creating a reference variable to a `Button` object. Notice that both words are highlighted in red indicating an error. Just as before, we need to import the Button class to make this code work. Use the *Alt + Enter* keyboard combination. Now click on **Import class** from the popped-up list of options. This will automatically add the required import directive at the top of our `MainActivity.java` file.

6. Now for something new. We will give the button the ability to *listen* to the user clicking on it. Type this immediately after the last line of code we entered:

```
buttonPlay.setOnClickListener(this);
```

7. Notice how the `this` keyword is highlighted in red indicating an error. This introduces another Java feature that will be more thoroughly explored in *Chapter 6, OOP – Using Other People's Hard Work*. Setting that aside, we need to make a modification to our code now in order to allow the use of an interface that is a special code element that allows us to add a functionality, such as listening for button clicks. Edit the line as follows. When prompted to import another class, click on **OK**:

```
public class MainActivity extends Activity {
```

to

```
public class MainActivity extends Activity implements View.
    OnClickListener{
```

Now we have the entire line underlined in red. This indicates an error but it's where we should be at this point. We mentioned that by adding `implements View.OnClickListener`, we have implemented an interface. We can think of this like a class that we can use but with extra rules. The rules of the `OnClickListener` interface state that we *must* implement/use one of its methods. Notice that until now, we have optionally overridden/used methods as and when they have suited us. If we wish to use the functionality this interface provides, namely listening for button presses, then we have to add/implement the `onClick` method.

8. This is how we do it. Notice the opening curly brace, {, and the closing curly brace, }. These denote the start and end of the method. Notice that the method is empty and it doesn't do anything, but an empty method is enough to comply with the rules of the `OnClickListener` interface, and the red line indicating that our code has an error has gone. The syntax of these methods we have been using, as promised, will be explained in the next chapter when we start to write our own methods. Make sure that you type the following code, outside the closing curly brace (}) of the `onCreate` method but inside the closing curly brace of our `MainActivity` class:

```
@Override
    public void onClick(View view) {


    }
```

9. Notice that we have an empty line between { and } of the `onClick` method. We can now add code in here to make the button actually do something. Type the following highlighted code between { and } of `onClick`:

```
@Override
    public void onClick(View view) {
        Intent i;
        i = new Intent(this, GameActivity.class);
        startActivity(i);
    }
```

10. OK, so that code is a bit of a mouthful to comprehend all at once. See if you can guess what is happening. The clue is in the method named `startActivity` and the hopefully familiar term, `GameActivity`. Notice that we are assigning something to `i`. We will quickly get our app working and then diagnose the code in full. Its understanding will be complete when we explore how classes work in *Chapter 6, OOP – Using Other People's Hard Work*.

11. Notice that we have an error: all instances of the word `Intent` are red. We can solve this by importing the classes required to make `Intent` work. As before press *Alt + Enter*.

12. Run the game in the emulator or on your device.

Our app will now work. This is what the new game screen looks like after pressing **Play** on the menu screen:

Almost every part of our code has changed a little and we have added a lot to it as well. Let's go over the contents of MainActivity.java and look at it line by line. For context, here it is in full:

```
package com.packtpub.mathgamechapter3a.mathgamechapter3a;

import android.app.Activity;
import android.content.Intent;
import android.os.Bundle;
import android.view.View;
```

```
import android.widget.Button;


public class MainActivity extends Activity implements View.
    OnClickListener{

    @Override
    protected void onCreate(Bundle savedInstanceState) {
        super.onCreate(savedInstanceState);
        setContentView(R.layout.activity_main);
        final Button buttonPlay =
            (Button)findViewById(R.id.buttonPlay);
        buttonPlay.setOnClickListener(this);
    }

    @Override
    public void onClick(View view) {
        Intent i;
        i = new Intent(this, GameActivity.class);
        startActivity(i);
    }

}
```

We have seen much of this code before, but let's just go over it a chunk at a time before moving on so that it is absolutely clear. The code works like this:

```
package com.packtpub.mathgamechapter3a.mathgamechapter3a;

import android.app.Activity;
import android.content.Intent;
import android.os.Bundle;
import android.view.View;
import android.widget.Button;
```

You would probably remember that this first block of code defines what our package is called and makes available all the Android API stuff we need for Button, TextView, and Activity.

From our `MainActivity.java` file, we have this:

```
public class MainActivity extends Activity implements View.
    OnClickListener{
```

Our `MainActivity` declaration with our new bit of code implements `View`. `OnClickListener` that gives us the ability to detect button clicks.

Next in our code is this:

```
@Override
    protected void onCreate(Bundle savedInstanceState) {
        super.onCreate(savedInstanceState);
        setContentView(R.layout.activity_main);
```

This previous bit of code hasn't changed since *Chapter 2, Getting Started with Android*. It is at the start of our `onCreate` method where we first ask the hidden code of `onCreate` to do its stuff using `super.onCreate(savedInstanceState);`. Then we set our UI to the screen with `setContentView(R.layout.activity_main);`.

Next, we get a reference to our button with an ID of `buttonPlay`:

```
Button buttonPlay = (Button)findViewById(R.id.buttonPlay);
buttonPlay.setOnClickListener(this);
```

Finally, our `onClick` method uses the `Intent` class to send the player to our `GameActivity` class and the related UI when the user clicks on the **Play** button:

```
@Override
    public void onClick(View view) {
        Intent i;
        i = new Intent(this, GameActivity.class);
        startActivity(i);
    }
```

If you run the app, you will notice that we can now click on the **Play** button and our math game will ask us a question. Of course, we can't answer it yet. Although we have very briefly looked at how to deal with button presses, we need to learn more of Java in order to intelligently react to them. We will also reveal how to write code to handle presses from several buttons. This will be necessary to receive input from our multiple-choice-centric `game_activity` UI.

Decisions in Java

We can now summon enough of Java prowess to ask a question but a real math game must obviously do much more than this. We need to capture the player's answer, and we are nearly there with that—we can detect button presses. From there, we need to be able to **decide** whether their answer is right or wrong. Then, based on this decision, we have to **choose** an appropriate course of action.

Let's leave the math game aside for now and look at how Java might help us by learning some more fundamentals and syntax of the Java language.

More operators

Let's look at some more operators: we can already add (+), take away (-), multiply (*), divide (/), assign (=), increment (++), compare (==), and decrement (--) with operators. Let's introduce some more super-useful operators, and then we will go straight to actually understanding how to use them in Java.

Don't worry about memorizing every operator given here. Glance at them and their explanations and then move quickly on to the next section. There, we will put some operators to use and they will become much clearer as we see a few examples of what they allow us to do. They are presented here in a list just to make the variety and scope of operators plain from the start. The list will also be more convenient to refer back to when not intermingled with the discussion about implementation that follows it.

- ==: This is a comparison operator we saw this very briefly before. It tests for equality and is either true or false. An expression like (10 == 9);, for example, is false.

- !: The logical NOT operator. The expression, ! (2+2==5).), is true because 2+2 is NOT 5.

- !=: This is another comparison operator, which tests if something is NOT equal. For example, the expression, (10 != 9);), is true, that is, 10 is not equal to 9.

- >: This is another comparison operator, which tests if something is greater than something else. The expression, (10 > 9);), is true. There are a few more comparison operators as well.

- <: You guessed it. This tests whether the value to the left is less than the value to the right or not. The expression, (10 < 9);, is false.

- >=: This operator tests whether one value is greater than or equal to the other, and if either is true, the result is true. For example, the expression, (10 >= 9);, is true. The expression, (10 >= 10);, is also true.

- <=: Like the preceding operator, this operator tests for two conditions but this time, less than and equal to. The expression, (10 <= 9);, is false. The expression, (10 <= 10);, is true.

- &&: This operator is known as logical AND. It tests two or more separate parts of an expression and all parts must be true in order for the result to be true. Logical AND is usually used in conjunction with the other operators to build more complex tests. The expression, ((10 > 9) && (10 < 11));, is true because both parts are true. The expression, ((10 > 9) && (10 < 9));, is false because only one part of the expression is true and the other is false.

- | |: This operator is called logical OR. It is just like logical AND except that only one of two or more parts of an expression need to be true for the expression to be true. Let's look at the last example we used but replace the && sign with | |. The expression, `((10 > 9) || (10 < 9));`, is now true because one part of the expression is true.

All of these operators are virtually useless without a way of properly using them to make real decisions that affect real variables and code. Let's look at how to make decisions in Java.

Decision 1 – If they come over the bridge, shoot them

As we saw, operators serve hardly any purpose on their own but it was probably useful to see just a part of the wide and varied range available to us. Now, when we look at putting the most common operator, ==, to use, we can start to see the powerful yet fine control that operators offer us.

Let's make the previous examples less abstract using the Java `if` keyword and a few conditional operators with a fun story and some code.

The captain is dying and, knowing that his remaining subordinates are not very experienced, he decides to write a Java program to convey his last orders after he has died. The troops must hold one side of a bridge while awaiting reinforcements.

The first command the captain wants to make sure his troops understand is this: If they come over the bridge, shoot them.

So how do we simulate this situation in Java? We need a Boolean variable `isComingOverBridge`. The next bit of code assumes that the `isComingOverBridge` variable has been declared and initialized.

We can then use it like this:

```
if(isComingOverBridge){
  //Shoot them
}
```

If the `isComingOverBridge` Boolean is true, the code inside the opening and closing curly braces will run. If not, the program continues after the `if` block without running it.

Decision 2 – Else, do this

The captain also wants to tell his troops what to do (stay put) if the enemy is not coming over the bridge.

Now we introduce another Java keyword, `else`. When we want to explicitly do something and the `if` block does not evaluate to true, we can use `else`.

For example, to tell the troops to stay put if the enemy is not coming over the bridge, we use `else`:

```
if(isComingOverBridge){
  //Shoot them
}else{
  //Hold position
}
```

The captain then realized that the problem wasn't as simple as he first thought. What if the enemy comes over the bridge and has more troops? His squad will be overrun. So, he came up with this code (we'll use some variables as well this time):

```
boolean isComingOverTheBridge;
int enemyTroops;
int friendlyTroops;
//Code that initializes the above variables one way or another

//Now the if
if(isComingOverTheBridge && friendlyTroops > enemyTroops){
  //shoot them
}else if(isComingOverTheBridge && friendlyTroops < enemyTroops) {
  //blow the bridge
}else{
  //Hold position
}
```

Finally, the captain's last concern was that if the enemy came over the bridge waving the white flag of surrender and were promptly slaughtered, then his men would end up as war criminals. The Java code needed was obvious. Using the `wavingWhiteFlag` Boolean variable he wrote this test:

```
if (wavingWhiteFlag){
  //Take prisoners
}
```

But where to put this code was less clear. In the end, the captain opted for the following nested solution and changing the test for wavingWhiteFlag to logical NOT, like this:

```
if (!wavingWhiteFlag){//not surrendering so check everything else
  if(isComingOverTheBridge && friendlyTroops > enemyTroops){
    //shoot them
  }else if(isComingOverTheBridge && friendlyTroops <
      enemyTroops) {
    //blow the bridge
  }
}else{//this is the else for our first if
  //Take prisoners
{
//Holding position
```

This demonstrates that we can nest if and else statements inside of one another to create even deeper decisions.

We could go on making more and more complicated decisions but what we have seen is more than sufficient as an introduction. Take the time to reread this if anything is unclear. Who knows, there might even be a tricky logic question in the self-test at the end of the chapter. It is also important to point out that very often, there are two or more ways to arrive at the solution. The *right* way will usually be the way that solves the problem in the clearest and simplest manner.

Switching to make decisions

We have seen the vast and virtually limitless possibilities of combining the Java operators with if and else statements. But sometimes a decision in Java can be better made in other ways.

When we have to make a decision based on a clear list of possibilities that doesn't involve complex combinations, then **switch** is usually the way to go.

We start a switch decision like this:

```
switch(argument){

}
```

In the previous example, an argument could be an expression or a variable. Then within the curly braces, we can make decisions based on the argument with case and break elements:

```
case x:
   //code to for x
   break;

case y:
   //code for y
   break;
```

You can see that in the previous example, each case states a possible result and each break denotes the end of that case as well as the point at which no further case statements should be evaluated. The first break encountered takes us out of the switch block to proceed with the next line of code.

We can also use **default** without a value to run some code if none of the case statements evaluate to true, like this:

```
default://Look no value
   //Do something here if no other case statements are true
break;
```

Supposing we are writing an old-fashioned text adventure game—the kind of game where the player types commands such as "Go East", "Go West", "Take Sword", and so on. In this case, switch could handle that situation like this example code and we could use default to handle the case of the player typing a command that is not specifically handled:

```
//get input from user in a String variable called command
switch(command){

   case "Go East":":
   //code to go east
   break;

   case "Go West":
   //code to go west
   break;
   case "Take sword":
   //code to take the sword
```

```
    break;

    //more possible cases

    default:
    //Sorry I don't understand your command
    break;

}
```

In the next section, we will use `switch` so that our `onClick` method can handle the different multiple-choice buttons of our math game.

 Java has even more operators than we have covered here. We have looked at all the operators we are going to need in this book and probably the most used in general. If you want the complete lowdown on operators, take a look at the official Java documentation at `http://docs.oracle.com/javase/tutorial/java/nutsandbolts/operators.html`.

Math game – getting and checking the answer

Here we will detect the right or wrong answer and provide a pop-up message to the player. Our Java is getting quite good now, so let's dive in and add these features. I will explain things as we go and then, as usual, dissect the code thoroughly at the end.

The already completed code is in the download bundle, in the following files that correspond to the filenames we will create/autogenerate in Android Studio in a moment:

- `Chapter3/MathGameChapter3b/java/MainActivity.java`
- `Chapter3/MathGameChapter3b/java/GameActivity.java`
- `Chapter3/MathGameChapter3b/layout/activity_main.xml`
- `Chapter3/MathGameChapter3b/layout/activity_game.xml`

As usual, I recommend following this tutorial step by step to see how we can create all of the code for ourselves.

1. Open the `GameActivity.java` file visible in the editor window.

2. Now we need to add the click detection functionality to our `GameActivity`, just as we did for our `MainActivity`. However, we will go a little further than the last time. So let's do it step by step as if it is totally new. Once again, we will give the buttons the ability to *listen* to the user clicking on them. Type this immediately after the last line of code we entered in the `onCreate` method but before the closing `}`. This time of course, we need to add some code to listen to three buttons:

   ```
   buttonObjectChoice1.setOnClickListener(this);
   buttonObjectChoice2.setOnClickListener(this);
   buttonObjectChoice3.setOnClickListener(this);
   ```

3. Notice how the `this` keyword is highlighted in red indicating an error. Again, we need to make a modification to our code in order to allow the use of an interface, the special code element that allows us to add functionalities such as listening to button clicks. Edit the line as follows. When prompted to import another class, click on **OK**. Consider this line of code:

   ```
   public class GameActivity extends Activity {
   ```

   Change it to the following line:

   ```
   public class GameActivity extends Activity implements
       View.OnClickListener{
   ```

4. Now we have the entire preceding line underlined in red. This indicates an error but it is where we should be at this point. We mentioned that by adding `implements View.OnClickListener`, we have implemented an interface. We can think of this like a class that we can use, but with extra rules. One of the rules of the `OnClickListener` interface is that we must implement one of its methods, as you might remember. Now we will add the `onClick` method.

5. Type the following code. Notice the opening curly brace, {, and the closing curly brace, }. These denote the start and end of the method. Notice that the method is empty; it doesn't do anything but an empty method is enough to comply with the rules of the OnClickListener interface and the red line that indicated an error has gone. Make sure that you type the following code outside the closing curly brace (}) of the onCreate method but inside the closing curly brace of our MainActivity class:

```
@Override
    public void onClick(View view) {


    }
```

6. Notice that we have an empty line between the { and } braces of our onClick method. We can now put some code in here to make the buttons actually do something. Type the following in between { and } of onClick. This is where things get different from our code in MainActivity. We need to differentiate between the three possible buttons that could be pressed. We will do this with the switch statement that we discussed earlier. Look at the case criteria; they should look familiar. Here is the code that uses the switch statements:

```
switch (view.getId()) {

            case R.id.buttonChoice1:
            //button 1 stuff goes here
                break;

            case R.id.buttonChoice2:
            //button 2 stuff goes here
                break;

            case R.id.buttonChoice3:
            //button 3 stuff goes here
                break;

    }
```

7. Each `case` element handles a different button. For each button case, we need to get the value stored in the button that was just pressed and see if it matches our `correctAnswer` variable. If it does, we must tell the player they got it right, and if not, we must tell them they got it wrong. However, there is still one problem we have to solve. The `onClick` method is separate from the `onCreate` method and the Button objects. In fact, all the variables are declared in the `onCreate` method. If you try typing the code from step 9 now, you will get lots of errors. We need to make all the variables that we need in `onClick` available in `onClick`. To do this, we will move their declarations from above the `onCreate` method to just below the opening `{` of `GameActivity`. This means that these variables become variables of the `GameActivity` class and can be seen anywhere within `GameActivity`. Declare the following variables like this:

```
int correctAnswer;
Button buttonObjectChoice1;
Button buttonObjectChoice2;
Button buttonObjectChoice3;
```

8. Now change the initialization of these variables within `onCreate` as follows. The actual parts of code that need to be changed are highlighted. The rest is shown for context:

```
//Here we initialize all our variables
int partA = 9;
int partB = 9;
correctAnswer = partA * partB;
int wrongAnswer1 = correctAnswer - 1;
int wrongAnswer2 = correctAnswer + 1;
```

and

```
TextView textObjectPartA =
    (TextView)findViewById(R.id.textPartA);

TextView textObjectPartB =
    (TextView)findViewById(R.id.textPartB);

buttonObjectChoice1 = (Button)findViewById(R.id.buttonChoice1);

buttonObjectChoice2 = (Button)findViewById(R.id.buttonChoice2);

buttonObjectChoice3 = (Button)findViewById(R.id.buttonChoice3);
```

9. Here is the top of our `onClick` method as well as the first `case` statement for our `onClick` method:

```
@Override
    public void onClick(View view) {
        //declare a new int to be used in all the cases
        int answerGiven=0;
        switch (view.getId()) {

            case R.id.buttonChoice1:
            //initialize a new int with the value contained in
            buttonObjectChoice1
            //Remember we put it there ourselves previously
                answerGiven = Integer.parseInt("" +
                    buttonObjectChoice1.getText());

            //is it the right answer?
            if(answerGiven==correctAnswer) {//yay it's the
            right answer
                Toast.makeText(getApplicationContext(),
                    "Well done!",
                    Toast.LENGTH_LONG).show();
            }else{//uh oh!
                Toast.makeText(getApplicationContext(),"Sorry
                    that's wrong", Toast.LENGTH_LONG).show();

            }
            break;
```

10. Here are the rest of the `case` statements that do the same steps as the code in the previous step except handling the last two buttons. Enter the following code after the code entered in the previous step:

```
            case R.id.buttonChoice2:
                //same as previous case but using the next button
                answerGiven = Integer.parseInt("" +
                    buttonObjectChoice2.getText());
                if(answerGiven==correctAnswer) {
                    Toast.makeText(getApplicationContext(), "Well
                        done!", Toast.LENGTH_LONG).show();
                }else{
                    Toast.makeText(getApplicationContext(),"Sorry
                        that's wrong", Toast.LENGTH_LONG).show();
                }
                break;

            case R.id.buttonChoice3:
```

```
//same as previous case but using the next button
answerGiven = Integer.parseInt("" +
    buttonObjectChoice3.getText());
if(answerGiven==correctAnswer) {
    Toast.makeText(getApplicationContext(), "Well
        done!", Toast.LENGTH_LONG).show();
}else{
    Toast.makeText(getApplicationContext(),"Sorry
        that's wrong", Toast.LENGTH_LONG).show();
}
break;

}
```

11. Run the program, and then we will look at the code carefully, especially that odd-looking `Toast` thing. Here is what happens when we click on the leftmost button:

This is how we did it: In steps 1 through 6, we set up handling for our multi-choice buttons, including adding the ability to listen to clicks using the `onClick` method and a `switch` block to handle decisions depending on the button pressed.

In steps 7 and 8, we had to alter our code to make our variables available in the `onClick` method. We did this by making them member variables of our `GameActivity` class.

When we make a variable a member of a class, we call it a **field**. We will discuss exactly when a variable should be a field and when it shouldn't in *Chapter 6, OOP – Using Other People's Hard Work.*

In steps 9 and 10, we implemented the code that actually does the work in our switch statement in `onClick`. Let's take a line-by-line look at the code that runs when `button1` is pressed.

```
case R.id.buttonChoice1:
```

First, the `case` statement is true when the button with an id of `buttonChoice1` is pressed. Then the next line of code to execute is this:

```
answerGiven = Integer.parseInt(""+ buttonObjectChoice1.getText());
```

The preceding line gets the value on the button using two methods. First, `getText` gets the number as a string and then `Integer.parseInt` converts it to an integer. The value is stored in our `answerGiven` variable. The following code executes next:

```
if(answerGiven==correctAnswer) {//yay it's the right answer
  Toast.makeText(getApplicationContext(), "Well done!",
    Toast.LENGTH_LONG).show();
}else{//uh oh!
    Toast.makeText(getApplicationContext(),"Sorry that's wrong",
      Toast.LENGTH_LONG).show();
              }
```

The `if` statement tests to see if the `answerGiven` variable is the same as `correctAnswer` using the `==` operator. If so, the `makeText` method of the `Toast` object is used to display a congratulatory message. If the values of the two variables are not the same, the message displayed is a bit more negative one.

The `Toast` line of code is possibly the most evil thing we have seen thus far. It looks exceptionally complicated and it does need a greater knowledge of Java than we have at the moment to understand. All we need to know for now is that we can use the code as it is and just change the message, and it is a great tool to announce something to the player. By the end of *Chapter 6, OOP – Using Other People's Hard Work*, the code for `Toast` will be clear. If you really want an explanation now, you can think of it like this: when we made button objects, we got to use all the button methods. But with Toast, we used the class directly to access its `makeText` method without creating an object first. We can do this process when the class and its methods are designed to allow it.

Finally, we break out of the whole `switch` statement as follows:

```
break;
```

Now that we have improved the project as far as we can with what we learned in this chapter, why not test your understanding of everything you've learned so far?

Self-test questions

Q1) What does this code do?

```
// setContentView(R.layout.activity_main);
```

Q2) Which of these lines causes an error?

```
String a = "Hello";
String b = " Vinton Cerf";
int c = 55;
a = a + b
c = c + c + 10;
a = a + c;
c = c + a;
```

Q3) We talked a lot about operators and how different operators can be used together to build complicated expressions. Expressions, at a glance, can sometimes make the code look complicated. However, when looked at closely, they are not as tough as they seem. Usually, it is just a case of splitting the expressions into smaller pieces to work out what is going on. Here is an expression that is more convoluted than anything else you will ever see in this book. As a challenge, can you work out: what will x be?

```
int x = 10;
int y = 9;
boolean isTrueOrFalse = false;
isTrueOrFalse = (((x <=y)||(x == 10))&&((!isTrueOrFalse) ||
(isTrueOrFalse)));
```

Summary

We covered a lot in this chapter. We went from knowing nothing about Java syntax to learning about comments, variables, operators, and decision making.

As with any language, mastery of Java can be achieved by simply practicing, learning, and increasing our vocabulary. At this point, the temptation might be to hold back until mastery of the current Java syntax has been achieved, but the best way is to move on to new syntax at the same time as revisiting what we have already begun to learn.

In the next chapter, we will finally finish our math game by adding random questions of multiple difficulties as well as using more appropriate and random wrong answers for the multiple choice buttons.

To enable us to do this, we will first learn some more Java.

4
Discovering Loops and Methods

In this chapter, we will learn how to repeatedly execute portions of our code in a controlled and precise way by looking at different types of loops in Java. These include `while` loops, `do-while` loops, and `for` loops. We will learn about the best occasions to use the different types of loops.

Then we will briefly cover the topic of random numbers. We will also see how the Java `Random` class can be used. This will obviously be of great help in enhancing our math game.

Next, we will look at **methods**. They allow us to compartmentalize our code into more manageable blocks. We will then see how to share data between methods and divide programming tasks to simplify problems.

We will then use all that we have learned about loops, random numbers and methods on our math game project. For example, we will make the game change the question after each time we attempt the answer.

We will also add question difficulty levels and random questions within a range appropriate for a given difficulty level. We will show and update our score. The score goes up faster depending upon the difficulty level of the question answered (correctly). Eventually, even the best mathematicians among us should be beaten by the game. Nevertheless, most of us will hopefully get a bit further than what is shown in the next screenshot.

If the player gets a question wrong, the difficulty goes back to the easiest level and the score to zero. This is what the game will look like when we are done:

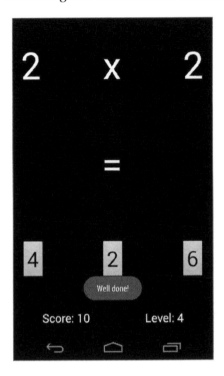

In this chapter we will:

- Learn about looping in multiple types of loops
- Learn how to generate random numbers in Java
- Learn everything about Java methods, including how to write and call them
- Significantly enhance our math game

Looping with loops

It would be completely reasonable to ask what loops have to do with programming, but they are exactly what the name implies. They are a way of performing the same part of the code more than once, or looping over the same part of code, but potentially for a different outcome each time.

This can simply mean doing the same thing until the code being looped over prompts the loop to end. It could prompt the loop after a predetermined number of times as specified by the loop code itself. It could also prompt the loop when a predetermined situation or **condition** is met. Or there could be a combination of more than one of these ways of prompting the loop to end. Along with if, else, and switch, loops are part of the Java **control flow statements**.

We will look at all the major types of loop that Java offers us to control our code, and after we have looked at methods, we will use some of them to implement the enhancements to our math game. Let's proceed to our first type of loop.

While loops

A while loop has the simplest syntax. Recollect the if statements in *Chapter 3, Speaking Java – Your First Game*. We can put virtually any combination of operators and variables in the conditional expression of the if statement. If the expression evaluated to true, then the code in the body of the if block is executed. Similarly, in the while loop, we put an expression that can evaluate to true or false, as shown in this code:

```
int x = 10;

while(x > 0){
  x--;
  //x decreases by one each pass through the loop
}
```

What is happening here is that outside the while loop, an integer, x, is declared and initialized to 10. Then the while loop begins. Its condition is x > 0, so it will continue looping through the code in its body until the condition evaluates to false. Hence, the code will execute 10 times.

On the first pass, x is equal to 10, then 9, then 8, and so on. But once x becomes equal to 0, it is obviously no longer greater than 0. So the program will exit the while loop and continue with the first line of code after the loop.

Just like an if statement, it is possible that the while loop will not execute even once. Take a look at this example of a while loop that never executes:

```
int x = 10;

while(x > 10){
  //more code here.
  //but it will never run unless x is greater than 10.
}
```

Moreover, there is no limit to the complexity of the condition expression or the amount of code that can be written in the loop body:

```
int playerLives = 3;
int alienShips = 10;

while(playerLives >0 && alienShips >0){
  //Entire game code here.
  //...
  //...
  //etc.
}
//continue here when either playerLives or alienShips = 0
```

The preceding `while` loop would continue to execute until either `playerLives` or `alienShips` becomes equal to or less than zero. As soon as one of these conditions occurs, the expression evaluates to `false` and the program continues to execute from the first line of code after the `while` loop.

It is worth noting that once the body of the loop has been entered, it will always complete, even if the expression evaluates to `false` somewhere in between, as the condition is not checked again until the code tries to start another pass:

```
int x = 1;

while(x > 0){
  x--;
  //x is now 0 so the condition is false
  //But this line still runs
  //and this one
  //and me!

}
```

The preceding loop body will execute exactly once. We can also set a `while` loop that will run forever (which is unsurprisingly called an **infinite loop**), like this:

```
int x = 0;

while(true){
  x++; //I am going to get mighty big!
}
```

Breaking out of a loop

We might use an infinite loop like the loop in the preceding example so that we can decide when to exit the loop from within its body. We would do this using the break keyword when we are ready to leave the loop body, as shown in the following code:

```
int x = 0;

while(true){
   x++; //I am going to get mighty big!
   break; //No you're not haha.
   //code doesn't reach here
}
```

You might have been able to guess that we can combine any of the decision making tools like if, else, and switch within our while loops and the rest of the loops we will look at in a minute:

```
int x = 0;
int tooBig = 10;

while(true){
   x++; //I am going to get mighty big!
   if(x == tooBig){
     break;
   } //No you're not haha.

   //code reaches here only until x = 10
}
```

It would be simple to go on for many more pages demonstrating the versatility of while loops, but at some point, we want to get back to doing some real programming. So here is one last concept, combined with while loops.

The continue keyword

The continue keyword acts in a way similar to break—up to a point. The continue keyword will break out of the loop body but will also check the condition expression afterwards, so the loop *could* run again. The following example will show the use of continue:

```
int x = 0;
int tooBig = 10;
int tooBigToPrint = 5;

while(true){
```

```
x++; //I am going to get mighty big!
if(x == tooBig){
   break;
} //No your not haha.

//code reaches here only until x = 10

if(x >= tooBigToPrint){
   //No more printing but keep looping
   continue;
}
//code reaches here only until x = 5

//Print out x


}
```

Do-while loops

A do-while loop is very much the same as a while loop with the exception that it evaluates its expression after the body. This means that a do-while loop will always execute at least once, as demonstrated in the following code:

```
int x= 0;
do{
   x++;
}while(x < 10);
//x now = 10
```

 The break and continue keywords can also be used in do-while loops.

For loops

A for loop has a slightly more complicated syntax than a while and do-while loop as it take three parts to initialize. Take a look at the following for loop first. Then we will break it apart:

```
for(int i = 0; i < 10; i++){
   //Something that needs to happen 10 times goes here
}
```

The apparently obscure form of the `for` loop is clearer when put like this:

```
for(declaration and initialization; condition; change after each pass
through loop)
```

To clarify further, we have the following in a `for` loop:

- **Declaration and initialization**: We create a new `int` variable, `i`, and initialize it to 0.

- **Condition**: Just like the other loops, this refers to the condition that must be evaluated to true for the loop to continue.

- **Change after each pass through loop**: In the preceding example, `i++` means that 1 is added to `i` on each pass. We could also use `i--` to reduce/decrement `i` on each pass, which is shown in the following code:

```
for(int i = 10; i > 0; i--){
    //countdown
}
//blast off i = 0
```

 Note that `break` and `continue` can also be used in `for` loops.

The `for` loop essentially takes control of initialization, condition evaluation, and the control variable on itself. We will be using a `for` loop to enhance our math game right after we take a look at random numbers and methods.

Random numbers in Java

Before we dive into methods, we will first take a look at how we can create random numbers because this is how we will generate our random questions.

All the hard work is done for us by the `Random` class. First we need to create an object of the `Random` type:

```
Random randInt = new Random();
```

Then we use our new object's `nextInt` method to generate a random number within a certain range:

```
int ourRandomNumber = randInt.nextInt(10);
```

The range for the number that we enter starts from zero. So the preceding line of code will generate a random number between 0 and 9. If we want a random number between 1 and 10, we just do this:

```
ourRandomNumber++;
```

 Often in these early chapters, we need to accept there is a bit of magic going on in objects like Random. In *Chapter 6, OOP – Using Other People's Hard Work*, we will be ripping open the black boxes and even making our own. We will be able to write our own classes and our own methods within those classes.

A good start is a look at regular vanilla methods, which we will do next.

Methods

So what exactly are Java methods? A method is a collection of variables, expressions, and control flow statements. We have already been using lots of methods; we just haven't looked inside any yet.

Learning about Java methods will be the last topic for this chapter before we get practical and use what we have learned to enhance our math game.

The structure of a method

The first part of a method that we write is called the **signature**. Here is a made-up example of a signature:

```
public boolean shootLazers(int number, string type)
```

Add an opening and closing pair of curly braces with some code that the method performs, and we have a complete method, or a **definition**. Here is a made-up but syntactically correct method:

```
private void setCoordinates(int x, int y){
  //code to set coordinates goes here
}
```

We could then use our new method from another part of our code, like this:

```
//I like it here

setCoordinates(4,6);//now I am going off to setCoordinates method

//Phew, I'm back again - code continues here
```

At the point where we call `setCoordinates`, our program's execution would branch to the code contained within that method, which would run until it reaches its end or is told to return. Then the code would continue running from the first line after the method call.

Here is another example of a method, complete with the code to make the method return to the code that called it:

```
int addAToB(int a, int b){
   int answer = a + b;
   return answer;
}
```

The call to use the preceding method could look like this:

```
int myAnswer = addAToB(2,4);
```

Clearly, we don't need to write methods to add two `int` variables together, but the preceding example helps us see a little more of the working of methods. First, we pass the values 2 and 4. In the signature of the method, the value, 2, is assigned to `int a` and the value, 4, is assigned to `int b`.

Within the method body, the `a` and `b` variables are added and used to initialize a new variable, which is the `int` answer. The `return answer` line does just that. It returns the value stored in `answer` to the calling code, causing `myAnswer` to be initialized with the value of 6.

Notice that each of the method signatures in the preceding examples varies a little. The reason for this is that the Java method signature is quite flexible, allowing us to build exactly the methods we require.

Exactly how the method signature defines how the method must be called and how a method must return a value, if it must, deserves further discussion. Let's give each part of that signature a name so that we can break it into chunks and learn about the parts separately.

Here is a method signature with its parts labeled and ready for discussion. You can also take a look at the following table to further identify which part of the signature is which. This will make the rest of our discussion on methods straightforward.

Modifier | return type | name of the method (parameters)

Here are a few examples that we have used so far so that you can clearly identify the part of the signature under discussion:

Part of signature	Examples
Modifier	`public`, `private`, and so on
Return type	`int`, `boolean`, `float`, and so on, or any Java type, expression, or object
Name of the method	`shootLazers`, `setCoordinates`, `addAToB`, and so on
Parameters	`(int number, string type)`, `(int x, int y)`, `(int a, int b)`, and so on

Modifier

In our previous examples, we only used a modifier twice, partly because the method doesn't have to use the modifier. The modifier is a way of specifying which code can use your method. Some of the types of modifiers are `public` and `private`. Actually, regular variables can have modifiers too, such as these:

```
//Most code can see me
public int a;

//Code in other classes can't see me
private string secret = "Shhh, I am private";
```

Modifiers (for methods and variables) are an essential Java topic but they are best dealt with when we discuss the other vital Java topic we have skirted around a few times so far—objects and classes.

 As previously promised, these mysterious objects will be revealed in *Chapter 6, OOP – Using Other People's Hard Work*. However, as we can see from our example methods and from the fact that all the examples we have written so far work just fine, modifiers are not necessary to facilitate our learning so far.

Return type

Next up is the `return` type. Like a modifier, a `return` type is also optional, although it is more immediately useful to us. So let's look a bit closer. We have seen that our methods can get anything done. But what if we need the result from what they have done? The simplest example of a return type we have seen so far was this:

```
int addAToB(int a, int b){
  int answer = a + b;
```

```
    return answer;
}
```

In this code, the `return` type in the signature is highlighted. So the `return` type is `int`. The `addAToB` method sends back (returns) to the code that called it a value that will fit in an `int` variable.

The `return` type can be any Java type we have seen so far. The method, however, does not have to return a value at all. In this case, the signature must use the `void` keyword as the `return` type. When the `void` keyword is used, the method body must not attempt to return a value as this will cause a compiler error. It can, however, use the `return` keyword without a value. Here are some combinations of return type and uses of the `return` keyword that are valid:

```
void doSomething(){
    //our code

    //I'm done going back to calling code here
    //no return is necessary
}
```

Another combination of `return` and `void` is as follows:

```
void doSomethingElse(){
    //our code

    //I can do this as long as I don't try and add a value
    return;
}
```

The following code is yet another combination of `return` and `void`:

```
void doYetAnotherThing(){
    //some code
    if(someCondition){
        //if someCondition is true returning to calling code
        //before the end of the method body
        return;
    }
    //More code that might or might not get executed

    return;
    //As I'm at the bottom of the method body
    //and the return type is void, I'm
    //really not necessary but I suppose I make it
    //clear that the method is over.
```

```
  }

String joinTogether(String firstName, String lastName){
   return firstName + lastName;
}
```

We can call each of the preceding methods one by one, like this:

```
//OK time to call some methods
doSomething();
doSomethingElse();
doYetAnotherThing();
String fullName = joinTogether("Jeff ","Minter")
//fullName now = Jeff Minter
//continue with code from here
```

 The preceding code would execute all the code statements in each method one by one. If the method signature had parameters, the code that calls the method would look slightly different.

Name of a method

When we design our own methods, the method name is arbitrary, but there is a convention to use verbs that clearly explain what the method will do. Another convention is of the first letter of the first word in the name being lower case, and the first letter of each of the subsequent words being uppercase. This is called **camel case** because the shape the name can form has a hump in it:

```
XGHHY78802c(){
   //code here
}
```

This name is perfectly legitimate and will work. However, let's take a look at a much clearer example that uses the conventions:

```
doSomeVerySpecificTask(){
   //code here
}

getMySpaceShipHealth(){
   //code here
}

startNewGame(){
   //code here
}
```

These are much clearer method names.

Now let's take a look at parameters.

Parameters

We know that a method can return a result to the calling code. What if we need to share some data values from the calling code with the method? Parameters allow us to share values with the method. We have already seen an example with parameters when looking at return types. We will look at the same example but a little more closely:

```
int addAToB(int a, int b){
    int answer = a + b;
    return answer;
}
```

The parameters in this code are highlighted. Notice that in the first line of the method body, we use a + b as if they are already declared and initialized. Well, that's because they are. The parameters of the method signature is their declaration, and the code that calls the method initializes them:

```
int returnedAnswer = addAToB(10,5);
```

Also, as we have partly seen in previous examples, we don't have to use int in our parameters. We can use any Java type, including types we design ourselves. We can mix and match types as well. We can also use as many parameters as necessary to solve our problem. An example of mixed Java types might help:

```
void addToAddressBook(char firstInitial, String lastName, String city,
    int age){
  //all the parameters are now living breathing,
  //declared and initialized variables

  //code to add details to address book goes here
}
```

It's now time to get serious about our body.

Getting things done in the method body

The body is the part we have been avoiding so far with comments like this:

```
//code here
    //some code
```

But actually, we know exactly what to do here already. Any Java syntax we have learned so far will work in the body of a method. In fact, if we look back, all of the code we have written so far has been in a method, albeit somebody else's method. For example, we wrote code in the `onCreate` and `onClick` methods.

The best thing we can do next is write some methods that actually do something in the body.

Using methods

We don't have to mess around with our math game project. We will quickly create a new blank project for each of the next two explorations into methods.

We also don't need to spend time making a UI. We will use the Android console to view the results and discuss the implications of our examples of methods. As we are using the Android console to view the results of our work with methods, we will need to run all of these examples on the Android emulator, not on a real device.

 It is possible to set up a real device to output to the console, but we have not covered that in this book. If you want to find out more about using your actual device for debugging, take a look at the article at `http://developer.android.com/tools/device.html`.

As usual, you can open the already typed code files in the usual way. The next two examples on methods can be found in the Packt Publishing code download in the `Chapter4` folder and the `AWorkingMethod` and `ExploringMethodOverloading` subfolders.

 The following is a quick reminder on how to create a new blank project.

1. Close any currently open projects by navigating to **File | Close Project**.
2. Click on **New Project...**.
3. The **Create New Project** configuration window will appear. Fill in the **Application name** field and **Company Domain** with `packtpub.com`, or you could use your own company website's name here instead.

4. Now click on the **Next** button. On the next screen, ensure that the **Phone and tablet** checkbox has a tick in it. Now we have to choose the earliest version of Android we want to build our app for. Go ahead and play with a few options in the drop-down selector. You will see that the earlier the version we select, the greater the percentage of devices our app can support. However, the trade-off here is that the earlier the version we select, the fewer cutting-edge Android features we can have in our apps. A good balance is to select **API 8: Android 2.2 (Froyo)**. Go ahead and do that now as shown in the next screenshot.

5. Click on **Next**. Now select **Blank Activity** and click on **Next** again.

6. On the next screen, simply change **Activity Name** to MainActivity and click on **Finish**.

7. As we did in *Chapter 2, Getting Started with Android*, to keep our code clear and simple, you can delete the two unneeded methods (onCreateOptionsMenu and onOptionsItemSelected) and their associated @override and @import statements, but this is not necessary for the example to work.

For a detailed explanation and images of creating a new project, see *Chapter 2, Getting Started with Android*.

A working method

First, let's make ourselves a simple working method, complete with return types and a fully functioning body.

This method will take three numbers as parameters and return a true or false value to the calling code depending upon whether one of the three numbers was randomly generated within the method or not:

1. Create a new blank project called A Working Method.

2. In this method, we will use the Random class we saw earlier and its randInt method as a part of the demonstration. Copy the code for this method after the closing bracket of onCreate but before the closing bracket of MainActivity. When you are prompted to import any classes, simply click on **OK**:

```
boolean guessANumber(int try1, int try2, int try3){
//all the Log.i lines print to the Android console
Log.i("info", "Hi there, I am in the method body");
//prove our parameters have arrived in the method
//By printing them in the console
Log.i("info", "try1 = " + try1);
Log.i("info", "try2 = " + try2);
Log.i("info", "try3 = " + try3);
```

3. Now we declare a Boolean variable called `found` and initialize it to `false`. We will change `found` to `true` if and when we guess the random number correctly. Next, we declare our random number and print some useful values to the console:

```
//we use the found variable to store our true or false
//setting it to false to begin with
boolean found = false;

//Create an object of the Random class so we can use it
Random randInt = new Random();
//Generate a random number between 0 and 5
int randNum = randInt.nextInt(6);
//show our random number in the console
Log.i("info", "Our random number = " + randNum);
```

4. The last portion of code in our method tests to see whether there is a match for any of our passed-in parameters, prints some output, and then returns `true` or `false` using the `found` variable to the calling code in the `onCreate` method:

```
//Check if any of our guesses are the same as randNum
if(try1 == randNum || try2 == randNum || try3 ==
    randNum){
    found = true;
    Log.i("info", "aha!");
}else{
    Log.i("info", "hmmm");
}

return found;
}
```

5. Now write this code just before the closing bracket of the `onCreate` method to call the code and print some values to the Android console:

```
//all the Log.i lines print to the Android console
Log.i("info", "I am in the onCreate method");

//Call guessANumber with three values
//and if true is returned output - Found it!
if(guessANumber( 1,2,3 )) {
    Log.i("info", "Found It!");
}else{//guessANumber returned false -didn't find it
```

```
    Log.i ("info", "Can't find it");
}

//continuing with the rest of the program now
Log.i("info", "Back in onCreate");
```

6. Launch an emulator.

7. Run the app on the emulator.

8. All our console messages have a tag called **info**. The console window will already have appeared underneath the editor window. We can filter its contents to only show our messages by typing info in the search box, as shown in the following screenshot:

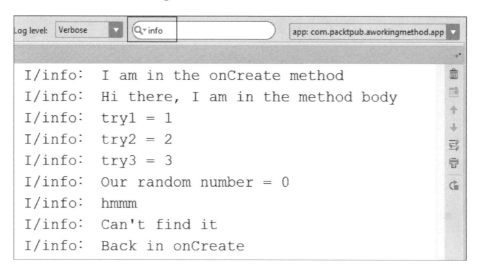

In the preceding screenshot, you can see the search filter and the console output. We will now run through the code and explain the output.

For clarity, here is the precise console output, without the extraneous date, time, and package name added to the beginning of each line. Remember that we are dealing with a random number, so your output may vary:

```
info: I am in the onCreate method
info:Hi there, I am in the method body
info:try1 = 1
info:try2 = 2
info:try3 = 3
info:Our random number = 0
```

```
info:hmmm
```

```
info:Can't find it
```

```
info:Back in onCreate
```

Here is what is happening. In step 2, we started writing our first method. We called it guessANumber. It has three int parameters and will return a Boolean. Remember that these three int parameters become fully initialized variables. First of all, however, in our method, we simply output the values of the new variables passed in as parameters as well as a message confirming that the code in our method is currently being executed:

```
boolean guessANumber(int try1, int try2, int try3){
    //all the Log.i lines print to the Android console
    Log.i("info", "Hi there, I am in the method body");
    //prove our parameters have arrived in the method
    //By printing them in the console
    Log.i("info", "try1 = " + try1);
    Log.i("info", "try2 = " + try2);
    Log.i("info", "try3 = " + try3);
```

In step 3, we added more code to our method. We declared and initialized a Boolean variable called found, which we will use to return a value to the calling code and let the calling code know whether one of the parameters passed in was the same as the random number:

```
//we use the found variable to store our true or false
//setting it to false to begin with
boolean found = false;
```

Next (still in step 3), we generated a random number in the same way as we did earlier in the chapter. We also used Log to output the random number so that we can examine what went on:

```
//Create an object of the Random class so we can use it
Random randInt = new Random();
//Generate a random number between 0 and 5
int randNum = randInt.nextInt(6);
//show our random number in the console
Log.i("info", "Our random number = " + randNum);
```

In step 4, we used an if statement with the logical OR operator to detect whether any of the passed-in parameters matches the random number we just generated, as shown in the following code:

```
//Check if any of our guesses are the same as randNum
if(try1 == randNum || try2 == randNum || try3 == randNum){
```

If the condition is true, that is, if any of `try1`, `try2`, or `try3` equals `randNum`, then the following code is run. Our `found` Boolean value is set to `true` and a message is printed:

```
found = true;
Log.i("info", "aha!");
```

If the condition is not true, the `else` statement is executed, a different message is printed, and the `found` variable is left the same as it was—`false`:

```
}else{
   Log.i("info", "hmmm");
}
```

Finally, in our method, we return the `found` variable, which will be either `true` or `false`, to the calling code:

```
   return found;
}
```

Now we look at step 5, which is the code in the `onCreate` method, which calls our `guessANumber` method in the first place. We start by simply printing a message saying that we are in `onCreate` at the moment:

```
//all the Log.i lines print to the Android console
Log.i("info", "I am in the onCreate method");
```

Then we make the call to `guessANumber` with the three parameters. In this case, we use 1, 2, and 3, but any `int` values would have worked. However, we wrap the call in an `if` statement. This means that the `return` value from the method will be used to evaluate the `if` statement. Simply put, if `true` is returned, the `if` statement will be executed and "**Found It!**" will be printed:

```
//Call guessANumber with three values
//and if true is returned output - Found it!
if(guessANumber(1,2,3)){
   Log.i("info", "Found It!");
   }
```

On the contrary, if `false` is returned, the `else` statement gets executed and "**Can't find it**" is printed:

```
else{//guessANumber returned false -didn't find it
   Log.i ("info", "Can't find it");
}

//continuing with the rest of the program now
Log.i("info", "Back in onCreate");
```

Remember that we are dealing with random numbers, so you might need to run it a few times before you see this output:

```
I am in the onCreate method
Hi there, I am in the method body
try1 = 1
try2 = 2
try3 = 3
Our random number = 3
aha!
Found It!
Back in onCreate
```

Of course, you should note that the guesses sent to the function as parameters are arbitrary. As long as all the numbers are between 0 and 5 and are not duplicated, they will together have a 50 percent chance of finding the random number.

On a closing note, if you've to read only one tip in this whole book, it should be this one.

 Printing variable values to the console is a great way to examine what is going on inside your game and to find bugs.

Let's look at another example of methods.

Exploring method overloading

As we are learning, methods are really diverse and deep as a topic, but hopefully, taking a step at a time, we will see they are not daunting in any way. We will be using what we have learned about methods when we enhance our math game. We will be exploring methods even more deeply in *Chapter 6, OOP – Using Other People's Hard Work*. For now, however, it will serve us well to look at one more topic on methods. Let's create a new project to explore **method overloading**.

As we will now see, we can create more than one method with the same name, provided the parameters are different. The code in this project is vastly simpler than that of the last project. It is how this code works that might appear slightly curious until we analyze it later:

1.   Create a new blank project called Exploring Method Overloading.

2. In the first method, we will simply call it `printStuff` and pass an `int` variable via a parameter to be printed. Copy the code for this method after the closing bracket of `onCreate` but before the closing bracket of `MainActivity`. When you are prompted to import any classes, simply click on **OK**:

```
void printStuff(int myInt){
  Log.i("info", "This is the int only version");
  Log.i("info", "myInt = "+ myInt);
}
```

3. We will also call the second method `printStuff` but pass a `string` variable to be printed. Copy the code for this method after the closing bracket of `onCreate` but before the closing bracket of `MainActivity`. Again, when you are prompted to import any classes, simply click on **OK**:

```
void printStuff(String myString){
  Log.i("info", "This is the String only version");
  Log.i("info", "myString = "+ myString);
}
```

4. Yet again, we will call this third method `printStuff` but pass a `string` variable and an `int` variable to be printed. As before, copy the code for this method after the closing bracket of `onCreate` but before the closing bracket of `MainActivity`:

```
void printStuff(int myInt, String myString){
  Log.i("info", "This is the combined int and String
    version");
  Log.i("info", "myInt = "+ myInt);
  Log.i("info", "myString = "+ myString);
}
```

5. Now write this code just before the closing bracket of the `onCreate` method to call the methods and print some values to the Android console:

```
//declare and initialize a String and an int
int anInt = 10;
String aString = "I am a string";

//Now call the different versions of printStuff
//The name stays the same, only the parameters vary
printStuff(anInt);
printStuff(aString);
printStuff(anInt, aString);
```

6. Launch an emulator.

7. Run the app on the emulator.

Here is the console output:

```
info: This is the int only version
info: myInt = 10
info: This is the String only version
info: myString = I am a string
info: This is the combined int and String version
info: myInt = 10
info: myString = I am a string
```

As you can see, Java has treated three methods with the same name as totally different methods. This, as we have just demonstrated, can be really useful. It is called **method overloading**.

Method overloading and overriding confusion

Overloading and overriding are defined as follows:

- Overloading occurs when we have more than one method with the same name but different parameters
- Overriding occurs when we essentially replace a method with the same name and the same parameter list

We know enough about overloading and overriding to complete this book, but if you are brave and your mind is wandering, you can override an overloaded method. However, that is something for another time.

This is how the preceding code works. In each of the three steps (2, 3, and 4), we create a method called `printStuff`, but each `printStuff` method has different parameters, so each is a different method that can be called individually:

```
void printStuff(int myInt){
...
}

void printStuff(String myString){
...
}

void printStuff(int myInt, String myString){
...
}
```

The body of each of the methods is simple. It just prints the passed-in parameters and confirms which version of the method is being called currently.

The next important part of our code is when we make it plain which method we want to call, using the appropriate parameters. In step 5, we call each of them in turn, using the appropriate parameters so that Java knows the exact method required:

```
printStuff(anInt);
printStuff(aString);
printStuff(anInt, aString);
```

Now we know more than enough about methods, loops, and random numbers to make some improvements to our math game.

Enhancing our math game

We are going to add some features to our math game using what we have just learned about methods and loops.

As usual, the code is available for copying in the `Chapter4` folder of the code download. The project is in the `MathGameChapter4` subfolder and encompasses all the remaining phases of improvement covered in this chapter, including enhancing the UI, amending our game activity, `setQuestion`, `updateScoreAndLevel`, `isCorrect`, and calling our new methods.

We will make the game change the question after each time we attempt the answer.

We will also add difficulty levels to questions and random questions but within a range appropriate for that difficulty level.

We will show and update our score. The score goes up faster depending on the difficulty level of the question answered correctly.

If the player gets a question wrong, the difficulty goes back to the easiest level and the score to zero.

Enhancing the UI

Let's get on with modifying our math game UI to incorporate our new game features. We will be adding a TextView to display the score and another TextView to display the level.

1. Open the `activity_game.xml` file in the editor window. We will add a new TextView to the very bottom of our UI for our score.

2. Drag a **Large Text** element from **Palette** and place it to the left, below our three answer buttons.

3. Now we need to change the **id** property so that we can access our new TextView from our Java code. Ensure that the new TextView is selected by clicking on it. Now, in the **Properties** window, change the **id** property to `textScore`.

4. For the sake of clarity (although this step serves no use in programming), change the **text** property to `Score:999`.

5. Now put another **Large Text** element to the right of the one we just configured and change the **id** property to `textLevel`. The lower part of our UI should now look like this:

6. Once again, for the sake of clarity (although this step serves no use in programming), change the **text** property to `Level:4`.

7. Save the project.

We have just added two new TextView elements and assigned them both an ID that we can refer to in our Java code.

> You have probably realized by now that the precise layout and size of our UI elements are unimportant as far as getting the game to work is concerned. This gives us a lot of flexibility in designing layouts for different screen sizes. As long as each layout for each screen size contains the same element types with the same IDs, the same Java code will work for different layouts. If you want to know more about designing for multiple screen sizes, take a look at `http://developer.android.com/training/multiscreen/screensizes.html`.

Now that we have our enhanced UI and an understanding of how the Java `Random` class works, we can add the Java code to implement our new features.

The new Java code

As previously explained, the project code is available in the Chapter4 folder of the downloadable code. The project is called MathGameChapter4 and encompasses all the improvements covered in this chapter.

In this phase, we will be adding lots of new code, moving some existing code, and modifying some existing code too. As so much is changing, we are going to approach the code from the very beginning. The new code will be explained completely, the code that has moved will be pointed out with a reason, and the code that has stayed the same and in the same place will have the least explanation.

We will first make some modifications and deletions to our existing code. We will then look at designing and implementing each of our new methods to improve our code and add our new features.

Amending GameActivity

First, let's perform the necessary amendments and deletions to our current code:

1. Open the GameActivity.java file in the editor window.

2. We now need to consider the scope of the objects that represent our UI elements. Both textObjectPartA and textObjectPartB need to be accessible from the methods we will be creating soon. So let's move their declarations, as we did with the multi-choice buttons in the previous chapter, out of the onCreate method so that they are accessible everywhere in our GameActivity class. The following code shows all our declarations so far. They are present immediately after the start of the GameActivity class. The recently added (or moved) declarations are highlighted. Notice that we have also added declarations for our two new TextViews and for the score and level displays. In addition, there are two new int variables that we can manipulate for our score and to keep track of our level. They are currentScore and currentLevel:

```
public class GameActivity extends Activity implements View.
OnClickListener{

    int correctAnswer;
    Button buttonObjectChoice1;
    Button buttonObjectChoice2;
    Button buttonObjectChoice3;
    TextView textObjectPartA;
    TextView textObjectPartB;
    TextView textObjectScore;
```

```
TextView textObjectLevel;

int currentScore = 0;
int currentLevel = 1;
```

3. All of the code that assigns text to our Buttons or TextViews objects, and the code that initializes the parts of our question and assigns the values for our wrong answers, are now going to change and move, so we need to delete it all. Everything shown in the following code is to be deleted:

```
//Here we initialize all our variables
int partA = 9;
int partB = 9;
correctAnswer = partA * partB;
int wrongAnswer1 = correctAnswer - 1;
int wrongAnswer2 = correctAnswer + 1;
```

4. The following code snippet needs to be deleted too:

```
//Now we use the setText method of the class on our objects
//to show our variable values on the UI elements.
textObjectPartA.setText("" + partA);
textObjectPartB.setText("" + partA);

//which button receives which answer, at this stage is arbitrary.
buttonObjectChoice1.setText("" + correctAnswer);
buttonObjectChoice2.setText("" + wrongAnswer1);
buttonObjectChoice3.setText("" + wrongAnswer2);
```

5. For clarity and context, here is the entire `onCreate` method as it currently stands. There is nothing new here, but you can see your code, which links our Button and TextView objects that we declared in step 2. Again, this code includes our two new TextViews, which are highlighted, but everything else, which is described in steps 3 and 4, is deleted. As before, there is a piece of code that makes our game listen to button clicks:

```
protected void onCreate(Bundle savedInstanceState) {
        super.onCreate(savedInstanceState);
        //The next line loads our UI design to the screen
        setContentView(R.layout.activity_game);


        /*Here we get a working object based on either the button
          or TextView class and base as well as link our new
          objects
```

```
                directly to the appropriate UI elements that we created
                previously*/
        textObjectPartA = (TextView)findViewById(R.id.textPartA);

        textObjectPartB = (TextView)findViewById(R.id.textPartB);

        textObjectScore = (TextView)findViewById(R.id.textScore);

        textObjectLevel = (TextView)findViewById(R.id.textLevel);

        buttonObjectChoice1 = (Button)findViewById(R.
            id.buttonChoice1);

        buttonObjectChoice2 = (Button)findViewById(R.
            id.buttonChoice2);

        buttonObjectChoice3 = (Button)findViewById(R.
            id.buttonChoice3);

        buttonObjectChoice1.setOnClickListener(this);
        buttonObjectChoice2.setOnClickListener(this);
        buttonObjectChoice3.setOnClickListener(this);

    }//onCreate ends here
```

6. Now we will delete some more code that we don't need because we are going to make it more efficient by compartmentalizing it into our new methods and adding our new features at the same time. So in our `onClick` method, in each case of our `switch` statement, we want to delete the `if` and the `else` statements. We will be completely rewriting these, but we will leave in place the code that initializes our `answerGiven` variable. Our `onClick` method will now look like this:

```
@Override
    public void onClick(View view) {
        //declare a new int to be used in all the cases
        int answerGiven=0;
        switch (view.getId()) {

            case R.id.buttonChoice1:
                //initialize a new int with the value contained in
                buttonObjectChoice1
                //Remember we put it there ourselves previously
```

```
            answerGiven = Integer.parseInt("" +
                buttonObjectChoice1.getText());

            break;

        case R.id.buttonChoice2:
            //same as previous case but using the next button
            answerGiven = Integer.parseInt("" +
                buttonObjectChoice2.getText());

            break;

        case R.id.buttonChoice3:
            //same as previous case but using the next button
            answerGiven = Integer.parseInt("" +
                buttonObjectChoice3.getText());

            break;

    }

}
```

7. Save your project.

Wow! That was a lot of code, but as we saw along the way, there were no new concepts. In step 2, we simply moved the initialization of our Button and TextView objects to a place where they will now be visible from anywhere within our class.

In steps 3 and 4, we did a fair bit of deletion because we will no longer be making the question or populating the multi-choice buttons in `onCreate`, as this is not flexible enough. We will soon see how we improve on this.

In step 6, we deleted the code that tested whether the answer was correct or incorrect. However, as we saw, we still initialized the `answerGiven` variable in the same way—in the appropriate case of our `switch` statement in the `onClick` method.

Great! Now we are ready to consider and design some new methods to compartmentalize our code, avoid repetitions in it, and add our extra features. Consider the following methods that we will soon implement.

The methods

We will now walk through writing some methods. As we will see, the methods will compartmentalize our code and prevent the implementation of our new features from causing the code to become too long and sprawling:

- We will write a `setQuestion` method to prepare a question of appropriate difficulty.
- We will write an `updateScoreAndLevel` method that will do just that. We will also write an `isCorrect` method that one of our other methods will use to evaluate the correctness of the answer.
- Then we will strategically place the code that calls our new methods.

We will do each of these tasks one at a time and explain the code along the way, as leaving the explanation to the end will make referring to individual steps cumbersome.

We will use many of the features of Java that we learned in this chapter and the previous chapter. These include the following:

- Methods
- A `for` loop
- The switch control structure

So let's get started with our first method.

The setQuestion method

We determined that we needed a method to prepare a question for us; `setQuestion` seems like a decent name for such a method. Every time our player gives an answer by tapping one of the three multi-choice buttons, a new question will need to be prepared.

This method will need to generate values for our `partA` and `partB` variables as well as show them in our TextViews referenced by the `textObjectPartA` and `textObjectPartB` objects. In addition, the method will need to assign the new correct answer to our `correctAnswer` variable, which will then be used to calculate some suitable incorrect answers. Finally, the method will show both the correct and incorrect answers on our multi-choice buttons.

Furthermore, our `setQuestion` method will need to take into account the level held in `currentLevel` to determine the range or difficulty of the question it will ask. Let's go through the code. If you want to type this code as we go, then just make sure you place it after the closing bracket of `onClick` but before the closing bracket of our `GameActivity` class:

1. First of all, we have the method signature and the opening curly brace before the body of our method:

```
void setQuestion(){
```

2. This tells us that the return type is `void`, so `setQuestion` will not return a value to the code that calls it. Also, there are no parameters here, so it does not need any value passed for it to work. Let's see what it does. Now we enter the code to generate the two parts of the question:

```
//generate the parts of the question
int numberRange = currentLevel * 3;
Random randInt = new Random();

int partA = randInt.nextInt(numberRange);
partA++;//don't want a zero value

int partB = randInt.nextInt(numberRange);
partB++;//don't want a zero value
```

3. In the previous step, we declared a new `int` variable, `numberRange`, and initialized it by multiplying the player's `currentLevel` value by 3. Then we got a new `Random` object called `randInt` and used it to generate new values based on `numberRange`. We did this to the `partA` and `partB` variables. As the value of `currentLevel` increases, so potentially does the difficulty of the question. Now, just as we have written in the past, we write this:

```
correctAnswer = partA * partB;
int wrongAnswer1 = correctAnswer-2;
int wrongAnswer2 = correctAnswer+2;

textObjectPartA.setText(""+partA);
textObjectPartB.setText(""+partB);
```

4. We assigned the answer of our new multiplication question to `correctAnswer`. Then we declared and assigned two incorrect answers to the new `int` variables, `wrongAnswer1` and `wrongAnswer2`. We also used the `setText` method of our TextView objects to display the question to the player. Notice that we have not yet displayed the correct and incorrect answers. Here it is. Try to work out what is happening here:

```
//set the multi choice buttons
```

```
//A number between 0 and 2
int buttonLayout = randInt.nextInt(3);
switch (buttonLayout){

case 0:
buttonObjectChoice1.setText(""+correctAnswer);
buttonObjectChoice2.setText(""+wrongAnswer1);
buttonObjectChoice3.setText(""+wrongAnswer2);
    break;


case 1:

buttonObjectChoice2.setText(""+correctAnswer);
buttonObjectChoice3.setText(""+wrongAnswer1);
buttonObjectChoice1.setText(""+wrongAnswer2);
    break;


case 2:
buttonObjectChoice3.setText(""+correctAnswer);
buttonObjectChoice1.setText(""+wrongAnswer1);
buttonObjectChoice2.setText(""+wrongAnswer2);
    break;
  }

}
```

5. In the preceding code, we used our `Random` object, `randInt`, to generate a number between 0 and 2, and assigned the value to a new `int` variable called `buttonLayout`. We then used `buttonLayout` to switch between all its possible values: 0, 1, or 2. Each `case` statement sets the correct and incorrect answers to the multi-choice buttons in a slightly different order, so the player can't just keep tapping the same button over and over to achieve a massive score. Notice the extra closing bracket after the closing bracket of the switch. This is the end of our `setQuestion` method.

We explained the code fairly thoroughly as we went through it but it might be worthwhile to just take a closer look at some parts again.

In step 1, we saw our method signature with a `void` return type and no parameters. In step 2, we generated some random numbers that will be within a certain range. This range isn't as obvious as it might seem at first. First, we assigned, declared, and initialized `numberRange` like this:

```
int numberRange = currentLevel * 3;
```

So if the player is at the first question, then `currentLevel` will hold the value `1` and `numberRange` will be initialized as `3`. Then we made a new `Random` object as previously discussed and entered this line of code:

```
int partA = randInt.nextInt(numberRange);
```

What occurs here is that the `nextInt` method of the `Random` object, `randInt`, will return a value of either 0, 1, or 2 because we have given it a seed of 3. We don't want any zeros in our game because they result in very easy multiplication, so we enter this:

```
partA++;//don't want a zero value
```

This operator, which you probably remember from *Chapter 3, Speaking Java – Your First Game*, when we discussed operators, adds 1 to `partA`. We then do exactly the same to our `partB` variable, which means that assuming that the player is still on level 1, they will have a question that will be one of the following:

1 x 1, 1 x 2, 1 x 3, 2 x 1, 2 x 2, 2 x 3, 3 x 1, 3 x 2, or 3 x 3

As the level increases, the potential range of the question increases significantly. So at level 2, the options are that either part of the question could be from 1 to 6; for level 3, from 1 to 9; and so on. It is still possible to get an easy question on a higher level but it becomes less likely as the levels advance. Finally in this step, we display the question to the player using the `setText` method.

In step 3, we have seen before but this time we varied it slightly. We calculate and assign a value for `correctAnswer`, and declare and assign values to `wrongAnswer1` and `wrongAnswer2`, which will hold the wrong answer choices for our buttons.

Part 3 varies very slightly from what we did in `onCreate` in the previous chapter because we subtract and add 2 to `wrongAnswer1` and `wrongAnswer2`, respectively. This makes guessing the answer to multiplication questions a little harder because you can't eliminate answers based on whether they are odd or even.

Step 4 simply randomizes which buttons the correct and incorrect answers will be placed on. We don't need to keep track of this because when the time comes to compare the value on the button pressed with the correct answer, we can simply use our Java code to discover it as we did in *Chapter 3, Speaking Java – Your First Game*.

The updateScoreAndLevel method

The name of this method speaks for itself. Because the keeping of the score is not simple and because we want higher levels to yield higher scores, we will compartmentalize the code to keep our program readable. If we then want to make modifications to the scoring system, they can all take place in there.

Let's write the code.

1. This code can go anywhere within the opening and closing braces of `GameActivity {}`, but it is good practice to place them in the approximate order they will be used. So why not start adding your code after the closing brace of `setQuestion` but obviously before the closing brace of `GameActivity`? Here is the method signature with the opening brace:

   ```
   void updateScoreAndLevel(int answerGiven){
   ```

2. This tells us that our method does not return a value but that it does receive an `int`, which it will require to do its stuff. The name of the parameter is a big clue to what we will be passing. We will see that in action in the body in a minute, but if passing the player's answer to this method instead of the `isCorrect` method is a bit confusing, we will see things become clearer in the next chunk of code. Here is the next part of the code to add:

   ```
   if(isCorrect(answerGiven)){
     for(int i = 1; i <= currentLevel; i++){
       currentScore = currentScore + i;
       }

     currentLevel++;
   }
   ```

3. There is a lot happening here, so we will dissect it more once we have the method completed. Basically, it calls the `isCorrect` method (which we will write soon) and if the response is `true`, adds to the player's score in a `for` loop. After that, the method adds 1 to `currentLevel`. Here comes the `else` part of the code in case the response from `isCorrect` is `false`:

   ```
   else{
     currentScore = 0;
     currentLevel = 1;
   }
   ```

4. If the response is `false`, that is, if the player got the answer wrong, the `currentScore` variable is set to `0` and the level back to `1`. Finally for this method, we type the following:

```
//Actually update the two TextViews
textObjectScore.setText("Score: " + currentScore);
textObjectLevel.setText("Level: " + currentLevel);
}
```

5. In the previous step, we updated the actual TextViews that the player sees with the newly determined score and level. The method then ended and the control of the program returned to the code that called `updateScoreAndLevel` to begin with. Save your project.

We explained most of the code as we went but it might be good to quickly review it and dig a bit deeper into certain parts, especially the call to `isCorrect` in that odd-looking `if` statement.

In step 1, we began with the method signature. Then in step 2, we began with the aforementioned curious `if`:

```
if(isCorrect(answerGiven)){
```

We have seen this type of statement before in the *A working method* example in the *Methods* section of this chapter. What is happening here is that the call to `isCorrect` is replacing the statement to be evaluated, or rather it *is* the statement to be evaluated. So `isCorrect` is called with the `answerGiven` variable. The `answerGiven` variable, as you might remember, was passed to `updateScoreAndLevel`. This time, it is passed to the `isCorrect` method, which will do some work with it and perhaps a few other things. Then it will return to the `if` statement a value of `true` or `false`. The value will be true if the question is answered correctly and false if not.

Assuming the `if` statement evaluates to true, the program runs this bit of code (also from step 2):

```
for(int i = 1; i <= currentLevel; i++){
  currentScore = currentScore + i;
}

currentLevel++;
```

The code enters a `for` loop where the starting variable `i` is initialized to 1 like this: `int i = 1;`. Furthermore, the loop is instructed to continue as long as `i` is less than or equal to our `currentLevel` variable. Then within the `for` loop, we add `i` to the current score. As an example, let's assume that the player has just got a question correct and we enter the `for` loop with `currentLevel` at 1. The player's score is still at 0 because this is their first correct answer.

At pass 1, we get the following:

- `i = 1`, so it is equal to `currentLevel`, which is also 1. So we enter the `for` loop
- `i = 1`, so `currentScore` equals 0
- We add `i`, which is 1, to `currentScore`
- Our `currentScore` variable is now equal to 1

At pass 2, the following steps take place:

- `i` is incremented to 2, so it is now greater than `currentLevel`, which is 1
- The `for` loop condition evaluates to `false` and we continue with the code after the `for` loop
- `currentLevel` is increased by 1 to 2

Now let's look at that `for` loop again assuming that the player gets the next question correct as well, and we are back in `updateScoreAndLevel`. This time, `isCorrect` has evaluated true and we enter the `for` loop but with a slightly different situation than the last time.

At pass 1, the following steps take place:

- `i = 1`, so `i` is less than `currentLevel` is 2 and we enter the `for` loop
- `i = 1`, `currentScore = 1`
- We add `i`, which is equal to 1, to `currentScore`
- Our `currentScore` variable is now equal to 2

At pass 2, we have the following steps happening:

- `i` is incremented to 2 and it is now equal to `currentLevel`, which is also 2
- `i = 2`, `currentScore = 2`
- We add `i`, which is now equal to 2, to `currentScore`
- Our `currentScore` variable is now equal to 4

At pass 3, the following steps take place:

- `i` is incremented to 3 and it is now greater than `currentLevel`, which is 2.
- The `for` loop condition evaluates to false and we continue with the code after the `for` loop.
- The value of `currentLevel` is increased by 1 to 3. So the next time, we will have an extra pass through our `for` loop.

What is happening is that with each level, the player is being rewarded with another pass through the for loop, and each pass through the for loop adds a greater value to their score. To summarize what happens in the for loop, here is a brief table of values showing how the player's score is increased based on the currentLevel variable:

currentLevel	Added to currentScore	currentScore after for loop
1	1	1
2	3 (1 + 2)	4
3	6 (1 + 2 + 3)	10
4	10 (1 + 2 + 3 + 4)	20
5	15 (1 + 2 + 3 + 4 + 5)	35

 Of course, we could have kept it really simple and not used a for loop. We could just use currentScore = currentScore + level perhaps, but that doesn't offer an ever increasing reward in the same way as our current solution does and we wouldn't have been able to practice our for loops either.

If if(isCorrect(answerGiven)) evaluates to false, it simply resets the score to 0 and the level to 1 in step 3. Step 4 then updates our TextViews for the score and the level using the variables we have just discussed.

Now we have just one more method to write. Of course, this is the isCorrect method, which we just called.

The isCorrect method

This method is nice and simple because we have seen all of the relevant code before. It is just the method signature and the return value that we need to look at carefully:

1. Enter the code just after the closing brace of the updateScoreAndLevel method but before the closing brace of the GameActivity class. Type the method signature like this:

   ```
   boolean isCorrect(int answerGiven){
   ```

2. Here we can see that the method must return a Boolean value, `true` or `false`. If it doesn't, then the program won't compile. This guarantees that when we use this method as the evaluation expression in the `updateScoreAndLevel` method, we will definitely get a result. It can be true or false. The signature also shows us the `answerGiven` variable passed in, ready for us to use. Type this code, which will determine that result:

```
boolean correctTrueOrFalse;
if(answerGiven == correctAnswer){//YAY!
  Toast.makeText(getApplicationContext(), "Well done!",
      Toast.LENGTH_LONG).show();
    correctTrueOrFalse=true;
}else{//Uh-oh!
    Toast.makeText(getApplicationContext(), "Sorry",
        Toast.LENGTH_LONG).show();
    correctTrueOrFalse=false;
}
```

3. We have seen almost all of the preceding code before. The exception is that we declare a Boolean variable, `correctTrueOrFalse`, which we assign to `true` if the player answers correctly and to `false` if not. We know whether the player is correct or not because we compare `answerGiven` to `correctAnswer` in the `if` statement. Notice that we have also triggered the appropriate Android pop-up toast message as we did before. Finally, we do this:

```
    return correctTrueOrFalse;
}
```

We just returned whatever value is contained within `correctTrueOrFalse`. So the critical `if` statement in `updateScoreAndLevel`, which we discussed in detail, will know what to do next.

To make sure we understand what is happening in `isCorrect`, let's go through the sequence of events in our code. In step 1 we have the method signature. We see that we will return a `true` or `false` value and receive `int`.

In step 2, we declare a Boolean variable called `correctTrueOrFalse` to hold the value we will soon return. Then we test for a right or wrong answer with `if(answerGiven == correctAnswer)`. If the two compared values match, a congratulatory message pops up and we assign `true` to our Boolean variable. Of course, if the `if` statement is `false`, we offer commiserations to the player and assign `false` to our important Boolean.

Finally in step 3, we send back `true` or `false` so that the `updateScoreAndLevel` method can proceed with its work.

We have now implemented all our methods. It's time to put them to work.

Calling our new methods

Of course, our shiny new methods won't do anything until we call them. So here is the plan to call these methods:

1. When the game starts, we want to set a new question for the player. Therefore, as the last line of code in our `onCreate` method, we can call our `setQuestion` method like this:

    ```
    setQuestion();

    }//onCreate ends here
    ```

2. Then we turn our attention to the `onClick` method, which already detects which button has been pressed and loads the player's answer into our `answerGiven` variable. So at the end of the `onClick` method, after the closing brace of the `switch` statement, we just call this function:

    ```
    updateScoreAndLevel(answerGiven);
    ```

3. This sends our player's attempted answer to `updateScoreAndLevel`, which evaluates the answer using `isCorrect`, adds points, and increments the score if the answer is correct or resets the score and level if not. All that we need now is another question. Add this line. It will ask another question:

    ```
    setQuestion();
    ```

So now what happens is that the player starts our math game by clicking on its icon on their Android device. Our `GameActivity` class declares a few variables that we need access to throughout:

```
int correctAnswer;
Button buttonObjectChoice1;
Button buttonObjectChoice2;
Button buttonObjectChoice3;
TextView textObjectPartA;
TextView textObjectPartB;
TextView textObjectScore;
TextView textObjectLevel;

int currentScore = 0;
int currentLevel = 1;
```

Then `onCreate` initializes some variables and gets our buttons ready to receive clicks from the player before asking the first question by calling `setQuestion`. The game then waits for the player to attempt an answer. When the player attempts an answer, it is dealt with by `onClick`, `updateScoreAndLevel`, and `isCorrect`. Then the program control comes back to `onClick` again, `setQuestion` is called again, and we wait for the player's answer once more.

Finishing touches

Our math game is coming along nicely. Unfortunately, we have to move on soon. The project has served its purpose to demonstrate some fundamentals of Java programming as well as some key Android features. Now we need to start introducing some more game-related topics.

Before we go on, there are two really easy things to make our game a bit more cool and complete. In case you are wondering about the High Scores button, we will see how that can be implemented when we look at our next game project in *Chapter 5, Gaming and Java Essentials*. You will then have enough information to easily come back and implement high scores on your own.

The other feature that would really round off our game and make it more playable is an overall or per question time limit. Perhaps even increasing the score based on how quickly the correct answer is given will help. We need some new Java tricks up our sleeves before we can do that, but we will see how we can measure and respond to time in *Chapter 5, Gaming and Java Essentials*, when we talk about threads.

Now we will quickly learn two improvements:

- Locking the screen orientation
- Changing the home screen image

Going full screen and locking orientation

You might have noticed that if you rotate your device while the app is running, not only does your game UI get distorted but the game progress is also lost. What goes wrong is that when the device is rotated, the `onPause` and `onStop` methods are called. Then the app is restarted. We could handle this by overriding the `onPause` method and saving our data. We will do this later. For now we don't want the screen to rotate anyway, so if we stop it we solve two problems in one.

While adding code to this file, Android Studio may try to "help" by adding extra formatting. If you get red error indicators, you can compare your `AndroidManifest.xml` file with the one in the code download in the `Chapter4/MathGameChapter4` folder. Alternatively, you can simply replace the contents of your file with the contents of the file in the download. The step-by-step changes are detailed in this guide just to highlight what is changing:

1. This is the first step in locking the app to portrait. Open the `AndroidManifest.xml` file. It is located directly below the `res` folder in the Project Explorer. Find the first opening `<activity` in the code.

2. Enter a new line as follows:

    ```
    android:screenOrientation="portrait"
    ```

3. Repeat step 2 after the second instance of `<activity`. We have now locked both the menu and game screens in portrait mode.

4. To make the game full screen, in the same file, find the following text and add the line in bold after it but before the closing `>` sign:

    ```
    <activity
    android:name="com.packtpub.mathgamechapter4.app.MainActivit
      y"
    android:label="@string/app_name"
    android:theme="@android:style/Theme.NoTitleBar.Fullscreen">

    </activity>
    ```

5. Make the same change to the `GameActivity` activity like this. Again, here is the code in context in order to avoid mistakes with these `>` signs:

    ```
    <activity
    android:name="com.packtpub.mathgamechapter4.app.GameActivit
      y"
    android:label="@string/title_activity_game"
    android:theme="@android:style/Theme.NoTitleBar.Fullscreen">
    </activity>
    ```

6. Save the project.

Now, when you rotate the device during gameplay, the portrait orientation will be fixed.

Adding a custom image (instead of the Android icon)

We probably don't want to have the Android image on our finished game home screen, so here is the procedure to change it. This quick guide relies on you having an image you would like to use:

1. First, we need to add the required image to the layout folder. Copy your image file by clicking on it in **Windows Explorer** and using *Ctrl + C*.

2. Now find the `drawable-mdpi` folder in the Android Studio Project Explorer. Click on the folder.

3. Paste the image to the folder using *Ctrl + V*.

4. Now the image is a part of our project. We simply need to choose it in the same way as we chose the image of the Android robot previously. Open `activity_main.xml` in the editor window and click on **ImageView** (currently an Android robot).

5. In the **Properties** window, find the **src** property. Click on it and then on **....**

6. Search for your image and select it.

7. Save your project.

8. You now have the image of your choice on the home screen.

Self-test questions

Q1) Guess what is wrong with this method:

```
void doSomething(){
    return 4;
}
```

Q2) What will x be equal to at the end of this code snippet?

```
int x=19;
do{
    x=11;
    x++;
}while(x<20)
```

Summary

We came a really long way in this chapter. You got a serious handle on Java loops and took your first, fairly deep look into Java methods and how to use them. You learned how to generate random numbers and significantly enhanced your math game using all of the knowledge you gained.

As the chapters proceed, the games will get more and more real-game-like. In the next chapter, we will make a game to test the player's memory. It will have sound, animation and will actually save the player's high scores too.

Congratulations on your progress so far but let's keep going.

5
Gaming and Java Essentials

In this chapter, we will cover a diverse and interesting range of topics. We will learn about Java arrays, which allow us to manipulate a potentially huge amount of data in an organized and efficient manner.

Then, we will look at the role threads can play in games, in order to do more than one thing apparently simultaneously.

If you thought that our math game was a bit on the quiet side, then we will look at adding sound effects to our games as well as introducing a cool open source app to generate authentic sound effects.

The last new thing we will learn will be persistence. This is what happens when the player quits our game or even turns off their Android device. What happens to the score then? How will we load the right level the next time they play?

Once we have done all this, we will use all the new techniques and knowledge along with what we already know to create a neat memory game.

In this chapter, we will cover the following topics:

- Java arrays—an array of variables
- Timing with threads
- Creating and using beeps 'n' buzzes—Android sound
- A look at life after destruction—persistence
- Building the memory game

Java arrays – an array of variables

You might be wondering what happens when we have a game with lots of variables to keep track of. How about a table of high scores with the top 100 scores? We could declare and initialize 100 separate variables like this:

```
int topScore1;
int topScore2;
int topScore3;
//96 more lines like the above
int topScore100;
```

Straightaway, this can seem unwieldy, and what about the case when someone gets a new top score and we have to shift the scores in every variable down one place? A nightmare begins:

```
topScore100 = topScore99;
topScore99 = topScore98;
topScore98 = topScore97;
//96 more lines like the above
topScore1 = score;
```

There must be a better way to update the scores. When we have a large set of variables, what we need is a Java **array**. An array is a reference variable that holds up to a fixed maximum number of elements. Each element is a variable with a consistent type.

The following line of code declares an array that can hold `int` type variables, even a high score table perhaps:

```
int [] intArray;
```

We can also declare arrays of other types, like this:

```
String [] classNames;
boolean [] bankOfSwitches;
float [] closingBalancesInMarch;
```

Each of these arrays would need to have a fixed maximum amount of storage space allocated before it is used, like this:

```
intArray = new int [100];
```

The preceding line of code allocates up to a maximum of 100 integer-sized storage spaces. Think of a long aisle of 100 consecutive storage spaces in our variable warehouse. The spaces would probably be labeled `intArray[0]`, `intArray[1]`, `intArray[2]`, and so on, with each space holding a single `int` value. Perhaps the slightly surprising thing here is that the storage spaces start off at 0, not 1. Therefore, in an array of size 100, the storage spaces would run from 0 to 99.

We can actually initialize some of these storage spaces like this:

```
intArray[0] = 5;
intArray[1] = 6;
intArray[2] = 7;
```

Note that we can only put the declared type into an array and the type that an array holds can never change:

```
intArray[3]= "John Carmack";//Won't compile
```

So when we have an array of `int` types, what are each of the `int` variables called? The array notation syntax replaces the name. We can do anything with a variable in an array that we could do with a regular variable with a name:

```
intArray[3] = 123;
```

Here is another example of array variables being used like normal variables:

```
intArray[10] = intArray[9] - intArray[4];
```

We can also assign a value from an array to a regular variable of the same type, like this:

```
int myNamedInt = intArray [3];
```

Note, however, that `myNamedInt` is a separate and distinct primitive variable, so any changes made to it do not affect the value stored in the `intArray` reference. It has its own space in the warehouse and is not connected to the array.

Arrays are objects

We said that arrays are reference variables. Think of an array variable as an address to a group of variables of a given type. Perhaps, using the warehouse analogy, `someArray` is an aisle number. So each of `someArray[0]`, `someArray[1]`, and so on is the aisle number followed by the position number in the aisle.

Arrays are also objects. This means that they have methods and properties that we can use:

```
int lengthOfSomeArray = someArray.length;
```

In the previous line of code, we assigned the length of `someArray` to the `int` variable called `lengthOfSomeArray`.

We can even declare an array of arrays. This is an array that, in each of its elements, stores another array, like this:

```
String[][] countriesAndCities;
```

In the preceding array, we could hold a list of cities within each country. Let's not go array-crazy just yet. Just remember that an array holds up to a predetermined number of variables of any predetermined type and their values are accessed using this syntax:

```
someArray[someLocation];
```

Let's actually use some arrays to try and get an understanding of how to use them in real code and what we might use them for.

A simple example of an array

Let's write a really simple working example of an array by performing the following steps. You can get the complete code for this example in the downloadable code bundle. It's at `Chapter5/SimpleArrayExample/MainActivity.java`:

1. Create a project with a blank activity, just as we did in *Chapter 2, Getting Started with Android*. Also, clean up the code by deleting the unnecessary parts, but this isn't essential.

2. First, we declare our array, allocate five spaces, and initialize some values to each of the elements:

```
//Declaring an array
int[] ourArray;

//Allocate memory for a maximum size of 5 elements
ourArray = new int[5];

//Initialize ourArray with values
//The values are arbitrary as long as they are int
//The indexes are not arbitrary 0 through 4 or crash!

ourArray[0] = 25;
ourArray[1] = 50;
```

```
ourArray[2] = 125;
ourArray[3] = 68;
ourArray[4] = 47;
```

3. We output each of the values to the **logcat** console. Notice that when we add the array elements together, we are doing so over multiple lines. This is fine because we have omitted a semicolon until the last operation, so the Java compiler treats the lines as one statement:

```
//Output all the stored values
Log.i("info", "Here is ourArray:");
Log.i("info", "[0] = "+ourArray[0]);
Log.i("info", "[1] = "+ourArray[1]);
Log.i("info", "[2] = "+ourArray[2]);
Log.i("info", "[3] = "+ourArray[3]);
Log.i("info", "[4] = "+ourArray[4]);

//We can do any calculation with an array element
//As long as it is appropriate to the contained type
//Like this:
int answer = ourArray[0] +
    ourArray[1] +
    ourArray[2] +
    ourArray[3] +
    ourArray[4];

Log.i("info", "Answer = "+ answer);
```

4. Run the example on an emulator.

Remember that nothing will happen on the emulator display because the entire output will be sent to our **logcat** console window in Android Studio. Here is the output of the preceding code:

```
info: Here is ourArray:
info: [0] = 25
info: [1] = 50
info: [2] = 125
info: [3] = 68
info: [4] = 47
info: Answer = 315
```

In step 2, we declared an array called `ourArray` to hold `int` variables, and allocated space for up to five variables of that type.

Next, we assigned a value to each of the five spaces in our array. Remember that the first space is `ourArray[0]` and the last space is `ourArray[4]`.

In step 3, we simply printed the value in each array location to the console. From the output, we can see that they hold the value we initialized in the previous step. Then we added each of the elements in `ourArray` and initialized their value to the `answer` variable. We then printed `answer` to the console and saw that all the values where added together, just as if they were plain old `int` types stored in a slightly different manner, which is exactly what they are.

Getting dynamic with arrays

As we discussed at the beginning of all this array stuff, if we need to declare and initialize each element of an array individually, there isn't a huge amount of benefit in an array over regular variables. Let's look at an example of declaring and initializing arrays dynamically.

Dynamic array example

Let's make a really simple dynamic array by performing the following steps. You can find the working project for this example in the download bundle. It is at `Chapter5/DynamicArrayExample/MainActivity.java`:

1. Create a project with a blank activity, just as we did in *Chapter 2, Getting Started with Android*. Also, clean up the code by deleting the unnecessary parts, but this isn't essential.

2. Type the following between the opening and closing curly braces of `onCreate`. See if you can work out what the output will be before we discuss it and analyze the code:

```
//Declaring and allocating in one step
int[] ourArray = new int[1000];

//Let's initialize ourArray using a for loop
//Because more than a few variables is allot of typing!
for(int i = 0; i < 1000; i++){
    //Put the value of ourValue into our array
    //At the position determined by i.
    ourArray[i] = i*5;

            //Output what is going on
            Log.i("info", "i = " + i);
            Log.i("info", "ourArray[i] = " + ourArray[i]);
}
```

3. Run the example on an emulator. Remember that nothing will happen on the emulator display because the entire output will be sent to our **logcat** console window in Android Studio. Here is the output of the preceding code:

```
info: i = 0
info: ourArray[i] = 0
info: i = 1
info: ourArray[i] = 5
info: i = 2
info: ourArray[i] = 10
```

I have removed 994 iterations of the loop for brevity:

```
info: ourArray[i] = 4985
info: i = 998
info: ourArray[i] = 4990
info: i = 999
info: ourArray[i] = 4995
```

All the action happened in step 2. We declared and allocated an array called `ourArray` to hold up to 1,000 `int` values. This time, however, we did the two steps in one line of code:

```
int[] ourArray = new int[1000];
```

Then we used a `for` loop that was set to loop 1,000 times:

```
(int i = 0; i < 1000; i++){
```

We initialized the spaces in the array from 0 to 999 with the value of `i` multiplied by `5`, as follows:

```
ourArray[i] = i*5;
```

To demonstrate the value of `i` and the value held in each position of the array, we output the value of `i` followed by the value held in the corresponding position in the array as follows:

```
Log.i("info", "i = " + i);
Log.i("info", "ourArray[i] = " + ourArray[i]);
```

All of this happened 1,000 times, producing the output we saw.

Entering the nth dimension with arrays

We very briefly mentioned that an array can even hold other arrays at each of its positions. Now, if an array holds lots of arrays that hold lots of some other type, how do we access the values in the contained arrays? And why would we ever need this anyway? Take a look at the next example of where multidimensional arrays can be useful.

An example of a multidimensional array

Let's create a really simple multidimensional array by performing the following steps. You can find the working project for this example in the download bundle. It is at `Chapter5/MultidimensionalArrayExample/MainActivity.java`:

1. Create a project with a blank activity, just as we did in *Chapter 2, Getting Started with Android*. Also, clean up the code by deleting the unnecessary methods, but this isn't essential.

2. After the call to `setContentView`, declare and initialize a two-dimensional array, like this:

```
//A Random object for generating question numbers later
Random randInt = new Random();
//And a variable to hold the random value generated
int questionNumber;

//We declare and allocate in separate stages for clarity
//but we don't have to
String[][] countriesAndCities;
//Here we have a 2 dimensional array

//Specifically 5 arrays with 2 elements each
//Perfect for 5 "What's the capital city" questions
countriesAndCities = new String[5][2];

//Now we load the questions and answers into our arrays
//You could do this with less questions to save typing
//But don't do more or you will get an exception
countriesAndCities [0][0] = "United Kingdom";
countriesAndCities [0][1] = "London";

countriesAndCities [1][0] = "USA";
countriesAndCities [1][1] = "Washington";

countriesAndCities [2][0] = "India";
```

```
countriesAndCities [2][1] = "New Delhi";

countriesAndCities [3][0] = "Brazil";
countriesAndCities [3][1] = "Brasilia";

countriesAndCities [4][0] = "Kenya";
countriesAndCities [4][1] = "Nairobi";
```

3. Now we output the contents of the array using a `for` loop and a `Random` class object. Note how we ensure that although the question is random, we can always pick the correct answer:

```
//Now we know that the country is stored at element 0
//The matching capital at element 1
//Here are two variables that reflect this
int country = 0;
int capital = 1;

//A quick for loop to ask 3 questions
for(int i = 0; i < 3; i++){
    //get a random question number between 0 and 4
    questionNumber = randInt.nextInt(5);

    //and ask the question and in this case just
    //give the answer for the sake of brevity
    Log.i("info", "The capital of "
      +countriesAndCities[questionNumber][country]);

    Log.i("info", "is "
      +countriesAndCities[questionNumber][capital]);

}//end of for loop
```

Run the example on an emulator. Once again, nothing will happen on the emulator display because the output will be sent to our **logcat** console window in Android Studio. Here is the output of the previous code:

```
info: The capital of USA
info: is Washington
info: The capital of India
info: is New Delhi
info: The capital of United Kingdom
info: is London
```

What just happened? Let's go through this chunk by chunk so that we know exactly what is going on.

We make a new object of the `Random` type, called `randInt`, ready to generate random numbers later in the program:

```
Random randInt = new Random();
```

We declare a simple `int` variable to hold a question number:

```
int questionNumber;
```

Then we declare `countriesAndCities`, our array of arrays. The outer array holds arrays:

```
String[][] countriesAndCities;
```

Now we allocate space within our arrays. The first outer array will be able to hold five arrays and each of the inner arrays will be able to hold two strings:

```
countriesAndCities = new String[5][2];
```

Next, we initialize our arrays to hold countries and their corresponding capital cities. Notice that with each pair of initializations, the outer array number stays the same, indicating that each country/capital pair is within one inner array (a string array). Of course, each of these inner arrays is held in one element of the outer array (which holds arrays):

```
countriesAndCities [0][0] = "United Kingdom";
countriesAndCities [0][1] = "London";

countriesAndCities [1][0] = "USA";
countriesAndCities [1][1] = "Washington";

countriesAndCities [2][0] = "India";
countriesAndCities [2][1] = "New Delhi";

countriesAndCities [3][0] = "Brazil";
countriesAndCities [3][1] = "Brasilia";

countriesAndCities [4][0] = "Kenya";
countriesAndCities [4][1] = "Nairobi";
```

To make the upcoming `for` loop clearer, we declare and initialize `int` variables to represent the country and the capital from our arrays. If you glance back at the array initialization, all the countries are held in position `0` of the inner array and all the corresponding capital cities are held at position `1`:

```
int country = 0;
int capital = 1;
```

Now we create a `for` loop that will run three times. Note that this number does not mean we access the first three elements of our array. It is rather the number of times we go through the loop. We could make it loop one time or a thousand times, but the example would still work:

```
for(int i = 0; i < 3; i++){
```

Next, we actually determine which question to ask, or more specifically, which element of our outer array. Remember that `randInt.nextInt(5)` returns a number between 0 and 4. This is just what we need as we have an outer array with five elements, from 0 to 4:

```
questionNumber = randInt.nextInt(5);
```

Now we can ask a question by outputting the strings held in the inner array, which in turn is held by the outer array that was chosen in the previous line by the randomly generated number:

```
Log.i("info", "The capital of "
    +countriesAndCities[questionNumber][country]);

Log.i("info", "is "
    +countriesAndCities[questionNumber][capital]);

}//end of for loop
```

For the record, we will not be using any multidimensional arrays in the rest of this book. So if there is still a little bit of murkiness around these arrays inside arrays, then that doesn't matter. You know they exist and what they can do, so you can revisit them if necessary.

Array-out-of-bounds exceptions

An array-out-of-bounds exception occurs when we attempt to access an element of an array that does not exist. Whenever we try this, we get an error. Sometimes, the compiler will catch it to prevent the error from going into a working game, like this:

```
int[] ourArray = new int[1000];
int someValue = 1;//Arbitrary value
ourArray[1000] = someValue;//Won't compile as compiler knows this
won't work.
//Only locations 0 through 999 are valid
```

Guess what happens if we write something like this:

```
int[] ourArray = new int[1000];
int someValue = 1;//Arbitrary value
int x = 999;
if(userDoesSomething){
   x++;//x now equals 1000
}
ourArray[x] = someValue;
//Array out of bounds exception if userDoesSomething evaluates to
true! This is because we end up referencing position 1000 when the
array only has positions 0 through 999

//Compiler can't spot it and game will crash on player - yuck!
```

The only way we can avoid this problem is to know the rule. The rule is that arrays start at zero and go up to the number obtained by subtracting one from the allocated number. We can also use clear, readable code where it is easy to evaluate what we have done and spot the problems.

Timing with threads

So what is a thread? You can think of threads in Java programming just like threads in a story. In one thread of a story, we have the primary character battling the enemy on the front line, and in another thread, the soldier's family are getting by, day to day. Of course, a story doesn't have to have just two threads. We could introduce a third thread. Perhaps the story also tells of the politicians and military commanders making decisions. These decisions subtly, or not so subtly, affect what happens in the other threads.

Threads in programming are just like this. We create parts/threads in our program and they control different aspects for us. We introduce threads to represent these different aspects because of the following reasons:

- They make sense from an organizational point of view
- They are a proven way of structuring a program that works
- The nature of the system we are working on forces us to use them

In Android, we use threads for all of these reasons simultaneously. It makes sense, it works, and we have to use it because of the design of the system.

In gaming, think about a thread that receives the player's button taps for "left", "right", and "shoot", a thread that represents the alien thinking where to move next, and yet another thread that draws all the graphics on the screen.

Programs with multiple threads can have problems. Like the threads of a story, if proper synchronization does not occur, then things go wrong. What if our soldier went into battle before the battle or even the war existed? Weird!

What if we have a variable, int x, that represents a key piece of data that say three threads of our program use? What happens if one thread gets slightly ahead of itself and makes the data "wrong" for the other two? This problem is the problem of **correctness**, caused by multiple threads racing to completion, oblivious of each other—because they are just dumb code after all.

The problem of correctness can be solved by close oversight of the threads and **locking**. Locking means temporarily preventing execution in one thread to ensure that things are working in a synchronized manner. It's like freezing the soldier from boarding a ship to war until the ship has actually docked and the plank has been lowered, avoiding an embarrassing splash.

The other problem with programs with multiple threads is the problem of **deadlock**, where one or more threads become locked, waiting for the right moment to access x, but that moment never comes and the entire program eventually grinds to a halt.

You might have noticed that it was the solution to the first problem (correctness) that is the cause of the second problem (deadlock). Now consider all that we have just been discussing and mix it in with the Android Activity lifecycle. It's possible that you start to feel a little nauseous with the complexity.

Fortunately, the problem has been solved for us. Just as we use the Activity class and override its methods to interact with the Android lifecycle, we can also use other classes to create and manage our threads. Just as with Activity, we only need to know how to use them, not how they work.

So why tell me all this stuff about threads when I didn't need to know, you would rightly ask. It's simply because we will be writing code that looks different and is structured in an unfamiliar manner. We will have no sweat writing our Java code to create and work within our threads if we can do the following:

- Accept that the new concepts we will introduce are what we need to work with in order to create an Android-specific solution to the problems related to working with threads

- Understand the general concept of a thread, which is mostly the same as a story thread that happens almost simultaneously

- Learn the few rules of using some of the Android thread classes

Notice that I said classes, plural, in the third bullet. Different thread classes work best in different situations. You could write a whole book on just threads in Android. We will use two thread classes in this book. In this chapter, we will use `Handler`. In *Chapter 7*, *Retro Squash Game*, and *Chapter 8*, *The Snake Game*, we will use the `Runnable` class. All we need to remember is that we will be writing parts of our program that run at almost the same time as each other.

 What do I mean by "almost"? What is actually happening is that the CPU switches between threads in turn. However, this happens so fast that we will not be able to perceive anything but simultaneity.

A simple thread timer example with the Handler class

After this example, we can heave a sigh of relief when we realize that threads are not as complicated as first feared. When using threads in a real game, we will have to add a bit of extra code alongside the code in this simple example, but it's not much, and we will talk about it when we get to it.

As usual, you can simply use the complete code from the download bundle. This project is located in `Chapter5/SimpleThreadTimer/MainActivity.java`.

As the name suggests, we will be creating a timer—quite a useful feature in a lot of games:

1. Create a project with a blank activity, just as we did in *Chapter 2*, *Getting Started with Android*. Also, clean up the code by deleting the unnecessary parts, but this isn't essential.

2. Immediately after the class declaration, enter the three highlighted lines:

```
public class MainActivity extends Activity {

    private Handler myHandler;
    boolean gameOn;
    long startTime;
```

3. Enter this code inside the onCreate method. It will create a thread with something else going on in the if(gameOn) block:

```
//How many milliseconds is it since the UNIX epoch
        startTime = System.currentTimeMillis();

        myHandler = new Handler() {
            public void handleMessage(Message msg) {
                super.handleMessage(msg);

                if (gameOn) {
                    long seconds = ((System.currentTimeMillis() -
                        startTime)) / 1000;
                    Log.i("info", "seconds = " + seconds);
                }

                myHandler.sendEmptyMessageDelayed(0, 1000);
            }

        };

        gameOn = true;
        myHandler.sendEmptyMessage(0);
    }
```

4. Run the app. Quit with the home or back button on the emulator. Notice that it is still printing to the console. We will deal with this anomaly when we implement our memory game.

When you run the example on an emulator, remember that nothing will happen on the emulator display because all of the output will be sent to our **logcat** console window in Android Studio. Here is the output of the previous code:

```
info: seconds = 1
info: seconds = 2
info: seconds = 3
info: seconds = 4
info: seconds = 5
info: seconds = 6
```

So what just happened? After 1-second intervals, the number of seconds elapsed was printed to the console. Let's learn how this happened.

First, we declare a new object, called myHandler, of the Handler type. We then declare a Boolean variable called gameOn. We will use this to keep track of when our game is running. Finally, the last line of this block of code declares a variable of the long type. You might remember the long type from *Chapter 3, Speaking Java – Your First Game*. We can use long variables to store very large whole numbers, and this is what we do here with startTime:

```
private Handler myHandler;
boolean gameOn;
long startTime;
```

Next, we initialized startTime using currentTimeMillis, a method of the System class. This method holds the number of milliseconds since January 1, 1970. We will see how we use this value in the next line of code.

```
startTime = System.currentTimeMillis();
```

Next is the important code. Everything up to if(gameOn) marks the code to define our thread. Certainly, the code is a bit of a mouthful, but it is not as bad as it looks at first glance. Also, remember that we only need to use the threads; we don't need to understand every aspect of how they do their work.

Let's dissect the preceding code to demystify it a bit. The myHandler = new Handler() line simply initializes our myHandler object. What is different from what we have seen before is that we go on to customize the object immediately afterwards. We override the handleMessage method (which is where we put our code that runs in the thread) and then we call super.handleMessage, which calls the default version of handleMessage before it runs our custom code. This is much like we do for the onCreate method every time we call super.onCreate.

Then we have the `if (gameOn)` block. Everything in that `if` block is the code that we want to run in the thread. The `if (gameOn)` block simply gives us a way to control whether we want to run our code at all. For example, we might want the thread up and running but only sometimes run our code. The `if` statement gives us the power to easily choose. Take a look at the code now. We will analyze what is happening in the `if` block later:

```
myHandler = new Handler() {
    public void handleMessage(Message msg) {
        super.handleMessage(msg);

        if (gameOn) {
          long seconds = ((System.currentTimeMillis() -
            startTime)) / 1000;
                Log.i("info", "seconds = " + seconds);
        }

        myHandler.sendEmptyMessageDelayed(0, 1000);
    }

};
```

Inside the `if` block, we declare and initialize another `long` variable called `seconds`, and do a little bit of math with it:

```
long seconds = ((System.currentTimeMillis() - startTime)) / 1000;
```

First, we get the current number of milliseconds since January 1, 1970, and then subtract `startTime` from it. This gives us the number of milliseconds since we first initialized `startTime`. Then we divide the answer by 1000 and get a value in seconds. We print this value to the console with the following line:

```
Log.i("info", "seconds = " + seconds);
```

Next, just after our `if` block, we have this line:

```
myHandler.sendEmptyMessageDelayed(0, 1000);
```

The previous line tells the Android system that we want to run the code in the `handleMessage` method once every 1000 milliseconds (once a second).

Back in `onCreate`, after the closing curly braces of the `handleMessage` method and the `Handler` class, we finally set `gameOn` to `true` so that it is possible to run the code in the `if` block:

```
gameOn = true;
```

Then, this last line of the code starts the flow of messages between our thread and the Android system:

```
myHandler.sendEmptyMessage(0);
```

It is worth pointing out that the code inside the `if` block can be as minimal or as extensive as we need. When we implement our memory game, we will see much more code in our `if` block.

All we really need to know is that the somewhat elaborate setup we have just seen allows us to run the contents of the `if` block in a new thread. That's it! Perhaps apart from brushing over that `System` class a bit quickly.

> The `System` class has many uses. In this case, we use it to get the number of milliseconds since January 1, 1970. This is a common system used to measure time in a computer. It is known as Unix time, and the first millisecond of January 1, 1970, is known as the Unix Epoch. We will bump into this concept a few more times throughout the book.

Enough on threads, let's make some noise!

Beeps n buzzes – Android sound

This section will be divided into two parts—creating and using sound FX. So let's get on with it.

Creating sound FX

Years ago, whenever I made a game, I would spend many hours trawling websites offering royalty-free sound FX. Although there are many good ones out there, the really great ones are always costly, and no matter how much you pay, they are never exactly what you want. Then a friend pointed out a simple open source app called Bfxr, and I have never wasted another moment looking for sound effects since. We can make our own.

Here is a very fast guide to making your own sound effects using Bfxr. Grab a free copy of Bfxr from www.bfxr.net.

Follow the simple instructions on the website to set it up. Try out a few of these examples to make cool sound effects:

 This is a seriously condensed tutorial. You can do much more with Bfxr. To learn more, read the tips on the website at the previous URL.

1. Run `bfxr.exe`:

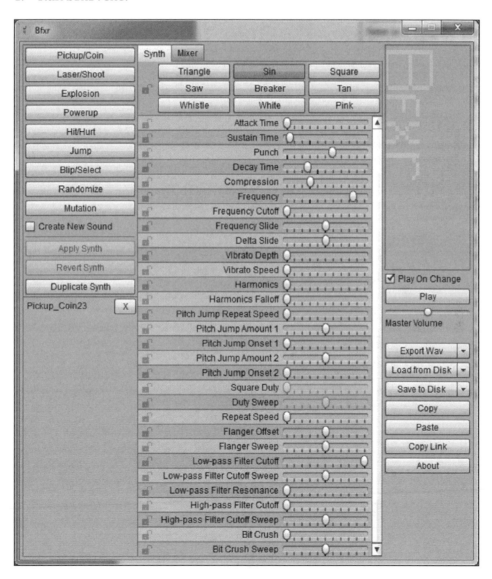

2. Try out all the preset types, which generate a random sound of that type. When you have a sound that is close to what you want, move to the next step:

3. Use the sliders to fine-tune the pitch, duration, and other aspects of your new sound:

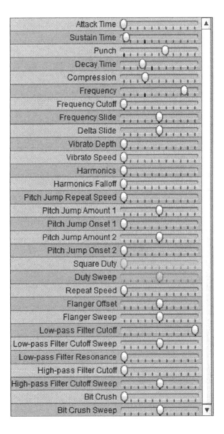

4. Save your sound by clicking on the **Export Wav** button. Despite the name of this button, as we will see, we can save in formats other than .wav.

5. Android likes to work with sounds in the OGG format, so when asked to name your file, use the .ogg extension on the end of whatever you decide to call it.

6. Repeat steps 2 to 5 as often as required.

 Every project in this book that requires sound samples comes with the sound samples provided, but as we have seen, it is much more fun to make our own samples. All you need to do is to save them with the same filename as the provided samples.

Playing sounds in Android

To complete this brief example, you will need three sound effects saved in the .ogg format. So if you don't have them to hand, go back to the *Creating sound FX* section to make some. Alternatively, you can use the sounds provided in the Chapter5/PlayingSounds/assets folder of the code bundle. As usual, you can view or use the already completed code at Chapter5/PlayingSounds/java/MainActivity.java and Chapter5/PlayingSounds/layout/activity_main.xml. Now perform the following steps:

1. Create a project with a blank activity, just as we did in *Chapter 2, Getting Started with Android*. Also, clean up the code by deleting the unnecessary parts, although this isn't essential.

2. Create three sound files and save them as sample1.ogg, sample2.ogg, and sample3.ogg.

3. In the main folder in the Project Explorer window, we need to add a folder called assets. So in the Project Explorer window, right-click on the **main** folder and navigate to **New | Directory**. Type assets in the **New Directory** dialog box.

4. Now copy and paste the three sound files to the newly created assets folder. Alternatively, select the three files, right-click on them, and click on **Copy**. Then click on the **assets** folder in the Android Studio Project Explorer. Now right-click on the **assets** folder and click on **Paste**.

5. Open `activity_main.xml` in the editor window and drag three button widgets onto your UI. It doesn't matter where they are or how they are aligned. When you look at the **id** property in the **Properties** window for any of our three new buttons, you will notice that they have automatically been assigned **id** properties. They are `button`, `button2`, and `button3`. As we will see, this is just what we need.

6. Let's enable our activity to listen to the buttons being clicked by implementing `onClickListener` as we have done in all our other examples with buttons. Open **MainActivity.java** in the editor window. Replace the `public class MainActivity extends Activity {` line with the following line of code:

   ```
   public class MainActivity extends Activity implements View.
       OnClickListener {
   ```

7. As before, we get an unsightly red underline on our new line of code. The last time this happened, we typed in the empty body of the `onClick` method that we must implement and all was well. This time, because we already know what is going on here, we will learn a shortcut. Hover your mouse cursor over the error and right-click on it. Now click on **Generate...** and then select **Implement methods....** In the **Select Methods To Implement** dialog box, **onClick(View):void** will already be selected:

8. Select this option by clicking on **OK**. Now scroll to the bottom of your code and see that Android Studio has very kindly implemented the `onClick` method for you and the error is also gone.

9. Type this code after the `MainActivity` declaration to declare some variables for our sound effects:

```
private SoundPool soundPool;
int sample1 = -1;
int sample2 = -1;
int sample3 = -1;
```

10. Type this code in the `onCreate` method to load our sounds into memory:

```
soundPool = new SoundPool(10, AudioManager.STREAM_MUSIC,0);
  try{
    //Create objects of the 2 required classes
        AssetManager assetManager = getAssets();
        AssetFileDescriptor descriptor;

        //create our three fx in memory ready for use
        descriptor = assetManager.openFd("sample1.ogg");
        sample1 = soundPool.load(descriptor, 0);

        descriptor = assetManager.openFd("sample2.ogg");
        sample2 = soundPool.load(descriptor, 0);


        descriptor = assetManager.openFd("sample3.ogg");
        sample3 = soundPool.load(descriptor, 0);


    }catch(IOException e){
        //catch exceptions here
    }
```

11. Now add the code to grab a reference to the buttons in our UI and listen to clicks on them:

```
//Make a button from each of the buttons in our layout
    Button button1 =(Button) findViewById(R.id.button);
    Button button2 =(Button) findViewById(R.id.button2);
    Button button3 =(Button) findViewById(R.id.button3);

    //Make each of them listen for clicks
    button1.setOnClickListener(this);
    button2.setOnClickListener(this);
    button3.setOnClickListener(this);
```

12. Finally, type this code in the `onClick` method that we autogenerated:

```
switch (view.getId()) {

    case R.id.button://when the first button is pressed
      //Play sample 1
            soundPool.play(sample1, 1, 1, 0, 0, 1);
            break;

            //Now the other buttons
            case R.id.button2:
            soundPool.play(sample2, 1, 1, 0, 0, 1);
            break;

            case R.id.button3:
            soundPool.play(sample3, 1, 1, 0, 0, 1);
            break;
    }
```

Run the example on an emulator or on a real Android device. Notice that by clicking on a button, you can play any of your three sound samples at will. Of course, sounds can be played at almost any time, not just on button presses. Perhaps they can be played from a thread as well. We will see more sound samples when we implement the memory game later in the chapter.

This is how the code works. We started off by setting up a new project in the usual way. In steps 2 to 5, however, we created some sounds with Bfxr, created an `assets` folder, and placed the files within it. This is the folder where Android expects to find sound files. So when we write the code in the next steps that refers to the sound files, the Android system will be able to find them.

In steps 6 to 8, we enabled our activity to listen to button clicks as we have done several times before. Only this time, we got Android Studio to autogenerate the `onClick` method.

Then we saw this code:

```
private SoundPool soundPool;
```

First, we create an object of the `SoundPool` type, called `soundPool`. This object will be the key to making noises with our Android device. Next, we have this code:

```
int sample1 = -1;
int sample2 = -1;
int sample3 = -1;
```

The preceding code is very simple; we declared three `int` variables. However, they serve a slightly deeper purpose than a regular `int` variable. As we will see in the next block of code we analyze, they will be used to hold a reference to a sound file that is loaded into memory. In other words, the Android system will assign a number to each variable that will refer to a place in memory where our sound file will reside.

We can think of this as a location in our variable warehouse. So we know the name of the `int` variable, and contained within it is what Android needs to find our sound. Here is how we load our sounds into memory and use the references we've just been discussing.

Let's break the code in step 10 into a few parts. Take a close look and then we will examine what is going on:

```
soundPool = new SoundPool(10, AudioManager.STREAM_MUSIC,0);
```

Here, we initialize our `soundPool` object and request up to 10 simultaneous streams of sound. We should be able to really mash the app buttons and get a sound every time. `AudioManager.STREAM_MUSIC` describes the type of stream. This is typical for applications of this type. Finally, the `0` argument indicates we would like default quality sound.

Now we see something new. Notice that the next chunk of code is wrapped into two blocks, `try` and `catch`. This means that if the code in the `try` block fails, we want the code in the `catch` block to run. As you can see, there is nothing but a comment in the `catch` block.

We must do this because of the way the `SoundPool` class is designed. If you try to write the code without the `try` and `catch` blocks, it won't work. This is typical of Java classes involved in reading from files. It is a fail-safe process to check whether the file is readable or even whether it exists. You could put a line of code to output to the console that an error has occurred.

If you want to experiment with `try/catch`, then put a line of code to output a message in the `catch` block and remove one of the sound files from the assets folder. When you run the app, the loading will fail and the code in the `catch` block will be triggered.

We will throw caution to the wind because we are quite sure that the files will be there and will work . Let's examine what is inside the `try` block. Take a close look at the following code and then we will dissect it:

```
try{
   //Create objects of the 2 required classes
         AssetManager assetManager = getAssets();
         AssetFileDescriptor descriptor;

         //create our three fx in memory ready for use
         descriptor = assetManager.openFd("sample1.ogg");
         sample1 = soundPool.load(descriptor, 0);

         descriptor = assetManager.openFd("sample2.ogg");
         sample2 = soundPool.load(descriptor, 0);


         descriptor = assetManager.openFd("sample3.ogg");
         sample3 = soundPool.load(descriptor, 0);


      }catch(IOException e){
          //catch exceptions here
      }
```

First, we create an object called `assetManager` of the `AssetManager` type and an `AssetFileDescriptor` object called `descriptor`. We then use these two objects combined to load our first sound sample like this:

```
descriptor = assetManager.openFd("sample1.ogg");
sample1 = soundPool.load(descriptor, 0);
```

We now have a sound sample loaded in memory and its location saved in our `int` variable called `sample1`. The first sound file, `sample1.ogg`, is now ready to use. We perform the same procedure for `sample2` and `sample3` and we are ready to make some noise!

In step 11, we set up our buttons, which we have seen several times before. In step 12, we have our switch block ready to perform a different action depending upon which button is pressed. You can probably see that the single action each button takes is the playing of a sound. For example, **Button1** does this:

```
soundPool.play(sample1, 1, 1, 0, 0, 1);
```

This line of code plays the sound that is loaded in memory at the location referred to by `int sample1`.

 The arguments of the method from left to right define the following: the sample to play, left volume, right volume, priority over other playing sounds, loop or not, rate of playback. You can have some fun with these if you like. Try setting the loop argument to 3 and the rate argument to perhaps 1.5.

We handle each button in the same way. Now let's learn something serious.

Life after destruction – persistence

Okay, this is not as heavy as it sounds, but it is an important topic when making games. You have probably noticed that the slightest thing can reset our math game, such as an incoming phone call, a battery that ran flat, or even tilting the device to a different orientation.

When these events occur, we might like our game to remember the exact state it was in so that when the player comes back, it is in exactly the same place as they left off. If you were using a word-processing app, you would definitely expect this type of behavior.

We are not going to go to that extent with our game, but as a bare minimum, shouldn't we at least remember the high score? This gives the player something to aim for, and most importantly, a reason to come back to our game.

An example of persistence

Android and Java have many different ways to achieve persistence of data, from reading and writing to files to setting up and using whole databases through our code. However, the neatest, simplest, and most suitable way for the examples in this book is by using the `SharedPreferences` class.

In this example, we will use the `SharedPreferences` class to save data. Actually, we will be reading and writing to files, but the class hides all of the complexity from us and allows us to focus on the game.

We will see a somewhat abstract example of persistence so that we are familiar with the code before we use something similar to save the high score in our memory game. The complete code for this example can be found in the code bundle at `Chapter5/Persistence/java/MainActivity.java` and `Chapter5/Persistence/layout/activity_main.xml`:

1. Create a project with a blank activity, just as we did in *Chapter 2, Getting Started with Android*. Also, clean up the code by deleting the unnecessary parts, but this isn't essential.

2. Open `activity_main.xml` in the editor window and click and drag one button from the palette to the design. The default ID of the button that is assigned is perfect for our uses, so no further work is required on the UI.

3. Open `MainActivity.java` in the editor window. Implement `View.onClickListener` and autogenerate the required `onClick` method, just as we did in steps 6 and 7 of the *Playing sound in Android* example previously.

4. Type the following code just after the `MainActivity` declaration. This declares our two objects that will do all the complex stuff behind the scenes: a bunch of strings that will be useful and a button:

```
SharedPreferences prefs;
SharedPreferences.Editor editor;
String dataName = "MyData";
String stringName = "MyString";
String defaultString = ":-(";
String currentString = "";//empty
Button button1;
```

5. Add the next block of code to the `onCreate` method after the call to `setContentView`. We initialize our objects and set up our button. We will look closely at this code once the example is done:

```
//initialize our two SharedPreferences objects
prefs = getSharedPreferences(dataName,MODE_PRIVATE);
editor = prefs.edit();

//Either load our string or
//if not available our default string
currentString = prefs.getString(stringName, defaultString);

 //Make a button from the button in our layout
 button1 =(Button) findViewById(R.id.button);

 //Make each it listen for clicks
```

```
button1.setOnClickListener(this);

//load currentString to the button
button1.setText(currentString);
```

6. Now the action takes place in our `onClick` method. Add this code, which generates a random number and adds it to the end of `currentString`. Then it saves the string and sets the value of the string to the button as well:

```
//we don't need to switch here!
//There is only one button
//so only the code that actually does stuff

//Get a random number between 0 and 9
Random randInt = new Random();
int ourRandom = randInt.nextInt(10);

//Add the random number to the end of currentString
currentString = currentString + ourRandom;

//Save currentString to a file in case the user
//suddenly quits or gets a phone call
editor.putString(stringName, currentString);
editor.commit();

//update the button text
button1.setText(currentString);
```

Run the example on an emulator or a device. Notice that each time you press the button, a random number is appended to the text of the button. Now quit the app, or even shut down the device if you like. When you restart the app, our cool `SharedPreferences` class simply loads the last saved string.

Here is how the code works. There is nothing we haven't seen several times before until step 4:

```
SharedPreferences prefs;
SharedPreferences.Editor editor;
```

Here, we declare two types of `SharedPreferences` objects called `prefs` and `editor`. We will see exactly how we use them in a minute.

Next, we declare the `dataName` and `stringName` strings. We do this because to use the facilities of `SharedPreferences`, we need to refer to our collection of data, as well as any individual pieces of data within it, using a consistent name. By initializing `dataName` and `stringName`, we can use them as a name for our data store as well as a specific item within that data store, respectively. The sad face in `defaultString` gets used any time the `SharedPreferences` object needs a default because either nothing has been previously saved or the loading process fails for some reason. The `currentString` variable will hold the value of the string we will be saving and loading as well as displaying to the user of our app. Our button is `button1`:

```
String dataName = "MyData";
String stringName = "MyString";
String defaultString = ":-(";
String currentString = "";//empty
Button button1;
```

In step 5, the real action starts with this code:

```
prefs = getSharedPreferences(dataName,MODE_PRIVATE);
editor = prefs.edit();


currentString = prefs.getString(stringName, defaultString);
```

The previous code does stuff that would take a lot more code if we didn't have the useful `SharedPreferences` class. The first two lines initialize the objects and the third loads the value from our data store item, whose name is contained in `stringName`, to our `currentString` variable. The first time this happens, it uses the `defaultString` value because nothing is stored there yet, but once there is a value stored, this single line of code that will load up our saved string.

At the end of step 5, we set up our button as we have done many times before. Moving on to step 6 in the `onClick` method, there is no `switch` block because there is only one button. So if a click is detected, it must be our button. Here are the first three lines from `onClick`:

```
Random randInt = new Random();
int ourRandom = randInt.nextInt(10);
currentString = currentString + ourRandom;
```

We generate a random number and append it to the `currentString` variable. Next, still in `onClick`, we do this:

```
editor.putString(stringName, currentString);
editor.commit();
```

This is like the opposite of the code that loaded our string in `onCreate`. The first of the previous two lines identifies the place in the data store to write the value to (`stringName`) and the value to be written there (`currentString`). The next line, `editor.commit();`, simply says, "go ahead and do it."

The following line displays `currentString` as text on our button so that we can see what is going on:

```
button1.setText(currentString);
```

 For more on persistence, take a look at the second question of the *Self-test questions* section at the end of this chapter.

The memory game

The code in the memory game shouldn't challenge us too much because we have done the background research on threads, arrays, sound, and persistence. There will be some new-looking code and we will examine it in detail when it crops up.

Here is a screenshot of our finished game:

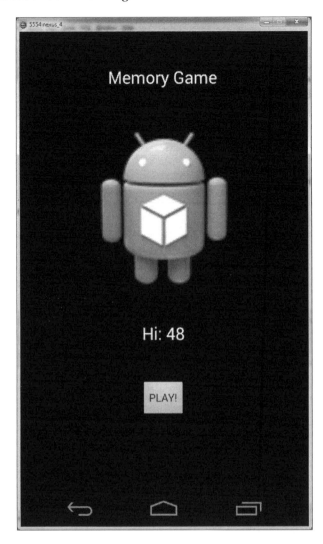

This is the home screen. It shows the high score, which persists between play sessions and when the device is shut down. It also shows a **Play** button, which will take the player to the main game screen. Take a look at the following screenshot:

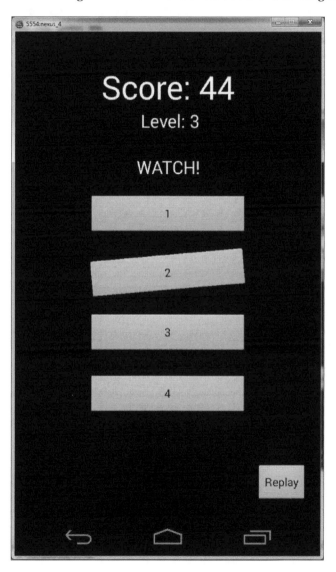

The game screen itself will play a sequence of sounds and numbers. The corresponding button will *wobble* in time with the corresponding sound. Then the player will be able to interact with the buttons and attempt to copy the sequence. For every part of the sequence that the player gets right, they will be awarded points.

If the sequence is copied in its entirety, then a new and longer sequence will be played and again the player will attempt to repeat the sequence. This continues until the player gets a part of a sequence wrong.

As the score increases, it is displayed in the relevant TextView, and when a sequence is copied correctly, the level is increased and displayed below the score.

The player can start a new game by pressing the **Replay** button. If a high score is achieved, it will be saved to a file and displayed on the home screen.

The implementation of the game is divided into five phases. The end of a phase would be a good place to take a break. Here are the different phases of the game:

- **Phase 1**: This implements the UI and some basics.
- **Phase 2**: This prepares our variables and presents the pattern (to be copied) to the player.
- **Phase 3**: In this phase, we will handle the player's response when they try to copy the pattern.
- **Phase 4**: Here, we will use what we just learned about persistence to maintain the player's high score when they quit the game or turn off their device.
- **Phase 5**: At the end of phase 4, we will have a fully working memory game. However, to add to our repertoire of Android skills, after we have discussed Android UI animations near the end of this chapter, we will complete this phase, which will enhance our memory game.

All the files containing the complete code and the sound files after all five stages can be found in the download bundle in the `Chapter5/MemoryGame` folder. In this project, however, there is a lot to be learned from going through each of the stages.

Phase 1 – the UI and the basics

Here, we will lay out a home menu screen UI and a UI for the game itself. We will also configure some IDs for some of the UI elements so that we can control them in our Java code later:

1. Create a new application called `Memory Game` and clean up the code if you wish.

2. Now we create a new activity and call it GameActivity. So right-click on the java folder in Project Explorer, navigate to **New | Activity**, then click on **Next**, name the activity as GameActivity, and click on **Finish**. For clarity, clean up this activity in the same way as we cleaned up all our others.

3. Make the game fullscreen and lock the orientation as we did in the *Going fullscreen and locking orientation* tutorial at the end of *Chapter 4, Discovering Loops and Methods*.

4. Open the activity_main.xml file from the res/layout folder.

Let's quickly create our home screen UI by performing the following steps:

1. Open activity_main.xml in the editor and delete the **Hello World** TextView.

2. Click and drag the following: **Large Text** to the top center (to create our title text), **Image** just below that, another **LargeText** below that (for our high score), and a **Button** (for our player to click to play). Your UI should look a bit like what is shown in the following screenshot:

3. Adjust the **text** properties of the two TextViews and the Button element to make it plain what each will be used for. As usual, you can replace the Android icon in the **ImageView** with any image you choose (as we did in *Chapter 4, Discovering Loops and Methods,* in the *Adding a custom image* tutorial).

4. Tweak the sizes of the elements in the usual way to suit the emulator or device you will be running the game on.

5. Let's make the ID for our **Hi Score** TextView more relevant to its purpose. Left-click to select the **Hi Score** TextView, find its **id** property in the **Properties** window, and change it to `textHiScore`. The IDs of the image and the title are not required, and the existing ID of the play button is `button`, which seems appropriate already. So there is nothing else to change here.

Let's wire up the **Play** button to create a link between the home and the game screens, as follows:

1. Open `MainActivity.java` in the editor.

2. Add `implements View.onClickListener` to the end of the `MainActivity` declaration so that it now looks like this:

    ```
    public class MainActivity extends Activity implements
       View.OnClickListener {
    ```

3. Now hover your mouse over the line you just typed and right-click on it. Now click on **Generate**, then on **Implement methods...**, and then on **OK** to have Android Studio autogenerate the `onClick` method we must implement.

4. At the end of our `onCreate` method, before the closing curly brace, enter the following code to get a reference to our **Play** button and listen to clicks:

    ```
    //Make a button from the button in our layout
    Button button =(Button) findViewById(R.id.button);

    //Make each it listen for clicks
    button.setOnClickListener(this);
    ```

5. Scroll down to our `onClick` method and enter the following code in its body to have the **Play** button take the player to our `GameActivity`, which we will design soon:

    ```
    Intent i;
    i = new Intent(this, GameActivity.class);
    startActivity(i);
    ```

At this point, the app will run and the player can click on the **Play** button to take them to our game screen. So let's quickly create our game screen UI:

1. Open `activity_game.xml` in the editor and delete the **Hello World** TextView.

2. Drag three **Large Text** elements one below the other and center them horizontally. Below them, add four buttons stacked one on top of the other, and finally, add another button below that but offset it to the right-hand side so that it looks like what is shown in the next screenshot. I have also adjusted the text properties for the UI elements to make it clear what each will be used for, but this is optional because our Java code will do all of the work for us. You can also tweak the sizes of the elements in the usual way to suit the emulator or device you will be running the game on.

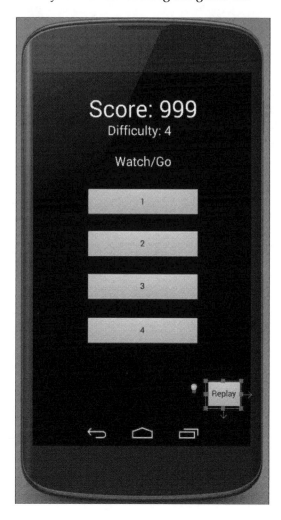

3. Now let's assign some useful IDs to our UI elements so that we can do some Java magic with them in the next tutorial. Here is a table that matches the UI elements shown in the last screenshot with the **id** property value that you need to assign. Assign the following **id** property values to the corresponding UI elements:

Purpose	Default id property	New id to assign
Score indicator	textView	textScore
Difficulty indicator	textView2	textDifficulty
Watch/go indicator	textView3	textWatchGo
Button 1	button	Leave at default
Button 2	button2	Leave at default
Button 3	button3	Leave at default
Button 4	button4	Leave at default
Replay button	button5	buttonReplay

Now that we have our game menu and actual game UI ready to go, we can start to make it work.

Phase 2 – preparing our variables and presenting the pattern

Here, we will set up a whole load of variables and objects for us to use, both in this phase and in the later phases. We will also implement the parts of the code that present a pattern to the player. We will add code that enables the player to respond in a later phase:

1. Open GameActivity.java in the editor window.

2. I made the sounds by finding a pleasing one then slowly increasing the **Frequency** slider for each subsequent sample. You can use my sound from the assets folder in the MemoryGame project or create your own sound using Bfxr.

3. In the main folder in the project explorer window, we need to add a folder called assets. So in the project explorer window, right-click on the main folder and navigate to **New | Directory**. Type assets in the **New Directory** dialog box.

4. Now copy and paste the four sound files to the newly created assets folder. You can do so like this: select the files, right-click on them, and then click on **Copy**. Then click on the assets folder in the Android Studio project explorer. Now right-click on the assets folder and click on **Paste**.

Let's prepare `GameActivity` to listen to button clicks just as we did for `MainActivity`, as follows:

1. Add `implementsView.onClickListener` to the end of the `GameActivity` declaration so that it now looks like this:

    ```
    public class GameActivity extends Activity implements
       View.OnClickListener {
    ```

2. Now hover your mouse over the line you just typed and right-click on it. Now click on **Generate**, then on **Implement methods...**, and then on **OK** to have Android Studio autogenerate the `onClick` method that we will use shortly.

3. Let's declare some objects that we need to reference our UI and our `int` references for the sound effects we will load soon. Write the code just after the declaration for `GameActivity`. By putting them here, they will be available to all parts of our code in `GameActivity.java`. Here is the code in context:

    ```
    public class GameActivity extends Activity implements
       View.OnClickListener {

    //Prepare objects and sound references

        //initialize sound variables
        private SoundPool soundPool;
        int sample1 = -1;
        int sample2 = -1;
        int sample3 = -1;
        int sample4 = -1;

        //for our UI
        TextView textScore;
        TextView textDifficulty;
        TextView textWatchGo;

        Button button1;
        Button button2;
        Button button3;
        Button button4;
        Button buttonReplay;
    ```

4. Now, after the last line of code from the previous step, enter the following code snippet, which will declare and initialize some variables for use in our thread. Notice that at the end, we also declare myHandler, which will be our thread, and gameOn to control whether our code within the thread is executed:

```
//Some variables for our thread
int difficultyLevel = 3;
//An array to hold the randomly generated sequence
int[] sequenceToCopy = new int[100];

private Handler myHandler;
//Are we playing a sequence at the moment?
boolean playSequence = false;
//And which element of the sequence are we on
int elementToPlay = 0;

//For checking the players answer
int playerResponses;
int playerScore;
boolean isResponding;
```

5. Just after our call to setContentView in the onCreate method, we make our sound effects ready to be played:

```
soundPool = new SoundPool(10, AudioManager.STREAM_MUSIC,0);
try{
  //Create objects of the 2 required classes
  AssetManager assetManager = getAssets();
  AssetFileDescriptor descriptor;

  //create our three fx in memory ready for use
  descriptor = assetManager.openFd("sample1.ogg");
  sample1 = soundPool.load(descriptor, 0);

        descriptor = assetManager.openFd("sample2.ogg");
        sample2 = soundPool.load(descriptor, 0);


        descriptor = assetManager.openFd("sample3.ogg");
        sample3 = soundPool.load(descriptor, 0);

        descriptor = assetManager.openFd("sample4.ogg");
        sample4 = soundPool.load(descriptor, 0);


        }catch(IOException e){
            //catch exceptions here
        }
```

6. Just after the code in the last step and still within the `onCreate` method, we initialize our objects and set click listeners for the buttons:

```
//Reference all the elements of our UI
//First the TextViews
textScore = (TextView)findViewById(R.id.textScore);
textScore.setText("Score: " + playerScore);
textDifficulty = (TextView)findViewById(R.id.textDifficulty);

textDifficulty.setText("Level: " + difficultyLevel);
textWatchGo = (TextView)findViewById(R.id.textWatchGo);

//Now the buttons
button1 = (Button)findViewById(R.id.button);
button2 = (Button)findViewById(R.id.button2);
button3 = (Button)findViewById(R.id.button3);
button4 = (Button)findViewById(R.id.button4);
buttonReplay = (Button)findViewById(R.id.buttonReplay);

//Now set all the buttons to listen for clicks
button1.setOnClickListener(this);
button2.setOnClickListener(this);
button3.setOnClickListener(this);
button4.setOnClickListener(this);
buttonReplay.setOnClickListener(this);
```

7. Now, after the last line of the code from the previous step, enter the code that will create our thread. We will add the details in the next step within the `if(playSequence)` block. Notice that the thread is run every nine-tenths of a second (900 milliseconds). Notice that we start the thread but do not set `playSequence` to `true`. So it will not do anything yet:

```
//This is the code which will define our thread
myHandler = new Handler() {
  public void handleMessage(Message msg) {
    super.handleMessage(msg);

        if (playSequence) {
        //All the thread action will go here

        }

        myHandler.sendEmptyMessageDelayed(0, 900);
  }
```

```
};//end of thread
```

```
myHandler.sendEmptyMessage(0);
```

8. Before we look at the code that will run in our thread, we need a way to generate a random sequence appropriate for the difficulty level. This situation sounds like a candidate for a method. Enter this method just before the closing curly brace of the GameActivity class:

```
public void createSequence(){
  //For choosing a random button
  Random randInt = new Random();
  int ourRandom;
  for(int i = 0; i < difficultyLevel; i++){
  //get a random number between 1 and 4
        ourRandom = randInt.nextInt(4);
        ourRandom ++;//make sure it is not zero
        //Save that number to our array
        sequenceToCopy[i] = ourRandom;
  }

}
```

9. We also need a method to prepare and start our thread. Type the following method after the closing curly brace of createSequence:

Actually, the order of implementation of the methods is unimportant. However, following along in order will mean our code will look the same. Even if you are referring to the downloaded code, the order will be the same.

```
public void playASequence(){
    createSequence();
    isResponding = false;
    elementToPlay = 0;
    playerResponses = 0;
    textWatchGo.setText("WATCH!");
    playSequence = true;
}
```

10. Just before we look at the details of the thread code, we need a method to tidy up our variables after the sequence has been played. Enter this method after the closing curly brace of `playASequence`:

```
public void sequenceFinished(){
        playSequence = false;
        //make sure all the buttons are made visible
        button1.setVisibility(View.VISIBLE);
        button2.setVisibility(View.VISIBLE);
        button3.setVisibility(View.VISIBLE);
        button4.setVisibility(View.VISIBLE);
        textWatchGo.setText("GO!");
        isResponding = true;
    }
```

11. Finally, we will implement our thread. There is some new code in this part, which we will go through in detail after we finish this phase of the project. Enter this code between the opening and closing curly braces of the `if(playSequence){ }` block:

```
if (playSequence) {
  //All the thread action will go here
  //make sure all the buttons are made visible
  button1.setVisibility(View.VISIBLE);
  button2.setVisibility(View.VISIBLE);
  button3.setVisibility(View.VISIBLE);
  button4.setVisibility(View.VISIBLE);

  switch (sequenceToCopy[elementToPlay]){
    case 1:
      //hide a button
button1.setVisibility(View.INVISIBLE);
       //play a sound
       soundPool.play(sample1, 1, 1, 0, 0, 1);
       break;

    case 2:
      //hide a button
button2.setVisibility(View.INVISIBLE)
       //play a sound
       soundPool.play(sample2, 1, 1, 0, 0, 1);
       break;

    case 3:
      //hide a button button3.setVisibility(View.INVISIBLE);
```

```
            //play a sound
            soundPool.play(sample3, 1, 1, 0, 0, 1);
            break;

        case 4:
            //hide a button
    button4.setVisibility(View.INVISIBLE);
            //play a sound
            soundPool.play(sample4, 1, 1, 0, 0, 1);
                break;
        }

        elementToPlay++;
        if(elementToPlay == difficultyLevel){
        sequenceFinished();
        }
    }

        myHandler.sendEmptyMessageDelayed(0, 900);

    }

    };
```

Just before the closing curly brace of onCreate, we could initiate a sequence by calling our playASequence method, like this:

```
    playASequence();
```

We could then run our app, click on **Play** on the home screen, and watch as a sequence of four random buttons and their matching sounds begins, with the sounds being played. In the next phase, we will wire up the **Replay** button so that the player can start the sequence when they are ready.

Phew! That was a long one. Actually, there is not much new there, but we did cram in just about everything we ever learned about Java and Android into one place, and we used it in new ways too. So we will look at it step by step and give extra focus to the parts that might seem tricky.

Let's look at each new piece of code in turn.

From steps 1 to 7, we initialized our variables, set up our buttons, and loaded our sounds as we have done before. We also put in the outline of the code for our thread.

In step 8, we implemented the `createSequence` method. We used a `Random` object to generate a sequence of random numbers between 1 and 4. We did this in a `for` loop, which loops until a sequence the length of `difficultyLevel` has been created. The sequence is stored in an array called `sequenceToCopy`, which we can later use to compare to the player's response:

```
public void createSequence(){
        //For choosing a random button
        Random randInt = new Random();
        int ourRandom;
        for(int i = 0; i < difficultyLevel; i++){
            //get a random number between 1 and 4
            ourRandom = randInt.nextInt(4);
            ourRandom ++;//make sure it is not zero
            //Save that number to our array
            sequenceToCopy[i] = ourRandom;
        }

    }
```

In step 9, we implemented `playASequence`. First, we call `createSequence` to load our `sequenceToCopy` array. Then we set `isResponding` to `false` because we don't want the player to bash buttons while the sequence is still playing. We set `elementToPlay` to `0` as this is the first element of our array. We also set `playerResponses` to `0`, ready to count the player's responses. Next, we set some text on the UI to `"WATCH!"` to make it clear to the player that the sequence is playing. Finally, we set `playSequence` to `true`, which allows the code in our thread to run once every 900 milliseconds. Here is the code we have just analyzed:

```
public void playASequence(){
        createSequence();
        isResponding = false;
        elementToPlay = 0;
        playerResponses = 0;
        textWatchGo.setText("WATCH!");
        playSequence = true;

    }
```

In step 10, we handle `sequenceFinished`. We set `playSequence` to `false`, which prevents the code in our thread from running. We set all the buttons back to visible because, as we will see in the thread code, we set them to invisible to emphasize which button comes next in the sequence. We set our UI text to **GO!** to make it clear. It is time for the player to try and copy the sequence. For the code in the `checkElement` method to run, we set `isResponding` to `true`. We will look at the code in the `checkElement` method in the next phase:

```
public void sequenceFinished(){
        playSequence = false;
        //make sure all the buttons are made visible
        button1.setVisibility(View.VISIBLE);
        button2.setVisibility(View.VISIBLE);
        button3.setVisibility(View.VISIBLE);
        button4.setVisibility(View.VISIBLE);
        textWatchGo.setText("GO!");
        isResponding = true;
    }
```

In step 11, we implement our thread. It's quite long but not too complicated. First, we set all the buttons to visible as this is quicker than checking which one of them is currently invisible and setting just that one:

```
if (playSequence) {
    //All the thread action will go here
    //make sure all the buttons are made visible
    button1.setVisibility(View.VISIBLE);
    button2.setVisibility(View.VISIBLE);
    button3.setVisibility(View.VISIBLE);
    button4.setVisibility(View.VISIBLE);
```

Then we switch based on what number is next in our sequence, hide the appropriate button, and play the appropriate sound. Here is the first case in the `switch` block for reference. The other case elements perform the same function but on a different button and with a different sound:

```
switch (sequenceToCopy[elementToPlay]){
  case 1:
    //hide a button
    button1.setVisibility(View.INVISIBLE);
        //play a sound
        soundPool.play(sample1, 1, 1, 0, 0, 1);
        break;

  //case 2, 3 and go here
  }
```

Now we increment `elementToPlay`, ready to play the next part of the sequence when the thread runs again in approximately 900 milliseconds:

```
elementToPlay++;
```

Next, we check whether we have played the last part of the sequence. If we have, we call our `sequenceFinished` method to set things up for the player to attempt their answer:

```
if(elementToPlay == difficultyLevel){
sequenceFinished();
}
}
```

Finally, we tell the thread when we would like to run our code again:

```
myHandler.sendEmptyMessageDelayed(0, 900);
}

};
```

When you ran a sequence (see the previous tip), did you notice an imperfection/bug with our game operation? This has to do with the way the last element of the sequence is animated. It is because our `sequenceFinished` method makes all the buttons visible so soon after the button has just been made invisible that looks like the button is never made invisible at all. We will solve the problem of the button that doesn't stay invisible long enough when we learn about UI animation in phase 5.

Now let's handle the player's response.

Phase 3 – the player's response

We now have an app that plays a random sequence of button flashes and matching sounds. It also stores that sequence in an array. So what we have to do now is enable the player to attempt to replicate the sequence and score points if successful.

We can do all of this in two phases. First, we need to handle the button presses, which can pass all the hard work to a method that will do everything else.

Let's write the code and look at it as we go. Afterwards, we will closely examine the less obvious parts:

1. Here is how we handle the button presses. We have the empty body of the `switch` statement with an extra `if` statement that checks whether there is a sequence currently being played. If there is a sequence, then no input is accepted. We will start to fill the code in the empty body in the next step:

    ```
    if(!playSequence) {//only accept input if sequence not playing
            switch (view.getId()) {
                //case statements here...
            }
    }
    ```

2. Now, here is the code that handles `button1`. Notice that it just plays the sound related to `button1` and then calls the `checkElement` method, passing a value of 1. This is all we have to do for the buttons 1 through 4: play a sound and then tell our new method (`checkElement`) which numbered button was pressed, and `checkElement` will do the rest:

    ```
    case R.id.button:
      //play a sound
        soundPool.play(sample1, 1, 1, 0, 0, 1);
        checkElement(1);
        break;
    ```

3. Here is the near-identical code for buttons 2 through 4. Notice that the value passed to `checkElement` and the sound sample that is played are the only differences from the previous step. Enter this code directly after the code in the previous step:

    ```
    case R.id.button2:
      //play a sound
        soundPool.play(sample2, 1, 1, 0, 0, 1);
        checkElement(2);
        break;

    case R.id.button3:
        //play a sound
        soundPool.play(sample3, 1, 1, 0, 0, 1);
        checkElement(3);
        break;

    case R.id.button4:
        //play a sound
        soundPool.play(sample4, 1, 1, 0, 0, 1);
        checkElement(4);
        break;
    ```

4. Here is the last part of the code in our `onClick` method. This handles the **Restart** button. The code just resets the score and the difficulty level and then calls our `playASequence` method, which does the rest of the work of starting the game again. Enter this code directly after the code in the previous step:

```
case R.id.buttonReplay:
    difficultyLevel = 3;
    playerScore = 0;
    textScore.setText("Score: " + playerScore);
    playASequence();
    break;
```

5. Finally, here is our do-everything method. This is quite a long method compared to most of our previous methods, but it helps to see its entire structure. We will break this down line by line in a minute. Enter the following code, after which you will actually be able to play the game and get a score:

```
public void checkElement(int thisElement){

if(isResponding) {
    playerResponses++;
    if (sequenceToCopy[playerResponses-1] == thisElement) { //
Correct
    playerScore = playerScore + ((thisElement + 1) * 2);
    textScore.setText("Score: " + playerScore);
    if (playerResponses == difficultyLevel) {//got the whole
sequence
    //don't checkElement anymore
    isResponding = false;
    //now raise the difficulty
    difficultyLevel++;
    //and play another sequence
    playASequence();
    }

} else {//wrong answer
    textWatchGo.setText("FAILED!");
    //don't checkElement anymore
    isResponding = false;
}
}
```

We covered the methods fairly comprehensively as we went through the tutorial. The one elephant in the room, however, is the apparent sprawl of code in the `checkElement` method. So let's go through all of the code in step 6, line by line.

First, we have the method signature. Notice that it does not return a value but it receives an int value. Remember that it is the onClick method that calls this method and it passes a 1, 2, 3, or 4, depending upon which button was clicked:

```
public void checkElement(int thisElement){
```

Next, we wrap the rest of this code into an if statement. Here is the if statement. We enter the block when the isResponding Boolean is true, and isResponding is set to true when the sequenceFinnished method completes, which is just what we need so that the player can't mash the buttons until it is time to do so and our game is ready to listen:

```
if(isResponding) {
```

Here is what happens inside the if block. We increment the number of the player's responses received in the playerResponses variable:

```
playerResponses++;
```

Now we check whether the number passed to the checkElement method and stored in thisElement matches the appropriate part of the sequence the player is trying to copy. If it matches, we increase playerScore by an amount relative to the number of correctly matched parts of the sequence so far. Then we set the score on the screen. Notice that if the response does not match, there is an else block to go with this if block that we will explain soon:

```
if (sequenceToCopy[playerResponses-1] == thisElement) {  //Correct
    playerScore = playerScore + ((thisElement + 1) * 2);
    textScore.setText("Score: " + playerScore);
```

Next, we have another if block. Note that this if block is nested inside the if block we just described. So it will only be tested and potentially run if the player's response was correct. This if statement checks whether it is the last part of the sequence, like this:

```
if (playerResponses == difficultyLevel) {
```

If it is the last part of the sequence, it executes the following lines:

```
//got the whole sequence
        //don't checkElement anymore
        isResponding = false;
        //now raise the difficulty
        difficultyLevel++;
        //and play another sequence
        playASequence();
    }
```

What is happening inside the nested `if` statement, which checks whether the whole sequence has been correctly copied, is the following: It sets `isResponding` to `false`, so the player gets no response from the buttons. It then raises the difficulty level by 1 so that the sequence is a bit tougher next time. Finally, it calls the `playSequence` method to play another sequence and the whole process starts again.

Here is the `else` block, which runs if the player gets part of the sequence wrong:

```
} else {
  //wrong answer
  textWatchGo.setText("FAILED!");
  //don't checkElement anymore
  isResponding = false;
  }
}
```

Here, we set some text on the screen and set `isResponding` to `false`.

Now let's use what we learned about the `SharedPreferences` class to preserve the high scores.

Phase 4 – preserving the high score

This phase is nice and short. We will use what we learned earlier in the chapter to save the player's score if it is a new high score, and then display the best score in the **hi-score** TextView in our `MainActivity`:

1. Open `MainActivity.java` in the editor window.

2. Then we declare our objects used to read from a file just after the class declaration, like this:

```
public class MainActivity extends Activity implements View.
OnClickListener{

    //for our hiscore (phase 4)
    SharedPreferences prefs;
    String dataName = "MyData";
    String intName = "MyString";
    int defaultInt = 0;
    //both activities can see this
    public static int hiScore;
```

3. Now, just after our call to `setContentView` in the `onCreate` method, we initialize our objects, read from our file, and set the result to our `hiScore` variable. We then display it to the player:

```
//for our high score (phase 4)
//initialize our two SharedPreferences objects
prefs = getSharedPreferences(dataName,MODE_PRIVATE);

//Either load our High score or
//if not available our default of 0
hiScore = prefs.getInt(intName, defaultInt);

//Make a reference to the Hiscore textview in our layout
TextView textHiScore =(TextView) findViewById(R.id.textHiScore);
//Display the hi score
textHiScore.setText("Hi: "+ hiScore);
```

4. Next, we need to go back to the `GameActivity.java` file.

5. We declare our objects to edit our file, this time like this:

```
//for our hiscore (phase 4)
SharedPreferences prefs;
SharedPreferences.Editor editor;
String dataName = "MyData";
String intName = "MyInt";
int defaultInt = 0;
int hiScore;
```

6. Just after the call to `setContentView` in the `onCreate` method, we instantiate our objects and assign a value to `hiScore`:

```
//phase 4
//initialize our two SharedPreferences objects
prefs = getSharedPreferences(dataName,MODE_PRIVATE);
editor = prefs.edit();
hiScore = prefs.getInt(intName, defaultInt);
```

7. The only thing that is different to what we have already learned is that we need to consider where we put the code to test for a high score and where to write to our file if appropriate. Consider this: eventually, every player must fail. Furthermore, the point at which they fail is the point when their score is at its highest, yet before it is reset when they try again. Place the following code in the `else` block, which handles a wrong answer from the player. The highlighted code is the new code; the rest is there to help you with the context:

```
} else {//wrong answer

    textWatchGo.setText("FAILED!");
      //don't checkElement anymore
      isResponding = false;

    //for our high score (phase 4)
    if(playerScore > hiScore) {
     hiScore = playerScore;
          editor.putInt(intName, hiScore);
          editor.commit();
          Toast.makeText(getApplicationContext(), "New Hi-
              score", Toast.LENGTH_LONG).show();
    }

}
```

Play the game and get a high score. Now quit the app or even restart the phone. When you come back to the app, your high score is still there.

The code we added in this phase is nearly the same as the code we wrote in our previous example of persistence, the only difference being that we wrote to the data store when a new high score was achieved instead of when a button was pressed. In addition, we used the `editor.putInt` method because we were saving an integer instead of `editor.putString` when we were saving a string.

Animating our game

Before we go ahead, let's just think about animation. What is it exactly? The word probably conjures up images of moving cartoon characters and in-game characters of a video game.

We need to animate our buttons (make them move) to make it clear when they are part of the sequence. We saw that simply making one disappear and then reappear was inadequate.

The thought of controlling the movement of UI elements might make us imagine complex `for` loops and per-pixel calculations.

Fortunately, Android provides us with the `Animation` class, which allows us to animate UI objects without any such per-pixel awkwardness. Here is how it works.

> Of course, to fully control the shape and size of in-game objects, we must eventually learn to manipulate individual pixels and lines. We will do so from *Chapter 7, Retro Squash Game*, onwards, when we make a retro pong-style squash game.

UI animation in Android

Animations in the Android UI can be divided into three phases:

- Describing the animation in a file using a special syntax we will see shortly
- Referencing that animation by creating an object of it in our Java code
- Applying the animation to a UI element when the animation is required to run

Let's take a look at some code that describes an animation. We will soon be reusing this same code in our memory game. The purpose of showing it is not so much that we understand each and every line of it. After all, learning Java should be enough of an accomplishment without mastering this too. Moreover, the purpose is to demonstrate that whatever animation you can describe can then be used in our games using the same Java.

We can quickly search the Web to find the code to perform the following:

- Fading in and out
- Sliding
- Rotating

- Expanding or shrinking

- Morphing color

Here is some code that causes a wobble effect. We will use it on a button, but you can also use it on any UI element or even the whole screen:

```xml
<?xml version="1.0" encoding="utf-8"?>
<rotate xmlns:android="http://schemas.android.com/apk/res/android"
    android:duration="100"
    android:fromDegrees="-5"
    android:pivotX="50%"
    android:pivotY="50%"
    android:repeatCount="8"
    android:repeatMode="reverse"
    android:toDegrees="5" />
```

The first line simply states that this is a file written in XML format. The next states that we will be performing a rotation. Then we state that the duration will be 100 milliseconds, the rotation will be from -5 degrees, the pivot will be on the *x* and *y* axes by 50 percent, repeat eight times, and reverse to positive 5 degrees.

This is quite a mouthful, but the point is that it is easy to grab a template that works and then customize it to fit our situation. We could save the preceding code with a filename like `wobble.xml`.

Then we could simply reference it as follows:

```
Animation wobble = AnimationUtils.loadAnimation(this, R.anim.wobble);
```

Now we can play the animation like this on our chosen UI object, in this case our `button1` object:

```
button1.startAnimation(wobble);
```

Phase 5 – animating the UI

Let's add an animation that causes a button to wobble when a button sound is played. At the same time, we can remove the code that makes the button invisible and the code that makes it reappear. That wasn't the best way to do it, but it served a purpose while developing the game:

1. We need to add a new folder to our project, called `anim`. So right-click on the `res` folder in the Project Explorer window. Navigate to **New | Android resource directory** and click on **OK** to create the new `anim` folder.

2. Now right-click on the `anim` folder and navigate to **New | Animation resource file**. Enter `wobble` in the **File name** field and click on **OK**. We now have a new file called **wobble.xml** open in the editor window.

3. Replace all but the first line of `wobble.xml` with this code:

```xml
<?xml version="1.0" encoding="utf-8"?>
<rotate xmlns:android="http://schemas.android.com/apk/res/android"
    android:duration="100"
    android:fromDegrees="-5"
    android:pivotX="50%"
    android:pivotY="50%"
    android:repeatCount="8"
    android:repeatMode="reverse"
    android:toDegrees="5" />
```

4. Now switch to `GameActivity.java`.

5. Add the following code just after the declaration of our `GameActivity` class:

```java
//phase 5 - our animation object
Animation wobble;
```

6. Just after the call to `setContentView` in our `onCreate` method, add this piece of code:

```java
//phase5 - animation
wobble = AnimationUtils.loadAnimation(this, R.anim.wobble);
```

7. Now, near the start of our thread code, find the calls to make our buttons reappear. Comment them out like this:

```java
//code not needed as using animations
//make sure all the buttons are made visible
//button1.setVisibility(View.VISIBLE);
//button2.setVisibility(View.VISIBLE);
//button3.setVisibility(View.VISIBLE);
//button4.setVisibility(View.VISIBLE);
```

8. Next, directly after our code in the previous step, within each of the four `case` statements, we need to comment out the lines that call `setVisibility` and replace them with our wobble animation. The following code is slightly abbreviated but shows exactly where to comment and where to add the new lines:

```java
switch (sequenceToCopy[elementToPlay]){
  case 1:
    //hide a button - not any more
    //button1.setVisibility(View.INVISIBLE);
    button1.startAnimation(wobble);
```

```
. . .
. . .
case 2:
    //hide a button - not any more
    //button2.setVisibility(View.INVISIBLE);
    button2.startAnimation(wobble);
    . . .
    . . .
case 3:
    //hide a button - not any more
    //button3.setVisibility(View.INVISIBLE);
    button3.startAnimation(wobble);
    . . .
    . . .
case 4:
    //hide a button - not any more
    //button4.setVisibility(View.INVISIBLE);
    button4.startAnimation(wobble);
```

9. Finally, in our `sequenceFinished` method, we can comment out all the `setVisibility` calls, just as we did in our thread, like this:

```
//button1.setVisibility(View.VISIBLE);
//button2.setVisibility(View.VISIBLE);
//button3.setVisibility(View.VISIBLE);
//button4.setVisibility(View.VISIBLE);
```

That was not too tough. We added the wobble animation to the `anim` folder, declared an animation object, and initialized it. Then we used it whenever it was required on the appropriate button.

There are obviously loads of improvements we could make to this game, especially to its appearance. I'm sure you can think of more. And certainly, if this was to be your app, you were trying to make it big on the Play Store. That is exactly what you should do.

Constantly improve all aspects and strive to be the best in your genre. If you feel the urge, then why not improve upon it?

Here are a few self-test questions that look at ways we could do more with some of the examples from this chapter.

Self-test questions

Q1) Suppose that we want to have a quiz where the question could be to name the president as well as capital city. How can we do this with multidimensional arrays?

Q2) In our *Persistence example* section, we saved a continually updating string to a file so that it persisted after the app had been shut down and restarted. This is like asking the user to click on a Save button. Summoning all your knowledge of *Chapter 2, Getting Started with Android*, can you think of a way to save the string without saving it in the button click but just when the user quits the app?

Q3) Other than increasing the difficulty level, how could we increase the challenge of our memory game for our players?

Q4) Using the plain Android UI with the dull grey buttons isn't very exciting. Take a look at the UI elements in the visual designer and try and work out how we could quickly improve the visual appearance of our UI.

Summary

That was a bit of a hefty chapter, but we learned lots of new techniques such as storing and manipulating with arrays, creating and using sound effects, and saving important data such as a high score, in our game. We also took a very brief look at the powerful but simple-to-use `Animation` class.

In the next chapter, we will be taking a more theoretical approach, but we will have plenty of working samples too. We will finally be opening the black box of Java classes so that we can gain an understanding of what is going on when we declare and use objects of a class.

6
OOP – Using Other People's Hard Work

OOP stands for **object-oriented programming**. In this chapter, you don't need to even try and remember everything. Why do I say this? Surely, that's what learning is. The more important thing is to grasp the concepts and begin to understand the *why* of OOP rather than memorize rules, syntax, and jargon.

The more important thing is to actually start to use some of the concepts, even though you might have to keep referring back and your code might not properly adhere to every OOP principal that we discuss. Neither does the code in this book. The code in this chapter is here to help you explore and grasp the concepts of OOP.

If you try to memorize this chapter, you will have to make a lot of room in your brain, and you will probably forget something really important in its place such as going to work or thanking the author for telling you not to try and memorize this stuff.

A good goal will be to try and almost get it. Then we will start to recognize examples of OOP in action so that our understanding becomes more rounded. You can then often refer back to this chapter for a refresher.

So what is all this OOP stuff we will learn about? Actually, we have already learned loads about OOP. Until now, we have been using classes such as `Button`, `Random`, and `Activity`, overriding methods of classes (mainly `onCreate`) and using an **interface** as well; remember implementing `onClickListener` a few times in the first five chapters?

This chapter just helps to make sense of OOP and expands our understanding, and finally, we will make our own classes.

Then we will be in a good position in the next two chapters to make two cool retro arcade games using lots of other people's hard work. This chapter will be mainly theory, but with a few practical console examples using LogCat so that we can see OOP in action.

In this chapter, we will do the following:

- Look at what OOP is.

- Write our first class.

- Look at what encapsulation is and how we achieve it as well as look more deeply at variables and the different types. We will also take a short break to throw out the garbage.

- Learn about inheritance and how we can extend and even improve upon a class before we use it.

- Take a look at polymorphism, which is a way of being more than one thing at a time and is really useful in programming.

What is OOP?

OOP is a way of programming that involves breaking our requirements down into chunks that are more manageable than the whole.

Each chunk is self-contained yet potentially reusable by other programs while working together as a whole with the other chunks.

These chunks are what we have been referring to as objects. When we plan an object, we do so with a class. A class can be thought of as the blueprint of an object.

We implement an object of a class. This is called an **instance** of a class. Think about a house blueprint. You can't live in it, but you can build a house from it, which means you build an instance of it. However, OOP is more than this. It is also a methodology that defines best practices such as the following:

- **Encapsulation**: This means keeping the internal workings of your code safe from interference from the programs that use it, and allowing only the variables and methods you choose to be accessed. This means your code can always be updated, extended, or improved without affecting the programs that use it, as long as the exposed parts are still accessed in the same way.

- **Inheritance**: Just like it sounds, inheritance means we can harness all the features and benefits of other people's hard work, including encapsulation and polymorphism, while refining their code specifically for our situation. Actually, we have done this already every time we used the `extends` keyword.

- **Polymorphism**: This allows us to write code that is less dependent on the types we are trying to manipulate, making our code clearer and more efficient. Some examples later in the chapter will make this clear.

 When we talk about using other people's hard work, we are not talking about a magical way to abuse copyright and get away with it. Some code is plain and simple, someone else's property. What we are taking about is the vast array of free-to-use code, particularly in the context of this book, in the Java and Android APIs. If you want some code that does a certain thing, it has probably been done before. We just have to find it, then use it or modify it.

Java was designed from the start with all of this in mind, so we are fairly significantly constrained to using OOP. However, this is a good thing because we learn how to use the best practices.

Why do it like this?

When written properly, all this OOP allows you to add new features without worrying as much about how they interact with existing features. When you do have to change a class, its self-contained nature means less, or perhaps zero, consequences for other parts of the program. This is the encapsulation part.

You can use other people's code without knowing or perhaps even caring how it works. Think about the Android lifecycle, buttons, threads, and so on. The `Button` class is quite complicated, with nearly 50 methods—do we really want to write all that just for a button?

OOP allows you to write apps for highly complex situations without breaking a sweat. You can create multiple similar yet different versions of a class without starting the class from scratch using inheritance, and you can still use the methods intended for the original type of object with your new object because of polymorphism.

Makes sense, really! Let's write some classes and then make some objects out of them.

Our first class and first object

So what exactly is a class? A class is a bunch of code that can contain methods, variables, loops, and all other types of Java syntax. A class is part of a package and most packages will normally have multiple classes. Usually, but not always, each new class will be defined in its own `.java` code file with the same name as the class.

Once we have written a class, we can use it to make as many objects from it as we need. Remember, the class is the blueprint, and we make objects based on the blueprint. The house isn't the blueprint just as the object isn't the class; it is an object made from the class.

Here is the code for a class. We call it a class implementation:

```
public class Soldier {
   int health;
   String soldierType;

   void shootEnemy(){
      //bang bang
   }


}
```

The preceding snippet of code is a class implementation for a class called `Soldier`. There are two variables, an `int` variable called `health` and a `string` variable called `soldierType`.

There is also a method called `shootEnemy`. The method has no parameters and a `void return` type, but class methods can be of any shape or size that we discussed in *Chapter 5, Gaming and Java Essentials*.

When we declare variables in a class, they are known as **fields**. When the class is instantiated into a real object, the fields become variables of the object itself, so we call them **instance** variables. Whichever fancy name they are referred to by, they are just variables of the class. However, the difference between fields and variables declared in methods (called the **local** variables) becomes more important as we progress. We will look at all types of variables again in the *Variables revisited* section.

Remember, this is just a class, not an object. It is a blueprint for a soldier, not an actual `soldier` object. This is how we make an object of the `Soldier` type from our `Soldier` class:

```
Soldier mySoldier = new Soldier();
```

In the first part of the code, `Soldier mySoldier` declares a new reference type variable of type `Soldier`, called `mySoldier`, and in the last part of the code, `new Soldier()` creates an actual `Soldier` object. Of course, the assignment operator, `=`, in the middle of the two parts assigns the result of the second part to that of the first. Just like regular variables, we could also have performed the preceding steps like this:

```
Soldier mySoldier;
mySoldier = new Soldier();
```

This is how we would assign and use the variables:

```
mySoldier.health = 100;
mySoldier.soldierType = "sniper";
//Notice that we use the object name mySoldier.
//Not the class name Soldier.
//We didn't do this:
// Soldier.health = 100; ERROR!
```

In the preceding code snippet, the dot operator, ., is used to access the variables of the class, and this is how we would call the method. Again, we use the object name and not the class name, followed by the dot operator:

```
mySoldier.shootEnemy();
```

 As a rough guide, a class's methods are what it can *do* and its instance variables are what it *knows* about itself.

We can also go ahead by making another `Soldier` object and accessing its methods and variables:

```
Soldier mySoldier2 = new Soldier();
mySoldier2.health = 150;
mySoldier2.soldierType = "special forces";
mySoldier2.shootEnemy();
```

It is important to realize that `mySoldier2` is a totally separate object with totally separate instance variables.

Also notice that everything is done on the object itself. We must create objects of classes in order to make them useful.

 As always, there are exceptions to this rule, but they are in the minority, and we will look at the exceptions later in the chapter. In fact, we have already seen an exception way back in *Chapter 3, Speaking Java – Your First Game*. Think of `Toast`.

Let's explore basic classes a little more deeply.

Basic classes

What happens when we want an army of `Soldier` objects? We will instantiate multiple objects. We will also demonstrate the use of the dot operator on variables and methods, and show that different objects have different instance variables.

You can get the working project for this example in the code download. It is in the `chapter6` folder and is called simply `BasicClasses`. Or read on to create your own working example:

1. Create a project with a blank activity, just as we did in *Chapter 2, Getting Started with Android*. Clean up the code by deleting the unnecessary parts, but this isn't essential. Call the application `BasicClasses`.

2. Now we create a new class called `Soldier`. Right-click on the `com.packtpub.basicclasses` folder in the Project Explorer window. Click on **New**, then on **Java Class**. In the **Name** field, type `Soldier` and click on **OK**. The new class is created for us, with a code template ready to put our implementation within, just like what is shown in the following screenshot:

```java
package com.packtpub.basicclasses.app;

/**
 * Created by John on 30/07/2014.
 */
public class Soldier {
}
```

3. Notice that Android Studio has put the class in the same package as the rest of our app. Now we can write its implementation. Write the following class implementation code within the opening and closing curly braces of the `Soldier` class:

```java
public class Soldier {
    int health;
    String soldierType;

    void shootEnemy(){
        //lets print which type of soldier is shooting
```

```
        Log.i(soldierType, " is shooting");
    }
}
```

4. Now that we have a class, a blueprint for our future objects of the `Soldier` type, we can start to build our army. In the editor window, click on the tab of **MainActivity.java**. We will write this code, as so often, within the `onCreate` method just after the call to `setContentView`:

```
//first we make an object of type soldier
    Soldier rambo = new Soldier();
    rambo.soldierType = "Green Beret";
    rambo.health = 150;// It takes a lot to kill Rambo

    //Now we make another Soldier object
    Soldier vassily = new Soldier();
    vassily.soldierType = "Sniper";
    vassily.health = 50;//Snipers have less armor

    //And one more Soldier object
    Soldier wellington = new Soldier();
    wellington.soldierType = "Sailor";
    wellington.health = 100;//He's tough but no green beret
```

> This is a really good time to start taking advantage of the autocomplete feature in Android Studio. Notice that after you have declared and created a new object, all you have to do is begin typing the object's name and all the autocomplete options will present themselves.

5. Now that we have our extremely varied and somewhat unlikely army, we can use it and also verify the identity of each object. Type the following code below the code in the previous step:

```
Log.i("Rambo's health = ", "" + rambo.health);
Log.i("Vassily's health = ", "" + vassily.health);
Log.i("Wellington's health = ", "" + wellington.health);

rambo.shootEnemy();
vassily.shootEnemy();
wellington.shootEnemy();
```

6. Now we can run our app on an emulator. Remember, all the output will be in the **LogCat** console window.

This is how the preceding pieces of code work. In step 2, Android Studio created a template for our new `Soldier` class. In step 3, we implemented our class in quite the same way that we have before—two variables, an `int` and a `string`, called `health` and `soldierType`, respectively.

We also have a method in our class called `shootEnemy`. Let's look at it again and examine what is going on:

```
void shootEnemy(){
        //lets print which type of soldier is shooting
        Log.i(soldierType, " is shooting");
    }
```

In the body of the method, we print the `soldierType` string to the console first, and then the arbitrary `" is shooting"` string. What's neat here is that the `soldierType` string will be different depending on which object we call the `shootEnemy` method on.

In step 4, we declared, created, and assigned three new objects of type `Soldier`. They where `rambo`, `vassily`, and `wellington`. In step 5, we initialized each with a different value for `health` as well as `soldierType`.

Here is the output:

```
Rambo's health =: 150
Vassily's health =: 50
Wellington's health =: 100
Green Beret: is shooting
Sniper: is shooting
Sailor: is shooting
```

Notice that each time we access the `health` variable of each `Soldier` object, it is printed to the value we assigned it, demonstrating that although the three objects are of the same type, they are completely separate individual objects.

Perhaps more interesting are the three calls to `shootEnemy`. One call by each of our `Soldier` objects' `shootEnemy` method is made, and we print the `soldierType` variable to the console. The method has the appropriate value for each individual object, further demonstrating that we have three distinct objects, albeit created from the same `Soldier` class.

More things we can do with our first class

We can treat a class much like other variables. Assuming we have already implemented our `Soldier` class, we can make an array of `Soldier` objects like this:

```
//Declare an array called myArmy to hold 10 Soldier objects
Soldier [] myArmy = new Soldier[10];

//Then we can add the Soldier objects
//We use the familiar array notation on the left
//And the newly learnt new Soldier() syntax on the right
myArmy[0] = new Soldier();
myArmy[1] = new Soldier();
myArmy[2] = new Soldier();
myArmy[3] = new Soldier();
//Initialize more here
//..
```

Then we can use an object from an array using the same style of array notation as we did for regular variables, like this:

```
myArmy[0].health = 125;
myArmy[0].soldierType = "Pilot";
myArmy[0].shootEnemy();
// Pilot: is shooting
```

We can also use a class as an argument in a method call. Here is a hypothetical call to a `healSoldier` method:

```
healSoldier(rambo);
//Perhaps healSoldier could add to the health instance variable
```

Of course, the preceding example might raise questions like should the `healSoldier` method be a method of a class?

```
someHospitalObjectPerhaps.healSoldier(rambo);
```

It could be or not (as shown in the previous example). It would depend upon what is the best solution for the situation. We will look at more OOP, and then the best solution for lots of similar conundrums should present themselves more easily.

As you might have come to expect by now, we can use an object as the return value of a method. Here is what the hypothetical `healSoldier` method might look like:

```
Soldier healSoldier(Soldier soldierToBeHealed){
    soldierToBeHealed.health++;

    return soldierToBeHealed;
}
```

All of this information will likely raise a few questions. OOP is like that, so to try and consolidate all this class stuff with what we already know, let's take another look at variables and encapsulation.

Encapsulation

So far, what we have really seen is what amounts to a kind of code-organizing convention, although we did discuss the wider goals of all this OOP stuff. Now we will take things further and begin to see how we actually manage to achieve encapsulation with OOP.

Definition of encapsulation

As we have learned encapsulation means keeping the internal workings of your code safe from interference from the programs that use it, allowing only the variables and methods you choose to be accessed. This means your code can always be updated, extended, or improved without affecting the programs that use it, as long as the exposed parts are still made available in the same way. It also allows the code that uses your encapsulated code to be much simpler and easier to maintain because much of the complexity of the task is encapsulated in your code.

But didn't I say that we don't have to know what is going on inside? So you might question what we have seen so far. If we are constantly setting the instance variables like this `rambo.health = 100;`, isn't it possible that eventually things could start to go wrong, perhaps like the following line of code?

```
rambo.soldierType = "ballerina";
```

Encapsulation protects your class from being used in a way that it wasn't meant to be. By strictly controlling the way that your code is used, it can only ever do what you want it to do, with values you can control. It can't be forced into errors or crashes. Also, you are then free to make changes to the way your code works internally, without breaking any programs that are using an older version of the code or the rest of your program:

```
weighlifter.legstrength = 100;
weighlifter.armstrength = -100;
weightlifter.liftHeavyWeight();
//one typo and weightlifter rips own arms off
```

We can encapsulate our classes to avoid this, and here is how.

Controlling the use of classes with access modifiers

The designer of the class controls what can be seen and manipulated by any program that uses their class. We can add an **access modifier** before the `class` keyword, like this:

```
public class Soldier{
  //Implementation goes here
}
```

There are two class access modifiers. Let's briefly look at each in turn:

- `public`: This is straightforward. A class declared as `public` can be seen by all other classes.

- `default`: A class has default access when no access modifier is specified. This will make it public but only to classes in the same package, and inaccessible to all others.

Now we can make a start with this encapsulation thing. However, even at a glance, the access modifiers described are not very fine-grained. We seem to be limited to complete lockdown to anything outside the package or a complete free-for-all.

Actually, the benefits here are easily taken advantage of. The idea would be to design a package that fulfills a set of tasks. Then all the complex inner workings of the package, the stuff that shouldn't be messed with by anybody but our package, should have default access (only accessible to classes within the package). We can then provide a careful selection of public classes that can be used by others (or other distinct parts of our program).

For the size and complexity of the games in this book, multiple packages are almost certainly overkill.

Class access in a nutshell

A well-designed app will probably consist of one or more packages, each containing only default or default and public classes.

In addition to class-level privacy controls, Java gives us very fine-grained controls, but to use these controls, we have to look at variables in more detail.

Controlling the use of variables with access modifiers

To build on class visibility controls, we have variable access modifiers. Here is a variable with the private access modifier being declared:

```
private int myInt;
```

Note also that all of our discussion of variable access modifiers applies to object variables too. For example, here is an instance of our Soldier class being declared, created, and assigned. As you can see, the access specified in this case is public:

```
public Soldier mySoldier = new Soldier();
```

Before you apply a modifier to a variable, you must first consider the class visibility. If class a is not visible to class b, say because class a has default access and class b is in another package, then it doesn't make any difference what access modifiers you use on the variables in class a; class b still can't see it.

Thus, it makes sense to show a class to another class when necessary, but you should only expose the variables that are needed—not everything.

We have a bit more to cover on access modifiers, and then we will look at a few examples to help clarify things. For now, here is an explanation of the different variable access modifiers. They are more numerous and fine-grained than the class access modifiers. Most of the explanations are straightforward, and the ones that might raise questions will become clearer when we look at an example.

The depth and complexity of access modification is not so much in the range of modifiers, but by using them in smart ways, we can combine them to achieve the worthy goals of encapsulation. Here are the variable access modifiers:

- `public`: You guessed it! Any class or method from any package can see this variable. Use `public` only when you are sure that this is what you want.

- `protected`: This is the next least restrictive modifier after `public`. `protected` Variables set as protected can be seen by any class and any method as long as they are in the same package.

- `default`: This doesn't sound as restrictive as `protected`, but it is more so. A variable has default access when no access is specified. The fact that `default` is restrictive perhaps implies that we should be thinking on the side of hiding our variables rather than exposing them. At this point, we need to introduce a new concept. Do you remember that we briefly discussed inheritance, and how we can quickly take on the attributes of a class and yet refine it using the `extends` keyword? Just for the record, default access variables are not visible to subclasses. This means that when we extend a class like we did with `Activity`, we cannot see its default variables. We will look at inheritance in more detail later in the chapter.

- `private`: These variables can only be seen within the class they are declared. Like default access, they cannot be seen by subclasses (inherited classes).

Variable access in a nutshell

A well-designed app will probably consist of one or more packages, each containing only default or default and public classes. Within these classes, variables will have carefully chosen and most likely varied access modifiers.

There's one more twist in all this access modification stuff before we get practical with it.

Methods have access modifiers too

It makes sense that methods are the things that our classes can do. We will want to control what users of our class can and can't do. The general idea here is that some methods will do things internally only and are therefore not needed by users of the class, and some methods will be fundamental to how users use your class.

The access modifiers for methods are the same as those for the class variables. This makes things easy to remember but suggests again that successful encapsulation is a matter of design rather than any specific set of rules.

As an example, the method in the following code snippet, provided in a public class, can be used by any other class:

```
public useMeEverybody(){
    //do something everyone needs to do here
}
```

However, the following method can only be used internally by the class that created it:

```
private secretInternalTask(){
    //do something that helps the class function internally
    //Perhaps, if it is part of the same class,
    //useMeEverybody could use this method...
    //On behalf of the classes outside of this class.
    //Neat!
}
```

The next method has default visibility with no access specified. It can be used only by other classes in the same package. If we extend the class containing this default access method, the class will not have access to this method:

```
fairlySecretTask(){
    //allow just the classes in the package
    //Not for external use
}
```

Here is a last example before we move on. It contains a `protected` method, only visible to the package, but usable by our classes that extend it:

```
protected familyTask(){
    //allow just the classes in the package
    //And you can use me if you extend me too
}
```

Method access in a nutshell

Method access should be chosen to best enforce the principles we have already discussed. It should provide the users of your class with just the access they need, and preferably nothing more. Thereby, we achieve our encapsulation goals such as keeping the internal workings of your code safe from interference from the programs that use it, for all the reasons we have discussed.

Accessing private variables with the getter and setter methods

So if it is best practice to hide our variables away as private, how do we allow access to them without spoiling our encapsulation? What if an object of the `Hospital` class wanted access to the `health` member variable from an object of type `Soldier` so that it could increase it? The `health` variable should be private, right?

In order to be able to make as many member variables as possible private and yet allow some kind of limited access to some of them, we use **getters** and **setters**. Getters and setters are methods that just get and set variable values.

This is not some special or new Java thing we have to learn. It is just a convention for the use of what we already know. Let's take a look at getters and setters using the example of our `Soldier` and `Hospital` classes.

In this example, each of our two classes are created in their own file but the same package. First of all, here is our hypothetical `Hospital` class:

```
class Hospital{
  private void healSoldier(Soldier soldierToHeal){
    int health = soldierToHeal.getHealth();
    health = health + 10;
    soldierToHeal.setHealth(health);
  }
}
```

Our implementation of the `Hospital` class has just one method, `healSoldier`. It receives a reference to a `Soldier` object as a parameter, so this method will work on whichever `Soldier` object is passed in: `vassily`, `wellington`, `rambo`, or whoever.

It also has a `health` variable. It uses this variable to temporarily hold and increase the soldier's health. In the same line, it initializes the `health` variable to the `Soldier` object's current health. The `Soldier` object's `health` is private, so the public getter method is used instead.

Then `health` is increased by 10 and the `setHealth` setter method loads the new `health` value back to the `Soldier` object.

The key here is that although a `Hospital` object can change a `Soldier` object's health, it does so within the bounds of the getter and setter methods. The getter and setter methods can be written to control and check for potentially erroneous or harmful values.

Next comes our hypothetical `Soldier` class, with the simplest implementation possible of it's getter and setter methods:

```
public class Soldier{
  private int health;
  public int getHealth(){
    return health;
  }

  public void setHealth(int newHealth){
    health = newHealth;
  }
}
```

We have one instance variable called `health` and it is private. Private means it can only be changed by methods of the `Soldier` class. We then have a public `getHealth` method, which unsurprisingly returns the value held in the private `health` variable of the `int` type. As this method is public, anyone with access to the `Soldier` class can use it.

Next, the `setHealth` method is implemented. Again it is public, but this time, it takes `int` as a parameter and assigns whatever value is passed to the private `health` variable. In a more life-like example, we would write some more code here to ensure that the value passed is within the bounds we expect.

Now we will declare, create, and assign to make an object of each of our two new classes and see how our getters and setters work:

```
Soldier mySoldier = new Soldier();
//mySoldier.health = 100;//Doesn't work private
//we can use the public setter setHealth()
mySoldier.setHealth(100);//That's better

Hospital militaryHospital = new Hospital();

//Oh no mySoldier has been wounded
mySoldier.setHealth(10);

//Take him to the hospital
//But my health variable is private
//And Hospital won't be able to access it
//I'm doomed - tell Laura I love her

//No wait- what about my public getters and setters?
```

```
//We can use the public getters and setters from another class

militaryHospital.healSoldier(mySoldier);

//mySoldiers private variable health has been increased by 10
//I'm feeling much better thanks!
```

We see that we can call our public `setHealth` and `getHealth` methods directly on our object of type `Soldier`. Not only that, we can also call the `healSoldier` method of the `Hospital` object, passing in a reference to the `Soldier` object, which can use the public getters and setters to manipulate the private `health` variable.

We see that the private `health` variable is simply accessible, yet totally within the control of the designer of the `Soldier` class.

If you want to play around with this example, there is a working app in the code bundle in the `Chapter6` folder, called `Getters And Setters`. I have added a few lines of code to print to the console. We deliberately covered this the way we did to keep the key parts of the code as clear as possible. We will soon build some real working examples that explore class, variable, and method access.

 Getters and setters are sometimes referred to by their more correct names, **Accessors** and **Mutators**. We will stick to getters and setters. Just thought you might like to know.

Yet again, our example and the explanation are probably raising more questions. That's good! Previously, I said that:

- There are two access modifiers for a class, default and public
- Objects of classes are a type of reference variable
- Variables (including objects) have even more access possibilities

We need to look more closely at reference and primitive variables as well as local and instance variables. We will do so in a moment in the *Variables revisited* section. In that section, we will consolidate our information further to get a tighter grip on this OOP stuff. First let's remind ourselves of a bit about encapsulation.

Using encapsulation features (such as access control) is like signing a really important deal about how to use and access a class, its methods, and its variables. The contract is not just an agreement about the present but an implied guarantee for the future. We will see that as we proceed through this chapter, there are more ways that we refine and strengthen this contract.

It is perfectly possible to rewrite every example in this book without thinking or caring about encapsulation. In fact, the projects in this book outside of this chapter are quite lax about encapsulation.

Use encapsulation where it is needed or, of course, if you are being paid to use it by an employer. Often encapsulation is overkill on small learning projects, such as the games in this book, except when the topic you are learning is encapsulation itself.

We are learning this Java OOP stuff under the assumption that you will one day want to write much more complex apps, whether on Android or some other platform that uses OOP.

Setting up our objects with constructors

With all of these private variables and their getters and setters, does it mean that we need a getter and a setter for every private variable? What about a class with lots of variables that need initializing at the start? Think about this:

```
mySoldier.name
mysoldier.type
mySoldier.weapon
mySoldier.regiment
...
```

We could go on like this. Some of these variables might need getters and setters, but what if we just want to set things up when the object is first created to make the object function correctly? Do we need two methods (a getter and a setter) for each?

For this, we have a special method called a constructor. Here, we create an object of type `Soldier` and assign it to an object called `mySoldier`:

```
Soldier mySoldier = new Soldier();
```

There's nothing new here, but look at the last part of that line of code:

```
...Soldier();
```

This looks suspiciously like a method.

We have called a special method called a constructor that has been supplied automatically for us by the compiler.

However (and this is getting to the point now), like a method, we can override it, which means we can do really useful things to set up our new object *before* it is used and any of its methods are placed on the stack:

```
public Soldier(){
  health = 200;
  //more setup here
}
```

This is a constructor. It has a lot of syntactical similarities to a method. It can only be run with the use of the new keyword. It is created for us automatically by the compiler unless we create our own like in the previous code.

Constructors have the following properties:

- They have no return type
- They have the same name as the class
- They can have parameters
- They can be overloaded

We will play with constructors in the next demo.

Variables revisited

You probably remember, back in the math game project, that we kept changing where we declared our variables. First, we declared some in onCreate, then we moved them to just below the class declaration, and then we were making them member or instance variables.

Because we didn't specify the access, they were of default access and visible to the whole class, and as everything took place in the one class, we could access them everywhere. For example, we could update our TextView type objects from onClick, but why couldn't we do that when they were declared in onCreate? Further explanation about when and how we can access different variables is probably going to be useful.

The stack and the heap

The VM inside every Android device takes care of memory allocation to our games. In addition, it stores different types of variables in different places.

Variables that we declare and initialize in methods are stored on the area of memory known as the stack. We can stick to our warehouse analogy when talking about the stack—almost. We already know how we can manipulate the stack.

Let's talk about the heap and what is stored there. All reference type objects, which include objects (of classes) and arrays, are stored in the heap. Think of the heap as a separate area of the same warehouse. The heap has lots of floor space for odd-shaped objects, racks for smaller objects, lots of long rows with smaller sized cube-shaped holes for arrays, and so on. This is where our objects are stored. The problem is that we have no direct access to the heap.

Let's look again at what exactly a reference variable is. It is a variable that we refer to and use via a reference. A reference can be loosely (but usefully) defined as an address or location. The reference (address or location) of the object is on the stack. When we use the dot operator, we are asking Dalvik to perform a task at a specific location as stored in the reference.

> Reference variables are just that—a reference. They are a way to access and manipulate the object (variables or methods), but they are not the actual variable. An analogy might be that primitives are right there (on the stack) but references are an address, and we say what to do at the address. In this analogy, all addresses are on the heap.

Why would we ever want a system like this? Just give me my objects on the stack already!

A quick break to throw out the trash

Remember way back in the first chapter when I said Java was easier to learn than some languages because it helps us manage the memory? Well, this whole stack and heap thing does that for us.

As we know, the VM keeps track of all our objects for us and stores them in the heap—a special area of our warehouse. Periodically, the VM will scan the stack, or the regular racks of our warehouse, and match references to objects. If it finds any objects without a matching reference, it destroys them. In Java terminology, it performs garbage collection. Think of a very discriminating refuse vehicle driving through the middle of our heap, scanning objects to match to references. No reference? You're garbage now! After all, if an object has no reference variable, we can't possibly do anything with it anyway. This system of garbage collection helps our games run more efficiently by freeing unused memory.

So variables declared in a method are local, on the stack, and only visible within the method they were declared. A member variable is on the heap and can be referenced from any place where there is a reference to it, provided the access specification allows the referencing.

Now we can take a closer look at the variable scope—what can be seen from where.

There are more twists and turns to be learned with regard to variables. In the next demo, we will explore all we have learned so far in this chapter and some new ideas too.

We will look at the following topics:

- Static variables that are consistent (the same) across every instance of a class
- Static methods of a class where you can use the methods of a class without an object of that class type
- We will demonstrate the scope of class and local variables, and where they can and can't be seen by different parts of the program
- We will look at the `this` keyword, which allows us to write code that refers to variables that belong to a specific instance of a class, but without keeping track of which instance we are currently using

The following is the demo.

Access, scope, this, static, and constructors demo

We have looked at the intricate way by which access to variables and their scope is controlled, and it would probably serve us well to look at an example of them in action. These will not be very practical real-world examples of variable use, but more of a demonstration to help understand access modifiers for classes, methods, and variables, alongside the different types of variables such as reference (or primitive) and local (or instance). Then we will cover the new concepts of static and final variables and the `this` keyword. The completed project is in the `Chapter6` folder of the code download. It is called `AccessScopeThisAndStatic`. We will now perform the following steps to implement it:

1. Create a new blank activity project and call it `AccessScopeThisAndStatic`.
2. Create a new class by right-clicking on the existing `MainActivity` class in the Project Explorer and navigating to **New** | **Class**. Name the new class `AlienShip`.
3. Now we declare our new class and some member variables. Note that `numShips` is private and static. We will soon see how this variable is the same across all instances of the class. The `shieldStrength` variable is `private` and `shipName` is `public`:

```
public class AlienShip {
private static int numShips;
private int shieldStrength;
public String shipName;
```

4. Next is the constructor. We can see that the constructor is public, has no return type, and has the same name as the class, as per the rules. In it, we increment the private static `numShips` variable. Remember that this will happen each time we create a new object of the `AlienShip` type. The constructor also sets a value for the `shieldStrength` private variable using the private `setShieldStrength` method:

```
public AlienShip(){
  numShips++;

  //Can call private methods from here because I am part
  //of the class
  //If didn't have "this" then this call might be less clear
  //But this "this" isn't strictly necessary
  this.setShieldStrength(100);
  //Because of "this" I am sure I am setting
  //the correct shieldStrength
}
```

5. Here is the public static getter method that classes outside `AlienShip` can use to find out how many `AlienShip` objects are there. We will also see the unusual way in which we use static methods:

```
public static int getNumShips(){
    return numShips;

}
```

6. The following code shows our private `setShieldStrength` method. We could have just set `shieldStrength` directly from within the class, but this code shows how we can distinguish between the `shieldStrength` local variable/parameter and the `shieldStrength` member variable using the `this` keyword:

```
private void setShieldStrength(int shieldStrength){
    //"this" distinguishes between the
    //member variable shieldStrength
    //And the local variable/parameter of the same name
    this.shieldStrength = shieldStrength;

}
```

7. This next method is the getter, so other classes can read but not alter the shield strength of each `AlienShip` object:

```
public int getShieldStrength(){
    return this.shieldStrength;
}
```

8. Now we have a public method that can be called every time an `AlienShip`
    object is hit. It just prints to the console and then checks whether that
    particular object's `shieldStrength` is zero. If it is zero, it calls the
    `destroyShip` method, which we look at next:

```
public void hitDetected(){

    shieldStrength -=25;
    Log.i("Incomiming: ","Bam!!");
    if (shieldStrength == 0){
        destroyShip();
    }

}
```

9. Finally, we will look at the `destroyShip` method for our `AlienShip` class.
    We print a message that indicates which ship has been destroyed, based on
    its `shipName`, as well as increment the `numShips` static variable so that we can
    keep track of the number of objects of the `AlienShip` type we have:

```
private void destroyShip(){
    numShips--;
    Log.i("Explosion: ", ""+this.shipName + " destroyed");
    }
}
```

10. Now we switch over to our `MainActivity` class and write some code that
    uses our new `AlienShip` class. All of the code goes in the `onCreate` method
    after the call to `setContentView`. First, we create two new `AlienShip` objects
    called `girlShip` and `boyShip`:

```
//every time we do this the constructor runs
AlienShip girlShip = new AlienShip();
AlienShip boyShip = new AlienShip();
```

11. Look how we get the value in `numShips`. We use the `getNumShips` method as
    we might expect. However, look closely at the syntax. We are using the class
    name and not an object. We can also access static variables with methods that
    are not static. We did it this way to see a static method in action:

```
//Look no objects but using the static method
Log.i("numShips: ", "" + AlienShip.getNumShips());
```

12. Now we assign names to our public `shipName` string variables:

```
//This works because shipName is public
girlShip.shipName = "Corrine Yu";
boyShip.shipName = "Andre LaMothe";
```

13. If we attempt to assign a value directly to a private variable, it won't work. Therefore, we use the public `getShieldStrength` getter method to print the value of `shieldStrength`, which was assigned to the constructor:

```
//This won't work because shieldStrength is private
//girlship.shieldStrength = 999;

//But we have a public getter
Log.i("girlShip shieldStrngth: ", "" + girlShip.
getShieldStrength());

Log.i("boyShip shieldStrngth: ", "" + boyShip.
getShieldStrength());

//And we can't do this because it's private
//boyship.setShieldStrength(1000000);
```

Finally, we get to blow some stuff up by playing with the `hitDetected` method and occasionally checking the shield strength of our two objects:

```
//let's shoot some ships
girlShip.hitDetected();
Log.i("girlShip shieldStrngth: ", "" + girlShip.
getShieldStrength());

Log.i("boyShip shieldStrngth: ", "" + boyShip.
getShieldStrength());

boyShip.hitDetected();
boyShip.hitDetected();
boyShip.hitDetected();

Log.i("girlShip shieldStrngth: ", "" + girlShip.
getShieldStrength());

Log.i("boyShip shieldStrngth: ", "" + boyShip.
getShieldStrength());

boyShip.hitDetected();//ahhh

Log.i("girlShip shieldStrngth: ", "" + girlShip.
getShieldStrength());

Log.i("boyShip shieldStrngth: ", "" + boyShip.
getShieldStrength());
```

14. When we think we have destroyed a ship, we again use our static `getNumShips` method to check whether our static variable `numShips` was changed by the `destroyShip` method:

```
Log.i("numShips: ", "" + AlienShip.getNumShips());
```

15. Run the demo and look at the console output.

Here is the output of the preceding blocks of code:

```
numShips:: 2
girlShip shieldStrngth:: 100
boyShip shieldStrngth:: 100
Incomiming:: Bam!!
girlShip shieldStrngth:: 75
boyShip shieldStrngth:: 100
Incomiming:: Bam!!
Incomiming:: Bam!!
Incomiming:: Bam!!
girlShip shieldStrngth:: 75
boyShip shieldStrngth:: 25
Incomiming:: Bam!!
Explosion:: Andre LaMothe destroyed
girlShip shieldStrngth:: 75
boyShip shieldStrngth:: 0
numShips:: 1
boyShip shieldStrngth:: 0
numShips:: 1
```

In the previous example, we saw that we can distinguish between local and member variables of the same name using the `this` keyword. We can also use the `this` keyword to write code that refers to the current object being acted upon.

We saw that a static variable, in this case `numShips`, is consistent across all instances. Moreover, by incrementing it in the constructor and decrementing it in our `destroyShip` method, we can keep track of the number of `AlienShip` objects we created.

We also saw that we can use static methods by writing the class name with the dot operator instead of an object.

Finally, we demonstrated how we could hide and expose certain methods and variables using an access specifier.

Let's take a look at a quick review of the stack and the heap before we move on to something new.

A quick summary on stack and heap

Let's look at what we learned about the stack and the heap:

- You don't delete objects but the VM sends the garbage collector when it thinks it is appropriate. This is usually done when there is no active reference to the object.

- Local variables and methods are on the stack, and local variables are local to the specific method within which they were declared.

- Instance or class variables are on the heap (with their objects) but the reference to the object (address) is a local variable on the stack.

- We control what goes inside the stack. We can use the objects on the heap but only by referencing them.

- The heap is maintained by the garbage collector.

- An object is garbage collected when there is no longer a valid reference to it. Therefore, when a reference variable, local or instance, is removed from the stack, then its related object becomes viable for garbage collection, and when the virtual machine decides the time is right (usually very promptly), it will free the RAM memory to avoid running out.

- If we try to reference an object that doesn't exist, we will get a **null pointer exception** and the game will crash.

Inheritance

We have seen how we can use other people's hard work by instantiating/creating objects from the classes of an API such as that of Android, but this whole OOP thing goes even further than that.

What if there is a class that has loads of useful functionality in it but not quite what we want? We can inherit from the class and then further refine or add to how it works and what it does.

You might be surprised to hear that we have done this already. In fact, we have done this with every single game and demo we looked at. When we use the extends keyword, we are inheriting, for example, in this line of code:

```
public class MainActivity extends Activity ...
```

Here, we are inheriting the Activity class along with all its functionality, or more specifically, all of the functionality that the class designers want us to have access to. Here are some of the things we can do to classes we have extended.

We can override a method and still rely in part on the overridden method in the class we inherit from. For example, we overrode the onCreate method every time we extended the Activity class, but we also called the default implementation provided by the class designers when we did this:

```
super.onCreate(...
```

In the next chapter, we will also be overriding some more methods of the Activity class. Specifically, we'll override the methods that handle the lifecycle.

If we or the designer of a class wants to force us to inherit before we use their class, they can declare a class as **abstract**. Then we cannot make an object from it. Therefore, we must extend it first and make an object from the subclass. We will do this in our inheritance example and discuss it further when we look at polymorphism.

We can also declare a method abstract, and that method must be overridden in any class that extends the class with the abstract method. We will do this as well in our inheritance example.

In our game projects, we will not be designing any classes that we will be extending. We have no need of that in the context of learning about building simple games. However, we will be extending classes designed by others in every future game.

We discuss inheritance mainly so that we understand what is going on around us and as the first step towards being able to eventually design useful classes that we or others can extend. With this in mind, let's make some simple classes and see how we can extend them, just to play around with the syntax as a first step, and also to be able to say we have done it. When we look at the last major topic of this chapter, polymorphism, we will also dig a little deeper into inheritance.

An example of inheritance

We have looked at the way we can create hierarchies of classes to model the system that fits our game or software project, so let's try out some simple code that uses inheritance. The completed project is in the Chapter6 folder of the code download. It is called InheritanceExample. We will now perform the following steps:

1. Create three new classes in the usual way. Call one AlienShip, another Fighter, and the last one Bomber.

2. Here is the code for the AlienShip class. It is very similar to our previous AlienShip class demo. The differences are that the constructor now takes an int parameter, which it uses to set the shield strength. The constructor also outputs a message to the console so that we can see when it is being used. The AlienShip class also has a new method, fireWeapon, that is declared abstract. This guarantees that any class that subclasses AlienShip must implement their own version of fireWeapon. Notice that the class has the abstract keyword as part of its declaration. We have to do this because one of its methods also uses the keyword abstract. We will explain the abstract method when discussing this demo and the abstract class when we talk about polymorphism:

```java
public abstract class AlienShip {
    private static int numShips;
    private int shieldStrength;
    public String shipName;

    public AlienShip(int shieldStrength){
        Log.i("Location: ", "AlienShip constructor");
        numShips++;
        setShieldStrength(shieldStrength);
    }

    public abstract void fireWeapon();//Ahh my body

    public static int getNumShips(){
        return numShips;
    }

    private void setShieldStrength(int shieldStrength){
        this.shieldStrength = shieldStrength;
    }


    public int getShieldStrength(){
        return this.shieldStrength;
```

```
        }

        public void hitDetected(){
            shieldStrength -=25;
            Log.i("Incomiming: ", "Bam!!");
            if (shieldStrength == 0){
                destroyShip();
            }

        }

        private void destroyShip(){
            numShips--;
            Log.i("Explosion: ", "" + this.shipName + " destroyed");
        }

    }
```

3. Now we will implement the Bomber class. Notice the call to super(100). This calls the constructor of the superclass with the value for shieldStrength. We could do further specific Bomber initialization in this constructor, but for now, we just print the location so that we can see when the Bomber constructor is being executed. We also implement a Bomber class-specific version of the abstract fireWeapon method because we must do so:

```
public class Bomber extends AlienShip {

    public Bomber(){
        super(100);
        //Weak shields for a bomber
        Log.i("Location: ", "Bomber constructor");
    }

    public void fireWeapon(){
        Log.i("Firing weapon: ", "bombs away");
    }
}
```

4. Now we will implement the `Fighter` class. Notice the call to `super(400)`. This calls the constructor of the superclass with the value of `shieldStrength`. We could do further `Fighter` class-specific initialization in this constructor, but for now, we just print the location so that we can see when the `Fighter` constructor is being executed. We also implement a `Fighter` specific version of the abstract `fireWeapon` method because we must do so:

```
public class Fighter extends AlienShip{

    public Fighter(){
        super(400);
        //Strong shields for a fighter
        Log.i("Location: ", "Fighter constructor");
    }

    public void fireWeapon(){
        Log.i("Firing weapon: ", "lasers firing");
    }

}
```

5. Here is our code in the `onCreate` method of `MainActivity`. As usual, we enter this code after the call to `setContentView`. This is the code that uses our three new classes. It looks quite ordinary, but there's nothing new; it is the output that is interesting:

```
Fighter aFighter = new Fighter();
Bomber aBomber = new Bomber();

//Can't do this AlienShip is abstract -
//Literally speaking as well as in code
//AlienShip alienShip = new AlienShip(500);

//But our objects of the subclasses can still do
//everything the AlienShip is meant to do
aBomber.shipName = "Newell Bomber";
aFighter.shipName = "Meier Fighter";

//And because of the overridden constructor
//That still calls the super constructor
//They have unique properties
Log.i("aFighter Shield:", ""+ aFighter.getShieldStrength());
```

```
Log.i("aBomber Shield:", ""+ aBomber.getShieldStrength());

        //As well as certain things in certain ways
        //That are unique to the subclass
        aBomber.fireWeapon();
        aFighter.fireWeapon();

        //Take down those alien ships
        //Focus on the bomber it has a weaker shield
        aBomber.hitDetected();
        aBomber.hitDetected();
        aBomber.hitDetected();
        aBomber.hitDetected();
```

Here is the output of the preceding snippets of code:

```
Location:: AlienShip constructor

Location:: Fighter constructor

Location:: AlienShip constructor

Location:: Bomber constructor

aFighter Shield:: 400

aBomber Shield:: 100

Firing weapon:: bombs away

Firing weapon:: lasers firing

Incomiming:: Bam!!

Incomiming:: Bam!!

Incomiming:: Bam!!

Incomiming:: Bam!!

Explosion:: Newell Bomber destroyed
```

We can see how the constructor of the subclass can call the constructor of the superclass. We can also clearly see that the individual implementations of the `fireWeapon` method work exactly as expected.

As if OOP where not useful enough already! We can now model real-world objects and design them to interact with each other. We have also seen how we can make OOP even more useful by subclassing/extending/inheriting from other classes. The terminology we might like to learn here is that the class that is extended from is the **superclass** and the class that inherits from the superclass is the **subclass**. We can also call them parent and child classes.

As usual, we might find ourselves asking this question about inheritance: Why? We can write common code once, in the parent class, and we can update that common code. All the classes that inherit from it are also updated. Furthermore, a subclass only inherits public instance variables and methods. When designed properly, this further enhances the goals of encapsulation.

Polymorphism

Polymorphism roughly means different forms. But what does it mean to us?

In the simplest words possible, any subclass can be used as a part of the code that uses the superclass.

For example, if we have an array of animals, we could put any object that is of a type that is a subclass of Animal in the Animal array, perhaps cats and dogs.

This means that we can write code that is simpler and easier to understand and modify:

```
//This code assumes we have an Animal class
//And we have a Cat and Dog class that extends Animal
Animal myAnimal = new Animal();
Dog myDog = new Dog();
Cat myCat = new Cat();
Animal [] myAnimals = new Animal[10];
myAnimals[0] = myAnimal;//As expected
myAnimals[1] = myDog;//This is OK too
myAnimals[2] = myCat;//And this is fine as well
```

We can also write code for the superclass and rely on the fact that no matter how many times it is subclassed, within certain parameters, the code will still work. Let's continue our previous example:

```
//6 months later we need elephants
//with its own unique aspects
//As long as it extends Animal we can still do this
Elephant myElephant = new Elephant();
myAnimals[3] = myElephant;//And this is fine as well
```

You can also write methods with polymorphic return types and arguments:

```
Animal feedAnimal(Animal animalToFeed){
  //Feed any animal here
  return animalToFeed;
}
```

So you can even write code *today* and make another subclass in a week, month, or year, and the very same methods and data structures will still work.

Further, we can enforce on our subclasses a set of rules as to what they can and cannot do, and also how they should do it. Thus, good design in one stage can influence our subclasses at other stages.

If you do suddenly find yourself with a flappy-bird-sized phenomenon, and you have a lot of OOP in your code, right from the start, it will be much easier to bring in hired help to move the project forward and still maintain control of the project.

What if you have an idea for a game with lots of features but you want to get a simple version of the game out as soon as possible? Smart, object-oriented design would certainly be the solution. It could enable you to write the working bare bones of a game and then gradually extend it.

Moving on, let's look at another OOP concept: abstract classes. We can now get to the bottom of what was going on with that `AlienShip` code:

```
public abstract class AlienShip{...
```

Abstract classes

An abstract class is a class that cannot be instantiated, or cannot be made into an object. We mentioned that `AlienShip` was abstract in the previous example. So is it a blueprint that will never be used then? But that's like paying an architect to design your home and then never building it! I kind of got the idea of an abstract method but this is just silly!

It might seem like this at first. We make a class abstract by declaring it with the `abstract` keyword, like this:

```
abstract class someClass{
   //All methods and variables here as usual
   //Just don't try and make an object out of me!
}
```

But why?

Sometimes, we want a class that can be used as a polymorphic type but we need to ensure that it can never be used as an object. For example, `Animal` doesn't really make sense on its own.

We don't talk about animals; we talk about types of animals. We don't say, "Ooh, look at that lovely, fluffy, white animal", or "Yesterday, we went to the pet shop and got an animal and an animal bed." It's just too abstract.

So an abstract class is like a template to be used by any class that extends it (inherits from it).

We might want a `Worker` class and extend to make classes such as `Miner`, `Steelworker`, `OfficeWorker`, and of course `Programmer`. But what exactly does a plain `Worker` class do? Why would we ever want to instantiate one?

The answer is that we wouldn't want to instantiate it, but we might want to use it as a polymorphic type so that we can pass multiple worker subclasses between methods and have data structures that can hold all types of workers.

We call this type of class an abstract class, and when a class has even one abstract method, like `AlienShip` did, it must be declared abstract itself. As we saw, all abstract methods must be overridden by any class that extends the abstract class. This means that the abstract class can provide some of the common functionality that would be available in all its subclasses. For example, the `Worker` class might have the `height`, `weight`, and `age` member variables.

It might have the `getPayCheck` method, which is the same in all the subclasses, and the `doWork` method, which is abstract and must be overridden because all the different types of worker do work very differently.

This leads us neatly on to another area of polymorphism that deserves an honorable mention because we have been using it in every game so far.

Interfaces

An interface is like a class. Phew! Nothing complicated here then. However, it's like a class that is always abstract and with only abstract methods.

We can think of an interface as an entirely abstract class with all its methods abstract too. Okay, so you can just about wrap your head round an abstract class because it can at least pass on some functionality in its methods that are not abstract and serve as a polymorphic type.

But seriously, this interface seems a bit pointless. Bear with me.

To define an interface, we type the following code:

```
public interface myInterface{
    void someAbstractMethod();//omg I've got no body
    int anotherAbstractMethod();//Ahh! Me too

    //Interface methods are always abstract and public implicitly
```

```
//but we could make it explicit if we prefer

   public abstract explicitlyAbstractAndPublicMethod();//still no body
   though



}
```

The methods of an interface have no body because they are abstract, but they can still have return types and parameters, or not.

To use an interface, we use the `implements` keyword after the class declaration. Yes, we already did this for `onClickListener` a few times:

```
public class someClass implements someInterface{

//class stuff here

//better implement the methods of the interface or the red error lines
will not go away
   public void someAbstractMethod(){
     //code here if you like but just an empty implementation will do
   }

   public int anotherAbstractMethod(){
     //code here if you like but just an empty implementation will do

     //Must have a return type though as that is part of the contract
     return 1;}
}
```

This enables us to use polymorphism with multiple different objects that are from completely unrelated inheritance hierarchies. As long as it implements an interface, the whole thing can be passed along as if it is that thing, which it is. We can even have a class implement multiple different interfaces at the same time. Just add a comma between each interface and list them after the `implements` keyword. Just be sure to implement all the necessary methods.

Let's go back to the `onClickListener` interface. Any thing might like to know when it is being clicked on; a Button, a TextView, and so on. We don't want different `onClick` methods for every type.

When using Android, for games or for more regular GUI-based apps (a bit like ours so far), 9 times out of 10, you will be implementing interfaces rather than writing your own. However, knowing what is happening is quite important, not so much from a point of view of technical awareness, as we have just seen that the interface specifies a contract and the compiler enforces it, but more as a matter of sanity in knowing what is actually happening when you use the `implements` keyword and write a method (or methods) with a name that you didn't choose.

More about OOP and classes

It is possible to write a whole book on OOP, and many authors have already done so, but the best way to learn OOP is probably to practice it; practice it *before* we have learned all of the theory. Anyway, before we get on with some more practical examples, here is one more slightly theoretical OOP example that will leave us scratching our heads later if not mentioned.

Inner classes

When we looked at our basic classes demo app, we declared and implemented the class in a separate file to our `MainActivity` class. That file had the same name as the class.

We can also declare and implement a class within a class. The only question remaining, of course, is why would we do this? When we implement an inner class, the inner class can access the member variables of the enclosing class and the enclosing class can access the members of the inner class. We will see this in action in the next two chapters.

If you are not modeling deep or real-world systems, then inner classes are often the way to go. In fact, all the classes we will write ourselves in the rest of this book will be extended inner classes. This means that we will extend a type to make our own class within our `Activity` class. This makes our code nice and simple.

Self-test questions

Q1) Find out what is wrong with this class declaration:

```
private class someClass{
   //class implementation goes here
}
```

Q2) What is encapsulation?

Q3) I don't get it all, and actually, I have more questions now than I had at the start of the chapter. What should I do?

Summary

In this chapter, we covered more theory than in any other chapter. If you haven't memorized everything, then you have succeeded completely. If you just understand that OOP is about writing reusable, extendable, and efficient code through encapsulation, inheritance, and polymorphism, then you have the potential to be a Java master. Simply put, OOP enables us to use other people's hard work even when those people were not aware of exactly what we would be doing at the time they did the work. All you have to do is keep practicing, so let's make a retro game in the next chapter.

7
Retro Squash Game

This chapter is where the fun starts. Although a retro squash game is obviously a step or two down from the latest big-budget game, it is the point when we start to look at some fundamentals—drawing, detecting when objects we have drawn bump into each other, and having animation that is actually controlled by us.

Once you can draw a pixel and move it, it only needs a bit of imagination and work and you have the potential to draw anything. Then, when we combine this knowledge with some really simple math to simulate the physics of collision and gravity, we will be close to being able to implement our squash game.

Sadly, this book does not have the time to go into the mathematics of turning a dot on the screen into realistic three-dimensional characters moving around in a three-dimensional world. Certainly, the technology and math behind big-budget titles is very advanced and complicated. However, the basics of turning pixels into lines and lines into triangles, texturing a triangle, building objects out of triangles, and positioning them in a three-dimensional world are within the grasp of anybody who has learned high-school-level math. Often, we hear that great graphics don't make a great game, which is true, but great graphics (at least for me) are one of the most exciting aspects of video games, even when they are displayed on a game that could be more fun to play by itself. If you want to see how to turn pixels into magical worlds, and start to appreciate what goes on behind the scenes of the top game engines and graphics libraries, you could start with *Computer Graphics: Mathematical First Steps, P.A. Egerton and W.S Hall, Prentice Hall.*

In this chapter, we will cover the following topics:

- Explore the Android `Canvas` class, which makes drawing easy and fun
- Write a simple Canvas demo app
- Learn about detecting touches on the screen
- Create the retro squash game
- Implement the retro squash game

Drawing with Android Canvas

So far, we have been using the Android UI designer to implement all our graphics. This is fine when all we need are objects such as buttons and text.

It is true that there is more to the Android UI elements than we have explored so far. For example, we know we can do a lot more with the `Animation` class, and we very briefly saw that we can assign any image we like to represent one of the UI elements.

As an example, we could assign game characters such as spaceships to UI elements and animate them.

However, if we want smoothly moving spaceships with accurate collision detection, cute characters, and gruesome baddies with multiframe, cartoon-like animation, then we are going to need to move away from predefined UI elements.

We are going to need to start looking at and designing with individual pixels, lines, bitmaps, and sprite sheets. Fortunately, as you might have guessed, Android has some classes to make this nice and easy for us. We will be learning how to get started with the `Canvas` and `Paint` classes.

Bitmaps and sprite sheets will be covered in the next chapter. In this chapter, we will learn how to draw pixels and lines to make a simple, smoothly moving pong-style game of squash.

To achieve this, we will learn about the coordinate system we use to draw our pixels and lines. Then we will look at the `Paint` and `Canvas` classes themselves.

The Android coordinate system

A pixel is the smallest graphical element we can manipulate using the `Paint` and `Canvas` classes. It is essentially a dot. If your device resolution is 1920 x 1080, like some of the newer Google-branded tablets or high-end Samsung phones, then we have 1920 pixels across the longest length of the device and 1080 pixels across the width.

We can therefore think of our screen on which we will be drawing as a grid. We draw using the `Canvas` and `Paint` classes on a virtual canvas. We will do so by plotting points (pixels), lines, shapes, and text using coordinates on this grid.

The coordinate system starts in the top-left corner of the screen.

As an example, take a look at this line of code:

```
drawPoint(0, 0); //Not actual syntax (but very close)
```

In this, we would plot a single pixel in the top-left corner of the screen. Now look at the following code:

```
drawPoint(1920, 1080); //Not actual syntax (but very close)
```

If we use it like this, we could draw a point in the bottom-right corner of one of these high-end devices (while in the landscape position).

We could also draw lines by specifying a start and end coordinate position, a bit like this:

```
drawLine(0,0,1920, 1080); //Not actual syntax (but very close)
```

This would draw a line from the top-left corner of the screen to the bottom right.

You might have noticed some potential problems. Firstly, not all Android devices have such a high resolution; in fact, most are significantly lower. Even devices with high resolution will have totally different coordinates when held in landscape or portrait positions. How will we write code that adapts to these devices regardless of the screen resolution? We will see the solution soon.

Animating our pixels

Drawing shapes, lines, and pixels is all very well, but how do we make them appear to move? We will be using the same animation trick used in cartoons, movies, and other video games:

1. Draw an object.

2. Rub it out.

3. Draw the object in its new position.

4. Repeat fast enough to trick the player's brain that the game objects are moving.

The theory makes all of this sound more complicated than it is. Let's take a quick look at the `Paint` and `Canvas` classes and a quick introductory demo app. Then we can implement our retro squash game for real.

Getting started with Canvas and Paint

The aptly named `Canvas` class provides just what you would expect—a virtual canvas to draw our graphics on.

We can make a virtual canvas using the `Canvas` class from any Android UI element. In our demo app, we will draw on an ImageView, and when we make our game, we will draw straight on a special type of view, which will bring some extra advantages, as we will see.

To get started, we need a view to draw on. We already know how to get a view from our UI layout using Java code:

```
ImageView ourView = (ImageView) findViewById(R.id.imageView);
```

This line of code grabs a reference to an ImageView placed in the UI design and assigns it to our object in our Java code. As we have seen, the ImageView in the UI design has an assigned ID of `imageView`, and our controllable ImageView object in our Java code is called `ourView`.

Now we need a bitmap. A bitmap itself has a coordinate system like the screen. We are creating a bitmap to turn it into a canvas:

```
Bitmap ourBitmap = Bitmap.createBitmap(300,600, Bitmap.Config.
ARGB_8888);
```

The previous line of code declares and creates an object of the `Bitmap` type. It will have a size of 300 by 600 pixels. We will keep this in mind when we draw on it shortly.

 The last argument in the `createBitmap` method, `Bitmap.Config.ARGB_8888`, is simply a format, and we can create some great games without getting into the different options for bitmap formats.

Now we can prepare our bitmap for drawing by creating a `Canvas` object from it:

```
Canvas ourCanvas = new Canvas(ourBitmap);
```

Next, we get ourselves an object of the `Paint` type. We can think of this object as the brush and the paint for our virtual canvas:

```
Paint paint = new Paint();
```

At this point, we are ready to use our `Paint` and `Canvas` objects to do some drawing. The actual code to draw a pixel in the top-left corner of the screen will look like this:

```
ourCanvas.drawPoint(0, 0, paint);//How simple is that?
```

Let's now look at a working example.

Android Canvas demo app

Let's make an app that uses the `Canvas` and `Paint` classes and do a bit of drawing. This example will be completely static (no animation), so we can clearly see how to use `Canvas` and `Paint` without cluttering the code with things we will learn later.

In this demo app, we use some conceptually helpful variable names to help us grasp the role that each object is playing, but we will go through the whole thing at the end to make sure we know exactly what is going on at each stage. Of course, you don't have to type all of this. You can open the completed code files from the `CanvasDemo` folder in the `Chapter7` folder of the download bundle:

1. Start a new project and call it `CanvasDemo`. Tidy up the unnecessary imports and overrides if you want to.

2. Open `activity_main.xml` in the editor. Drag an **ImageView** from the palette to the layout. The ImageView has an ID by default, which is `imageView`. Now we will use this ID in our code.

3. Switch to `MainActivity.java` in the editor. First, we will create our `Bitmap`, `Canvas`, and `Paint` objects as we discussed earlier. Here is the first part of the code. Enter it directly after the call to the `setContentView` method:

```
//Get a reference to our ImageView in the layout
ImageView ourFrame = (ImageView) findViewById(R.id.imageView);

//Create a bitmap object to use as our canvas
Bitmap ourBitmap = Bitmap.createBitmap(300,600, Bitmap.Config.
ARGB_8888);
Canvas ourCanvas = new Canvas(ourBitmap);

//A paint object that does our drawing, on our canvas
Paint paint = new Paint();
```

4. Here, we try out some of the cool things we can draw. Enter the code directly after the code in the previous step:

```
//Set the background color
ourCanvas.drawColor(Color.BLACK);

//Change the color of the virtual paint brush
paint.setColor(Color.argb(255, 255, 255, 255));

//Now draw a load of stuff on our canvas
ourCanvas.drawText("Score: 42 Lives: 3 Hi: 97", 10, 10, paint);
ourCanvas.drawLine(10, 50, 200, 50, paint);
ourCanvas.drawCircle(110, 160, 100, paint);
ourCanvas.drawPoint(10, 260, paint);

//Now put the canvas in the frame
   ourFrame.setImageBitmap(ourBitmap);
```

5. Run the demo on an emulator or a device.

Your output will look like what is shown in the following screenshot:

Let's go through the code again. In steps 1 and 2, we created a new project and placed an ImageView object with an ID of `imageView` on our UI layout.

In step 3, we started by getting a reference to the `ImageView` object in our layout. However, we have done this often, usually with TextViews and Buttons. We named our ImageView `ourFrame` because it will hold our canvas:

```
ImageView ourFrame = (ImageView) findViewById(R.id.imageView);
```

Then we created a bitmap to be used to make a canvas:

```
Bitmap ourBitmap = Bitmap.createBitmap(300,600, Bitmap.Config.
ARGB_8888);
Canvas ourCanvas = new Canvas(ourBitmap);
```

After that, we created our new `Paint` object:

```
Paint paint = new Paint();
```

In step 4, we were ready to draw, and we did so in a few different ways. First, we painted the entire canvas black:

```
ourCanvas.drawColor(Color.BLACK);
```

Then we chose the color with which we will be painting. `(255, 255, 255, 255)` is a numerical representation of white with full opacity (no transparency):

```
paint.setColor(Color.argb(255, 255, 255, 255));
```

Now we see something new, but it is quite easy to understand. We can also draw strings of text to the screen and position that text at precise screen coordinates, just like we can with a pixel.

You will notice that with the `drawText` method and all other drawing methods of the `Canvas` class, we always pass our `Paint` object as an argument. Just to make what is going on in the next line of code absolutely clear, I am stating that `"Score: 42 Lives:3 Hi: 97"` is the string that will be drawn on the screen, `10, 10` are the screen coordinates, and `paint` is our `Paint` object:

```
ourCanvas.drawText("Score: 42 Lives: 3 Hi: 97", 10, 10, paint);
```

Next, we draw a line. The argument list here can be described as follows: (start x coordinate, start y coordinate, end x coordinate, end y coordinate, our `Paint` object):

```
ourCanvas.drawLine(10, 50, 200, 50, paint);
```

Now we see that we can draw circles. We can also draw other shapes. The argument list here can be described as follows: (start x coordinate, start y coordinate, radius of circle, our `Paint` object):

```
ourCanvas.drawCircle(110, 160, 100, paint);
```

Then we draw a humble, lonely pixel (point). The arguments we use are in this format: (*x* coordinate, *y* coordinate, `Paint` object):

```
ourCanvas.drawPoint(10, 260, paint);
```

Finally, we place our bitmap canvas on our ImageView frame:

```
ourFrame.setImageBitmap(ourBitmap);
```

We still need to get smarter with managing screen resolution and orientation, and we will do so in our retro squash game. Also, we need to look for a system that will allow us to rub out and redraw our images at a set interval to create the illusion of movement. Actually, we already know one such system. Think about how we might use threads to achieve this illusion. First of all, let's take a look at how the player will control the game. After all, we are not going to have any handy UI buttons to press for this game.

Detecting touches on the screen

In our retro squash game, we will have no UI buttons, so we cannot use the `OnClickListener` interface and override the `onClick` method. This is not a problem, however. We will just use another interface to suit our situation. We will use `OnTouchListener` and override the `onTouchEvent` method. It works a bit differently, so let's take a look at implementing it before we dive into the game code.

We must implement the `OnTouchListener` interface for the activity we want to listen to touches in, like this:

```
public class MainActivity extends Activity implements View.
OnTouchListener{
```

Then we can override the `onTouchEvent` method, perhaps a bit like this.

```
@Override
public boolean onTouchEvent(MotionEvent motionEvent) {
  float x = motionEvent.getX();
  float y = motionEvent.getY();
  //do something with the x and y values
  return false;
}
```

The x variable will hold the horizontal value of the position on the screen that was touched, and y will hold the vertical position. It is worth noting that the motionEvent object parameter contains lots of information as well as the *x* and *y* location, for example, whether the screen was touched or released. We can make some really useful switch statements with this information, as we will see later.

Knowing exactly how we use this to achieve our goals in the squash game requires us to first consider the design of the game.

Preparing to make the retro squash game

Now we are ready to discuss the making of our next game. We actually know everything we need to. We just need to think about how to use the different techniques we have learned.

Let's first look at exactly what we want to achieve so that we have something to aim for.

The design of the game

Let's look at a screenshot of the game as a good starting point. When you design your own games, drawing sketches of the in-game objects and mechanics of the game will be an invaluable part of the design process. Here, we can cheat a bit by taking a look at the end result.

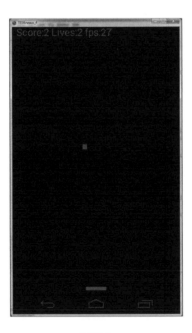

The UI

Starting from the top, we have **Score**. Every time the player successfully hits the ball, a point is added. Next, we have **Lives**. The player starts with three lives, and every time they let a ball go past their racket, they lose one life. When the player has zero lives, their score is set to zero, lives are set back to three, and the game begins again. Next to this, we have **FPS**. FPS stands for frames per second. It would be nice if we monitor on the screen the number of times our screen is being redrawn every second, as this is the first time we are animating our very own graphics.

Approximately in the middle of the previous screenshot is the ball. It is a square ball, in keeping with the traditional pong style. Squares are also easier when you have to perform realistic-looking collision detection.

Physics

We will detect when the ball hits any of the four sides of the screen as well as when it hits the racket. Depending on what the ball hits and its current direction at the time of the collision, we will determine what happens to the ball. Here is a rough outline of what each type of collision will do:

- **Hit the top of the screen**: The ball will maintain the same horizontal (x) direction of travel but reverse the vertical (y) direction of travel.

- **Hit either side of the screen**: The ball will maintain its y direction of travel but reverse its x direction.

- **Hit the bottom of the screen**: The ball will disappear and restart at the top of the screen with a downward y direction of travel and a random x direction of travel.

- **Hit the player's racket**: We will check whether the ball has hit the left or the right of the racket and alter the x direction of travel to match. We will also reverse the y direction of travel to send the ball back to the top again.

By enforcing these crude virtual rules of physics, we can simply create a ball that behaves almost as we would expect a real ball to do. We will add a few properties such as slightly increasing the ball speed after hitting the racket. These rules will work just as well in portrait or landscape orientations.

The player's racket will be a simple rectangle that the player can slide left by holding anywhere on the left half of the screen, and right by holding anywhere on the right of the screen.

For brevity, we will not be making a main menu screen to implement high scores. In our final game, which we start in the next chapter, we will go ahead and have an animated menu screen, online high scores, and achievements. However, this squash game will simply restart when the player reaches zero lives.

The structure of the code

Here, we will take a quick theoretical look at some aspects of the implementation that might be raising questions. When we finally get down to the implementation, we should find most of the code quite straightforward, with only a few bits that might need extra explanation.

We have discussed everything we need to know, and we will also discuss specifics in the code as we go through the implementation. We will go over the trickier parts of the code at the end of each phase of implementation.

As usual, all the completed code files can be found in the download bundle. The files encompassing all the phases of this project are in the `Chapter7/RetroSquash` folder.

We have learned that in an application using classes and their methods, different parts of the code will be dependent on other parts. Therefore, rather than jumping back and forth in the code, we will lay it out from the first line to the last in order. Of course, we will also refer to the related parts of code as we go along. I definitely recommend studying the code in its entirety to fully grasp what is going on and which parts of the code call which other parts.

To prevent this implementation from spreading into an enormous to-do list, it has been broken into four phases. This should provide convenient places to stop and take a break.

There is no layout file and only one `.java` file. This file is called `MainActivity.java`. The `MainActivity.java` file has a structure as indicated in the following overview of the code. I have indented some parts to show what parts are enclosed within others. This is a high-level view, and it omits quite a lot of detail:

```
Package name and various import statements
MainActivity class starts{
    Declare some member variables
    OnCreate method{
      Initialization and setup
    }
    SquashCourtView class{
      Constructor
```

```
        Multiple methods of SquashCourtView
    }
    Some Android lifecycle method overrides
}
```

As previously stated, we can see that everything is in the `MainActivity.java` file. As usual, at the top of our file, we will have a package name and a load of imports for the different classes we will be using.

Next, as per all our other projects, we have the `MainActivity` class. It encompasses everything else, even the `SquashCourtView` class. This makes the `SquashCourtView` class an inner class and will therefore be able to access the member variables of the `MainActivity` class, which will be essential in this implementation.

Before the `SquashCourtView` class, however, comes the declaration of all the member variables in the `MainActivity` class, followed by a fairly in-depth `onCreate` method.

We could implement the other Android lifecycle methods next, and you are welcome to do so. However, the code within the other Android lifecycle methods will make more sense once we have seen the code in the `SquashCourtView` class methods.

After `onCreate`, we will implement the `SquashCourtView` class. This has some fairly long methods in it, so we will break it into phases 2 and 3.

Finally, we will implement the remaining Android lifecycle methods. They are short but important.

The four implementation phases in detail

Let's take an even closer look at the implementation before we actually get to it. Here is how we will divide the implementation into the four phases, this time with a bit more detail as to what to expect in each:

- **Phase 1 – MainActivity and onCreate**: In this phase, we will create the project itself as well as implement the following steps:

    ° We will add our imports and create the body of our `MainActivity` class

    ° Within this, we will declare the member variables that the game needs

    ° We will implement our `onCreate` method, which does loads of setup work but nothing that is hard to understand

- **Phase 2 – SquashCourtView part 1**: In this phase, we will start work on our key class, SquashCourtView. Specifically, we will:
  - Implement the declaration of the SquashCourtView class and its member variables.
  - Write a simple constructor.
  - Implement the run method to control the flow of the game.
  - Implement the lengthy but fairly easy-to-understand updateCourt method. This is the method that handles collision detection and keeps track of our ball and racket.

- **Phase 3 – SquashCourtView part 2**: In this phase, we will finish the SquashCourtView class by implementing the following:
  - The drawCourt method, which unsurprisingly does all the drawing
  - The controlFPS method, which makes the game run at similar speeds on devices that have different CPUs
  - Next, we will quickly write a couple of methods that help the Android lifecycle methods with similar names—the pause and resume methods
  - Finally for this phase, we will easily handle the touch controls of the game by overriding the onTouchEvent method we looked at earlier

- **Phase 4 – Remaining lifecycle methods**: In this short phase we will add the finishing touches:
  - Quickly implement what happens in the onPause, onResume, and onStop methods by overriding them
  - We will also handle what happens when the player presses the back button on their phone or tablet

Phase 1 – MainActivity and onCreate

Now that we have seen what we will do in each of the phases, let's actually get started with building our game by performing the following steps:

1. Create a new project, just as we have before, but with one slight difference. This time, on the **New Project** dialog, change **Minimum required SDK** to **API 13: Android 3.2 (Honeycomb)**. Call the project RetroSquash. Delete the unnecessary overridden methods if you like.

2. Edit the `AndroidManifest.xml` file, just as we did at the end of *Chapter 4, Discovering Loops and Methods*, to make the app use the full screen. Check back for full details if needed. Note that we are *not* locking orientation because this game is fun in both portrait and landscape. Here is the line of code to add:

```
android:theme="@android:style/Theme.NoTitleBar.Fullscreen">
```

3. Make some sound effects using Bfxr, as we did in *Chapter 5, Gaming and Java Essentials*. Four will be enough, but there is nothing stopping you from adding more sounds. For authentic 1970s-style sounds, try the **Blip/Select** button shown in the following screenshot. Name the samples `sample1.ogg`, `sample2.ogg`, `sample3.ogg`, and `sample4.ogg`. Or you can just use my samples. They are in the `assets` folder of the folder named `RetroSquash` in the code bundle.

4. In Project Explorer, create a directory called `assets` within the `main` directory. Copy the four sound files you created in the previous step to the newly created `assets` folder.

5. Type the following import statements at the top of the `MainActivity.java` file but just after your package name, as shown in the following code:

```
package com.packtpub.retrosquash.app;

import android.app.Activity;
import android.content.Context;
import android.content.res.AssetFileDescriptor;
import android.content.res.AssetManager;
import android.graphics.Canvas;
import android.graphics.Color;
import android.graphics.Paint;
import android.graphics.Point;
import android.media.AudioManager;
import android.media.SoundPool;
import android.os.Bundle;
import android.view.Display;
import android.view.KeyEvent;
import android.view.MotionEvent;
import android.view.SurfaceHolder;
import android.view.SurfaceView;
import java.io.IOException;
import java.util.Random;
```

6. Now type your class declaration and declare the following member variables. We will discuss the member variables in detail at the end of this phase:

```java
public class MainActivity extends Activity {

    Canvas canvas;
    SquashCourtView squashCourtView;

    //Sound
    //initialize sound variables
    private SoundPool soundPool;
    int sample1 = -1;
    int sample2 = -1;
    int sample3 = -1;
    int sample4 = -1;

    //For getting display details like the number of pixels
    Display display;
    Point size;
    int screenWidth;
    int screenHeight;

    //Game objects
    int racketWidth;
    int racketHeight;
    Point racketPosition;

    Point ballPosition;
    int ballWidth;

    //for ball movement
    boolean ballIsMovingLeft;
    boolean ballIsMovingRight;
    boolean ballIsMovingUp;
    boolean ballIsMovingDown;

    //for racket movement
    boolean racketIsMovingLeft;
    boolean racketIsMovingRight;

    //stats
    long lastFrameTime;
    int fps;
    int score;
    int lives;
```

7. Next, we will enter the `onCreate` method in its entirety. We are initializing many of the member variables that we declared in the previous step, as well as creating an object from our `SquashCourtView` class, which we will begin to implement in the next phase. Perhaps the most notable line in this block of code is the somewhat different call to `setContentView`. Look at the argument for `setContentView`. We will learn more about this argument at the end of this phase. This phase also sets up `SoundPool` and loads the sound samples. Type the first part of the `onCreate` code:

```
protected void onCreate(Bundle savedInstanceState) {
        super.onCreate(savedInstanceState);
        squashCourtView = new SquashCourtView(this);
        setContentView(squashCourtView);

        //Sound code
        soundPool = new SoundPool(10,
          AudioManager.STREAM_MUSIC, 0);
        try {
            //Create objects of the 2 required classes
            AssetManager assetManager = getAssets();
            AssetFileDescriptor descriptor;

            //create our three fx in memory ready for use
            descriptor =
              assetManager.openFd("sample1.ogg");
            sample1 = soundPool.load(descriptor, 0);

            descriptor =
              assetManager.openFd("sample2.ogg");
            sample2 = soundPool.load(descriptor, 0);


            descriptor =
              assetManager.openFd("sample3.ogg");
            sample3 = soundPool.load(descriptor, 0);

            descriptor =
              assetManager.openFd("sample4.ogg");
            sample4 = soundPool.load(descriptor, 0);


        } catch (IOException e) {
            //catch exceptions here
        }
```

8. Now we initialize the variables we created earlier. Notice that there are some good potential candidates for a bit of encapsulation. However, to keep the code readable, we will not do so at this stage. Enter this code:

```
//Could this be an object with getters and setters
//Don't want just anyone changing screen size.
//Get the screen size in pixels
display = getWindowManager().getDefaultDisplay();
size = new Point();
display.getSize(size);
screenWidth = size.x;
screenHeight = size.y;


//The game objects
racketPosition = new Point();
racketPosition.x = screenWidth / 2;
racketPosition.y = screenHeight - 20;
racketWidth = screenWidth / 8;
racketHeight = 10;

ballWidth = screenWidth / 35;
ballPosition = new Point();
ballPosition.x = screenWidth / 2;
ballPosition.y = 1 + ballWidth;

lives = 3;

}
```

Phase 1 code explained

Let's look at what we did. From steps 1 to 4, we simply created a project and some sound files. Then we added the sound files to the `assets` folder as we have done before on other projects. In step 5, we added all the necessary imports for the classes we will be using.

In step 6, we created a whole load of member variables. Let's take a closer look at them. We declared an object of the `Canvas` type called `canvas`. We will use this object to set up our drawing system. We also declared an instance of `SquashCourtView` called `squashCourtView`. This will be underlined as an error because we haven't implemented the class yet.

Here, we declared and initialized variables to be references to our sound files, just as we did in other projects. After this, we did something new:

```
//For getting display details like the number of pixels
Display display;
Point size;
int screenWidth;
int screenHeight;
```

We declared a `Display` object and a `Point` object. We see these in action in our `onCreate` method in a minute, alongside the two `int` variables, `screenWidth` and `screenHeight`. We use them to get the screen size in pixels so that we can make our game work on a screen with any resolution.

Here, we declared some variables whose purpose is plain from their names. Their actual usage becomes clearer when we initialize them in step 8 and use them throughout our `SquashCourtView` class:

```
//Game objects
int racketWidth;
int racketHeight;
Point racketPosition;

Point ballPosition;
int ballWidth;
```

Here, we have a bunch of Boolean variables to control the logic of the movement of both the racket and the ball. Notice that there is a variable for each possible direction for both the racket and the ball. Notice also that the racket can move in two directions — left and right — and the ball in four. Of course, the ball can travel in two directions at the same time. All will become clear when we write the `updateCourt` method in phase 2. Here is that code again:

```
//for ball movement
boolean ballIsMovingLeft;
boolean ballIsMovingRight;
boolean ballIsMovingUp;
boolean ballIsMovingDown;

//for racket movement
 boolean racketIsMovingLeft;
 boolean racketIsMovingRight;
```

In the last part of step 6, we declared two fairly obvious variables, `lives` and `score`. But what about `lastFrameTime` and `fps`? These will be used in the `controlFPS` method, which we will write in phase 3. They will be used along with some local variables to measure how fast our game loop runs. We can then lock it to run at a consistent rate so that players on devices with different CPU speeds get a similar experience.

In step 7, we entered the `onCreate` method, but this time, things are different. We initialize `squashCourtView` as a new `SquashCourtView` object. It's fine so far, but then we seem to be telling `setContentView` to make this the entire view that the player will see, instead of the usual view created in the Android Studio designer, which we have become used to. We are not using any Android UI components in this game, so the visual designer and all of its generated XML are of no use to us. As you will see right at the start of phase 2, our `SquashCourtView` class extends (inherits from) `SurfaceView`.

We created an object with all the facilities of a `SurfaceView`. We will just customize it to play our squash game. Neat! Therefore, it is perfectly acceptable and logical to set our `squashCourtView` object as the entire view that the player will see:

```
squashCourtView = new SquashCourtView(this);
setContentView(squashCourtView);
```

We then set up our sound effects as we have done before.

In step 8, we initialized many of the variables that we declared in step 6. Let's look at the values and the order in which we initialized them. You might have noticed that we don't initialize every variable here; some will be initialized later. Remember that we don't have to initialize member variables and that they also have default values.

In the following code, we get the number of pixels (wide and high) for the device. The `display` object holds the details of the display after the first line has been executed. Then we create a new object called `size` of the `Point` type. We send `size` as an argument to the `display.getSize` method. The `Point` type has an `x` and `y` member variable, and so does the `size` object, which now holds the width and height (in pixels) of the display. These values are then assigned to `screenWidth` and `screenHeight` respectively. We will use `screenWidth` and `screenHeight` quite extensively in the `SquashCourtView` class:

```
display = getWindowManager().getDefaultDisplay();
size = new Point();
display.getSize(size);
screenWidth = size.x;
screenHeight = size.y;
```

Next, we initialize the variables that determine the size and position of the ball and racket. Here, we initialize our `racketPosition` object, which is of the `Point` type. Remember that it has an `x` and a `y` member variable:

```
racketPosition = new Point();
```

We initialize `racketPosition.x` to be whatever the current screen width in pixels might be, but divided by two, so the racket will start in a horizontal and central position regardless of the resolution of the screen:

```
racketPosition.x = screenWidth / 2;
```

In the next line of code, `racketPosition.y` is put at the bottom of the screen with a small 20-pixel gap:

```
racketPosition.y = screenHeight - 20;
```

We make the width of the racket to one-eighth the width of the screen. We will see when we get to run the game that this is a fairly effective size, but we could make it bigger by dividing it by a lower number, or smaller by dividing it by a larger number. The point is that it will be the same fraction of `screenWidth` regardless of the resolution of the device:

```
racketWidth = screenWidth / 8;
```

In the following line of code, we choose an arbitrary height for our racket:

```
racketHeight = 10;
```

Then we make our ball as small as 1/35th of the screen. Again, we could make it larger or smaller:

```
ballWidth = screenWidth / 35;
```

In the next line of code, we will create a new point object to hold the position of the ball:

```
ballPosition = new Point();
```

As we did with the racket, we start the ball in the center of the screen, like this:

```
ballPosition.x = screenWidth / 2;
```

However, we set it to start at the top of the screen just far enough to see the top of the ball:

```
ballPosition.y = 1 + ballWidth;
```

The player starts the game with three lives:

```
lives = 3;
```

Phew! That was a fairly chunky section. Take a break if you like, and then we will move on to phase 2.

Phase 2 – SquashCourtView part 1

Finally, we get to the secret weapon of our game—the SquashCourtView class. The first three methods are presented here, and explained more fully once we have implemented them:

1. Here is a class declaration that extends SurfaceView, giving our class all the methods and properties of SurfaceView. It also implements Runnable, which allows it to run in a separate thread. As you will see, we will put the bulk of the functionality in the run method. After the declaration, we have a constructor. Remember that the constructor is a method that has the same name as the class and is called when we initialize a new object of its type. The code in the constructor initializes some objects and then sends the ball off in a random direction. We will look at that part in detail after we have implemented this phase. Enter the following code before the closing curly brace of the MainActivity class:

```
class SquashCourtView extends SurfaceView implements Runnable {
        Thread ourThread = null;
        SurfaceHolder ourHolder;
        volatile boolean playingSquash;
        Paint paint;

        public SquashCourtView(Context context) {
            super(context);
            ourHolder = getHolder();
            paint = new Paint();
            ballIsMovingDown = true;

            //Send the ball in random direction
            Random randomNumber = new Random();
            int ballDirection = randomNumber.nextInt(3);
            switch (ballDirection) {
                case 0:
                    ballIsMovingLeft = true;
                    ballIsMovingRight = false;
```

```
            break;

        case 1:
            ballIsMovingRight = true;
            ballIsMovingLeft = false;
            break;

        case 2:
            ballIsMovingLeft = false;
            ballIsMovingRight = false;
            break;
        }


    }
```

2. Now we have this short and sweet overriding of the run method. Remember that the `run` method contains the functionality of the thread. In this case, it has three calls, one to each of `updateCourt`, `drawCourt`, and `controlFPS`, the three key methods of our class. Enter this code:

```
@Override
    public void run() {
        while (playingSquash) {
            updateCourt();
            drawCourt();
            controlFPS();

        }

    }
```

3. We will implement just one more method in this phase (`updateCourt`), but it is quite long. We will split it into chunks and briefly mention what is going on in each chunk before we type the code. We will perform a closer examination of how it works when the phase is implemented. In this next chunk of code, we handle the left and right movement of the racket as well as detecting and reacting when the ball hits either the left or the right of the screen. Enter the following code after the code from the previous step:

```
public void updateCourt() {
        if (racketIsMovingRight) {
            racketPosition.x = racketPosition.x + 10;
        }

        if (racketIsMovingLeft) {
```

```
                    racketPosition.x = racketPosition.x - 10;
            }


            //detect collisions

            //hit right of screen
            if (ballPosition.x + ballWidth > screenWidth) {
                ballIsMovingLeft = true;
                ballIsMovingRight = false;
                soundPool.play(sample1, 1, 1, 0, 0, 1);
            }

            //hit left of screen
            if (ballPosition.x < 0) {
                ballIsMovingLeft = false;
                ballIsMovingRight = true;
                soundPool.play(sample1, 1, 1, 0, 0, 1);
            }
```

4. In this next chunk of code, we check whether the ball has hit the bottom of the screen, that is, the player has failed to return the ball. Enter this code directly after the code in the previous step:

```
//Edge of ball has hit bottom of screen
            if (ballPosition.y > screenHeight - ballWidth) {
                lives = lives - 1;
                if (lives == 0) {
                    lives = 3;
                    score = 0;
                    soundPool.play(sample4, 1, 1, 0, 0, 1);
                }
                ballPosition.y = 1 + ballWidth;//back to top of
                screen

                //what horizontal direction should we use
                //for the next falling ball
                Random randomNumber = new Random();
                int startX =
                   randomNumber.nextInt(screenWidth -
                   ballWidth) + 1;
                ballPosition.x = startX + ballWidth;

                int ballDirection =
                   randomNumber.nextInt(3);
                switch (ballDirection) {
```

```
            case 0:
                ballIsMovingLeft = true;
                ballIsMovingRight = false;
                break;

            case 1:
                ballIsMovingRight = true;
                ballIsMovingLeft = false;
                break;

            case 2:
                ballIsMovingLeft = false;
                ballIsMovingRight = false;
                break;
        }
    }
```

5. In this chunk of code, we handle whether the ball has hit the top of the screen. We also calculate all the possible movements of the ball for this frame. Now type the following code:

```
//we hit the top of the screen
        if (ballPosition.y <= 0) {
            ballIsMovingDown = true;
            ballIsMovingUp = false;
            ballPosition.y = 1;
            soundPool.play(sample2, 1, 1, 0, 0, 1);
        }

        //depending upon the two directions we should
        //be moving in adjust our x any positions
        if (ballIsMovingDown) {
            ballPosition.y += 6;
        }

        if (ballIsMovingUp) {
            ballPosition.y -= 10;
        }

        if (ballIsMovingLeft) {
            ballPosition.x -= 12;
        }

        if (ballIsMovingRight) {
            ballPosition.x += 12;
        }
```

6. Finally, we handle collision detection and the reaction of the racket and the ball. We also close the updateCourt method, and this is the last chunk of code for this phase. Enter the following after your code from the previous step:

```
//Has ball hit racket
            if (ballPosition.y + ballWidth >=
                (racketPosition.y - racketHeight / 2)) {
                int halfRacket = racketWidth / 2;
                if (ballPosition.x + ballWidth >
                   (racketPosition.x - halfRacket)
                   && ballPosition.x - ballWidth <
                      (racketPosition.x + halfRacket)) {
                   //rebound the ball vertically and play a sound
                   soundPool.play(sample3, 1, 1, 0, 0, 1);
                   score++;
                   ballIsMovingUp = true;
                   ballIsMovingDown = false;
                   //now decide how to rebound the ball
                   horizontally
                   if (ballPosition.x > racketPosition.x) {
                       ballIsMovingRight = true;
                       ballIsMovingLeft = false;

                   } else {
                       ballIsMovingRight = false;
                       ballIsMovingLeft = true;

                   }

                }
            }
        }
    }
```

Phase 2 code explained

The code in this phase was lengthy, but there is nothing too challenging when we break it down. Possibly, the only challenge is in unravelling some of those nested if statements. We will do this now.

In step 1, we declare our SquashCourView class. This implements the Runnable interface. You might remember from *Chapter 5, Gaming and Java Essentials*, that Runnable provides us with a thread. All we need to do is override the run method, and whatever is within it will work in a new thread.

Then we created a new `Thread` object called `ourThread`, and a `SurfaceHolder` object to hold our surface and enable us to control or lock our surface for use within our thread. Next, we have `playingSquash` of the `boolean` type. This wraps the inside of our overridden `run` method to control when the game is running. The odd-looking `volatile` modifier means that we will be able to change its value from the outside and inside of our thread.

Lastly, for the currently discussed block of code, we declare an object of the `Paint` type, called `paint`, to do our painting:

```
class SquashCourtView extends SurfaceView implements Runnable {
        Thread ourThread = null;
        SurfaceHolder ourHolder;
        volatile boolean playingSquash;
        Paint paint;
```

Next, we implemented the constructor of our class, so that when we initialized a new `SquashCourtView` object back in `onCreate`, this is the code that runs. First, we see that we run the constructor of the superclass. Then we initialize `ourHolder` using the `getHolder` method. Next, we initialize our `paint` object:

```
public SquashCourtView(Context context) {
        super(context);
        ourHolder = getHolder();
        paint = new Paint();
```

Now, still within the constructor, we get things moving. We set our `ballIsMovingDown` variable to `true`. At the start of each game, we always want the ball to be moving down. We will see soon that the `updateCourt` method will perform the ball movement. Next, we send the ball in a random horizontal direction. This is achieved by getting a random number between 0 and 2. We then switch for each possible case: 0, 1, or 2. In each case statement, we set the Boolean variables that control horizontal movement differently. In `case 0`, the ball moves left, and in `case 1` and `case 3`, the ball will move right and straight down, respectively. Then we close our constructor:

```
        ballIsMovingDown = true;

        //Send the ball in random direction
        Random randomNumber = new Random();
        int ballDirection = randomNumber.nextInt(3);
        switch (ballDirection) {
            case 0:
                ballIsMovingLeft = true;
                ballIsMovingRight = false;
```

```
                break;


        case 1:
            ballIsMovingRight = true;
            ballIsMovingLeft = false;
            break;

        case 2:
            ballIsMovingLeft = false;
            ballIsMovingRight = false;
            break;
    }



}
```

In step 2, we have some really simple code, but this is the code that runs everything else. The overridden run method is what ourThread calls at defined intervals. As you can see, the code is wrapped in a while block controlled by our playingSquash variable of the boolean type. Then the code simply calls updateCourt, which controls movement and collision detection; drawCourt, which will draw everything; and controlFPS, which will lock our game to a consistent frame rate. That's it for run:

```
    @Override
        public void run() {
            while (playingSquash) {
                updateCourt();
                drawCourt();
                controlFPS();

            }


        }
```

Then in step 3, we begin the updateCourt method. It was quite long, so we broke it down into a few manageable chunks. The first two if blocks check to see whether either the racketIsMovingRight or the racketIsMovingLeft Boolean variables is true. If one of them is true, the blocks add 10 to or subtract 10 from racketPosition.x. The effect of this will be seen by the player when the racket is drawn in the drawCourt method. How the Boolean variables are manipulated in the onTouchEvent method will be discussed soon:

```
    public void updateCourt() {
            if (racketIsMovingRight) {
                racketPosition.x = racketPosition.x + 10;
```

```
}

if (racketIsMovingLeft) {
    racketPosition.x = racketPosition.x - 10;
}
```

Now, still in the `updateCourt` method, we detect and handle collisions with the left and right side of the screen. Checking whether `ballPosition.x` is larger than `screenWidth` would be enough to see whether the ball bounces back the other way. However, by being a bit more precise and testing for `ballPosition.x + ballWidth > screenWidth`, we are testing whether the right edge of the ball hits the right side of the screen. This creates a much more pleasing effect as it looks more *real*. When a collision occurs with the right side, we simply reverse the direction of our ball and play a sound. The reason that the `if` code for the left-side detection is simpler is because we have drawn the ball using `drawRect`, so `ballPosition.x` is the precise left side of the ball. When the ball collides with the left side, we simply reverse its direction and play a beep sound:

```
//detect collisions

//hit right of screen
if (ballPosition.x + ballWidth > screenWidth) {
    ballIsMovingLeft = true;
    ballIsMovingRight = false;
    soundPool.play(sample1, 1, 1, 0, 0, 1);
}

//hit left of screen
if (ballPosition.x < 0) {
    ballIsMovingLeft = false;
    ballIsMovingRight = true;
    soundPool.play(sample1, 1, 1, 0, 0, 1);
}
```

In step 4, we implemented what happens when the ball hits the bottom of the screen. This occurs when the player fails to return the ball, so a fair few things need to happen here. However, there is nothing overly complicated in this section. First comes the collision test. We check whether the underside of the ball has hit the bottom of the screen:

```
//Edge of ball has hit bottom of screen
if (ballPosition.y > screenHeight - ballWidth) {
```

If it has hit, we deduct a life. Then we check whether the player has lost all their lives:

```
lives = lives - 1;
if (lives == 0) {
```

If all lives are lost, we start the game again by resetting lives to 3 and score to 0. We also play a low beep sound:

```
lives = 3;
score = 0;
soundPool.play(sample4, 1, 1, 0, 0, 1);
}
```

As of now, we are still within the `if` block because the ball hit the bottom of the screen, but outside the `if` block for the player who has zero lives. Whether the player has zero lives or still has some lives left, we need to put the ball back at the top of the screen and send it in a downward trajectory and a random horizontal direction. This code is similar to but not the same as the code we have seen in the constructor to start the ball moving at the beginning of the game:

```
ballPosition.y = 1 + ballWidth;//back to top of screen
//what horizontal direction should we use
//for the next falling ball
Random randomNumber = new Random();
int startX = randomNumber.nextInt(screenWidth - ballWidth) + 1;
            ballPosition.x = startX + ballWidth;

            int ballDirection = randomNumber.nextInt(3);
            switch (ballDirection) {
                case 0:
                    ballIsMovingLeft = true;
                    ballIsMovingRight = false;
                    break;

                case 1:
                    ballIsMovingRight = true;
                    ballIsMovingLeft = false;
                    break;

                case 2:
                    ballIsMovingLeft = false;
                    ballIsMovingRight = false;
                    break;
            }
        }
```

In step 5, we handle the event of the ball hitting the top of the screen. Reverse the values held by `ballIsMovingDown` and `ballIsMovingUp` to reverse the direction of the ball. Tweak the ball position with `ballPosition.y = 1`. This stops the ball from getting stuck and plays a nice beep:

```
//we hit the top of the screen
        if (ballPosition.y <= 0) {
            ballIsMovingDown = true;
            ballIsMovingUp = false;
            ballPosition.y = 1;
            soundPool.play(sample2, 1, 1, 0, 0, 1);
        }
```

Now, after all this collision detection and switching around of our Boolean variables, we actually move the ball. For each direction that is true, we add to or subtract from the `ballPosition.x` and `ballPosition.y` accordingly. Notice that the ball travels up faster than it travels down. This is done to shorten the time the player is waiting to get back into the action, and also crudely simulates the act of acceleration after the ball is hit by the racket:

```
        //depending upon the two directions we should be
        //moving in adjust our x any positions
        if (ballIsMovingDown) {
            ballPosition.y += 6;
        }

        if (ballIsMovingUp) {
            ballPosition.y -= 10;
        }

        if (ballIsMovingLeft) {
            ballPosition.x -= 12;
        }

        if (ballIsMovingRight) {
            ballPosition.x += 12;
        }
```

 You might have noticed that by hardcoding the number of pixels the ball moves, we create an inconsistent speed for the ball between high-resolution and low-resolution screens. Take a look at the self-test questions at the end of the chapter to see how we can solve this.

We have one last bit of collision detection to do. Has the ball hit the racket? This detection is done in a couple of stages. First, we check whether the underside of the ball has reached or gone past the top side of the racket:

```
if (ballPosition.y + ballWidth >= (racketPosition.y - racketHeight /
    2)) {
```

If this condition is true, we perform some more tests. First, we declare and initialize an `int` variable called `halfRacket` to hold half the width of the racket. We will use this in the upcoming tests:

```
int halfRacket = racketWidth / 2;
```

The next `if` block checks whether the right-hand side of the ball is greater than the far left corner of the racket, and whether it is touching it. Using the AND operator (`&&`), the block verifies that the ball's left edge is not past the far right of the racket. If this condition is true, we definitely have a hit and can think about how to handle the rebound:

```
if (ballPosition.x + ballWidth > (racketPosition.x - halfRacket)
   && ballPosition.x - ballWidth < (racketPosition.x + halfRacket)) {
```

The first bit of code inside the `if` block, which determined a definite hit, is simple. Play a sound, increase the score, and set the ball on an upwards trajectory, like this:

```
//rebound the ball vertically and play a sound
                soundPool.play(sample3, 1, 1, 0, 0, 1);
                score++;
                ballIsMovingUp = true;
                ballIsMovingDown = false;
```

Now we have an `if-else` condition, which simply checks whether the left-hand edge of the ball is past the center of the racket. If it is, we send the ball to the right. Otherwise, we send the ball to the left:

```
                //now decide how to rebound the ball horizontally
                if (ballPosition.x > racketPosition.x) {
                    ballIsMovingRight = true;
                    ballIsMovingLeft = false;

                } else {
                    ballIsMovingRight = false;
                    ballIsMovingLeft = true;
                }

            }
        }
    }
```

Phase 3 – SquashCourtView part 2

In this phase, we will complete our `SquashCourtView` class. There are two methods remaining that are called from the `run` method, `drawCourt` and `controlFPS`. Then there are a few short methods to interact with the Android lifecycle methods that we will implement in the fourth and final phase:

1. Here is the code that draws, in the following order, the text at the top of the screen, the ball, and the bat. All is contained within the `drawCourt` method, which is called from the `run` method, right after the call to `updateCourt`. Here is the code for `drawCourt`. Type the following code before the closing curly brace of the `SquashCourtView` class:

```
public void drawCourt() {

        if (ourHolder.getSurface().isValid()) {
            canvas = ourHolder.lockCanvas();
            //Paint paint = new Paint();
            canvas.drawColor(Color.BLACK);//the background
            paint.setColor(Color.argb(255, 255, 255,
                255));
            paint.setTextSize(45);
            canvas.drawText("Score:" + score + "
              Lives:" + lives + " fps:" + fps, 20, 40,
              paint);


            //Draw the squash racket
            canvas.drawRect(racketPosition.x -
              (racketWidth / 2),
               racketPosition.y - (racketHeight / 2),
                 racketPosition.x + (racketWidth / 2),
                   racketPosition.y + racketHeight,
                     paint);

            //Draw the ball
            canvas.drawRect(ballPosition.x,
              ballPosition.y,
                    ballPosition.x + ballWidth, ballPosition.y
                      + ballWidth, paint);


            ourHolder.unlockCanvasAndPost(canvas);
        }

    }
```

2. And now the `controlFPS` method locks our frame rate to something smooth and consistent. We will soon go through its exact working. Type the following code after the code in the previous step:

```
public void controlFPS() {
        long timeThisFrame =
          (System.currentTimeMillis() - lastFrameTime);
        long timeToSleep = 15 - timeThisFrame;
        if (timeThisFrame > 0) {
            fps = (int) (1000 / timeThisFrame);
        }
        if (timeToSleep > 0) {

            try {
                ourThread.sleep(timeToSleep);
            } catch (InterruptedException e) {
            }

        }

        lastFrameTime = System.currentTimeMillis();
    }
```

3. Next, we write the code for `pause` and `resume`. These are called by their related Android lifecycle methods (`onPause` and `onResume`). We ensure that our thread is ended or started safely when the player has finished or resumed our game, respectively. Now type this code after the code in the previous step:

```
public void pause() {
        playingSquash = false;
        try {
            ourThread.join();
        } catch (InterruptedException e) {
        }

    }

    public void resume() {
        playingSquash = true;
        ourThread = new Thread(this);
        ourThread.start();
    }
```

4. Finally, we have the method that controls what happens when the player touches our customized `SurfaceView`. Remember that when we discussed the design of the game, we said that a press anywhere on the left of the screen would move the racket to the left, and a press anywhere on the right will move the racket to the right. Type the following code after the code in the preceding step:

```java
@Override
        public boolean onTouchEvent(MotionEvent motionEvent) {

            switch (motionEvent.getAction() &
               MotionEvent.ACTION_MASK) {
               case MotionEvent.ACTION_DOWN:

                   if (motionEvent.getX() >= screenWidth /
                      2) {
                      racketIsMovingRight = true;
                      racketIsMovingLeft = false;
                   } else {
                      racketIsMovingLeft = true;
                      racketIsMovingRight = false;
                   }

                   break;


            case MotionEvent.ACTION_UP:
                   racketIsMovingRight = false;
                   racketIsMovingLeft = false;
                   break;
            }
            return true;
        }


    }
```

Phase 3 code explained

In step 1, we do all the drawing. We have seen what all the different drawing methods of the Canvas class can do, and their names are self-explanatory as well. However, the manner in which we arrived at the coordinates needs some explanation. First, inside drawCourt, we use ourHolder to get a drawing surface, and we check its validity (usability). Then we initialize our canvas and paint objects:

```
public void drawCourt() {

        if (ourHolder.getSurface().isValid()) {
            canvas = ourHolder.lockCanvas();
            //Paint paint = new Paint();
```

Next, we clear the screen from the previous frame of drawing:

```
        canvas.drawColor(Color.BLACK);//the background
```

Now we set the paint color to white:

```
        paint.setColor(Color.argb(255, 255, 255, 255));
```

This is new but simple to explain—we set a size for our text:

```
        paint.setTextSize(45);
```

Now we can draw a line of text at the top of the screen. It shows the score and lives variables. We have already seen how to control their values. It also shows the value of the fps variable. We will see how we can assign a value to that when we look at the next method, controlFPS:

```
        canvas.drawText("Score:" + score + " Lives:" + lives + " fps:" +
            fps, 20, 40, paint);
```

Then we draw the racket. Notice that we calculate the x start position by subtracting half the racket width from racketPosition.x, and the x end position by adding the width to x. This makes our collision detection code simple because racketPosition.x refers to the center of the racket:

```
    //Draw the squash racket
    canvas.drawRect(racketPosition.x - (racketWidth / 2),
                    racketPosition.y - (racketHeight / 2),
                    racketPosition.x + (racketWidth / 2),
                    racketPosition.y + racketHeight, paint);
```

Next, we draw the ball. Notice that the starting *x* and *y* coordinates are the same as the values held in `ballPosition.x` and `ballPosition.y`. Therefore, these coordinates correspond to the top-left corner of the ball. This is just what we need for our simple collision detection code:

```
//Draw the ball
canvas.drawRect(ballPosition.x, ballPosition.y,
    ballPosition.x + ballWidth, ballPosition.y +
    ballWidth, paint);
```

This final line draws what we have just done to the screen:

```
ourHolder.unlockCanvasAndPost(canvas);
    }


    }
```

In step 2, we essentially pause the game. We want to decide the number of times we recalculate the position of our objects and redraw them. Here is how it works.

First, we enter the `controlFPS` method when it is called from the `run` method. We declare and initialize a `long` variable with the time in milliseconds, and then take away the time that the last frame took in milliseconds. The time is calculated in the previous run through this method, at the end, as we will see:

```
public void controlFPS() {
long timeThisFrame = (System.currentTimeMillis() - lastFrameTime);
```

We then calculate how long we want to pause between frames, and initialize that value to `timeToSleep`, a new long variable. Here is how the calculation works: 15 milliseconds of pause gives us around 60 frames per second, which works well for our game and provides a very smooth animation. Therefore, `15 - timeThisFrame` equals the number of milliseconds we should pause for to make the frame last for 15 milliseconds:

```
long timeToSleep = 15 - timeThisFrame;
```

Of course, some devices will not cope with this speed. Neither do we want to pause for a negative number, nor do we want to calculate the frames per second when `timeThisFrame` is equal to zero. Next, we wrap the calculation of frames per second within an `if` statement that prevents us from dividing by zero or a negative number:

```
if (timeThisFrame > 0) {
    fps = (int) (1000 / timeThisFrame);
}
```

Likewise, we wrap the instruction to our thread to pause within a similar cautionary
`if` statement:

```
if (timeToSleep > 0) {

    try {
        ourThread.sleep(timeToSleep);
    } catch (InterruptedException e) {
    }

}
```

Finally, we see how we initialize `lastFrameTime`, ready for the next time
`controlFPS` is called:

```
lastFrameTime = System.currentTimeMillis();
}
```

In step 3, we quickly implement two methods. They are `pause` and `resume`.
These are not to be confused with the Android Activity lifecycle methods called
`onPause` and `onResume`. However, the `pause` and `resume` methods are called from
their near-namesakes. They handle stopping and starting `ourThread`, respectively.
We should always clean up our threads. Otherwise, they can keep running even after
the activity has finished:

```
public void pause() {
    playingSquash = false;
    try {
        ourThread.join();
    } catch (InterruptedException e) {
    }

}

public void resume() {
    playingSquash = true;
    ourThread = new Thread(this);
    ourThread.start();
}
```

In step 4, we handle touches on the screen. This is how we initialize our
`racketIsMovingLeft` and `racketIsMovingRight` Boolean variables, which the
`updateCourt` method uses to decide whether to slide the player's racket left or right,
or to keep it still. We have talked about the `onTouchEvent` method before, but let's
see how we set the values in those variables.

First, we override the method and switch to get the type of event and the *x, y* coordinates of the event:

```
@Override
    public boolean onTouchEvent(MotionEvent motionEvent) {

    switch (motionEvent.getAction() & MotionEvent.ACTION_MASK) {
```

If the event type is `ACTION_DOWN`, that is, the screen has been touched, we enter this case:

```
        case MotionEvent.ACTION_DOWN:
```

Then we handle the coordinates. If the player has touched a position on the screen with an x coordinate greater than `screenWidth / 2`, then it means they have touched the right-hand side of the screen, so we set `isMovingRight` to `true` and `isMovingLeft` to `false`. The `updateCourt` method will handle changes in the necessary coordinates, and the `drawCourt` method will draw the racket in the appropriate place:

```
        if (motionEvent.getX() >= screenWidth / 2) {
            racketIsMovingRight = true;
            racketIsMovingLeft = false;
```

The `else` statement sets our two Boolean variables in the opposite manner because a touch must have occurred on the left of the screen:

```
        } else {
            racketIsMovingLeft = true;
            racketIsMovingRight = false;
        }

        break;
```

Now we handle the case for the `ACTION_UP` event. But why do we care about two events? With the buttons, we just cared about a click and that was all, but by handling the `ACTION_UP` event, we can enable the functionality that allows our player to hold the screen to slide left or right, just as we discussed in the section *The design of the game* of this chapter. Thus, the `ACTION_DOWN` case sets the racket moving one way or the other, and the `ACTION_UP` case simply stops the slide completely:

```
        case MotionEvent.ACTION_UP:
            racketIsMovingRight = false;
            racketIsMovingLeft = false;
            break;
    }
```

```
            return true;
        }



    }
```

Notice that we don't care about the *y* coordinate. Anywhere on the left we go left, anywhere on the right we go right.

Notice also that all of the code will work whether a device is held in the portrait or landscape form, and will function the same regardless of the resolution of the device. However (and it is quite an important "however"), the game will be slightly harder on low-resolution screens. The solution to this problem is quite complicated and will not be discussed until the final chapter, but it might well help us make some decisions about the future path to learn Android, gaming, and Java.

Phase 4 – Remaining lifecycle methods

We are nearly there; just a few more steps and we will have a working retro squash game. I can almost smell the nostalgia! As these remaining methods are quite straightforward, we will explain them as we write them:

1. As we previously learned, the `onStop` method is called by the Android system when the app is stopped. It is implemented for us already. The only reason we override it here is to ensure that our thread is stopped. We do so with the line highlighted. Enter the following code before the closing curly brace of the `MainActivity` class:

```
@Override
    protected void onStop() {
        super.onStop();

        while (true) {
            squashCourtView.pause();
            break;
        }

        finish();
    }
```

2. The `onPause` method is called by the Android system when the app is paused. This too is implemented for us already, and the only reason we override it here is to ensure that our thread is stopped. We do so with the line highlighted. Enter this code after the preceding code:

```
@Override
    protected void onPause() {
        super.onPause();
        squashCourtView.pause();
    }
```

3. The `onResume` method is called by the Android system when the app is resumed. Again, this method is implemented for us already. The only reason we override it here is to ensure that our thread is resumed, and we do so with the line highlighted. Enter the following code after the code in the previous step:

```
@Override
    protected void onResume() {
        super.onResume();
        squashCourtView.resume();
    }
```

4. Finally, we do something completely new. We handle what happens should the player press the back button on their device. As you might have guessed, there is a method we can override to achieve this— `onKeyDown`. We pause our thread, just as we did in the overridden lifecycle methods, and then call `finish()`, which ends the activity and our app. Enter this code after the code in the previous step:

```
public boolean onKeyDown(int keyCode, KeyEvent event) {
        if (keyCode == KeyEvent.KEYCODE_BACK) {
            squashCourtView.pause();
            finish();
            return true;
        }
        return false;
    }
```

We covered the code in this phase as we went through it, and this was the shortest phase so far. So why didn't we encapsulate everything?

Good object-oriented design

Perhaps simple games are not the best way to demonstrate good object-oriented design in action, but a simple code design with fewer private variables actually enhances the project. It certainly makes the teaching aspects of coding games simpler to explain.

However, when a game becomes more complex and more people work on the code, principles of object-oriented programming become more necessary.

Self-test questions

Q1) Can you explain how to make ball speed relative between different screen resolutions?

Summary

I hope you enjoyed animating your first game. You achieved a lot to get to this point. You learned not only all the Java topics but also the way the different classes of Android can be used to make games relatively simple.

In the next chapter, we will move on to a new, more complex game. I hope you are ready.

8
The Snake Game

In this chapter, we will get straight down to designing and implementing a clone of the highly addictive *Snake* game. We will look at the design of the game and learn how to animate some bitmaps. Then we will look at a few aspects of the code that are new, such as our coordinate system. After that, we will whiz through the implementation of the game. Finally, we will look at how we could enhance our game.

In this chapter, we will cover the following topics:

- Examine the design of our game
- Look at the coordinate system of our *Snake* game
- Examine the code structure so that when we come to implement the game, it will be more straightforward
- Learn about animation with sprite sheets at the same time as implementing the home screen of our game
- Break the code for the *Snake* game into manageable chunks and run through its full implementation
- Enhance the game a little

Game design

If you haven't played the excellent *Snake* game before, here is an explanation of how it works. You control a very small snake. In our version, there is just a head, one body segment, and a tail. Here is a screenshot of our snake, made out of three segments:

The following screenshot shows the three segments individually:

Now, here is the thing; our snake is very hungry and also a very quick grower. Every time he eats an apple, he grows a body segment. This is a screenshot of the apple:

Life is great! Our snake just eats and grows! The problem that the player of our game needs to solve is that the snake is a little hyperactive. It never stops moving! What exacerbates this problem is that if the snake touches the side of the screen, it dies.

At first, this doesn't seem like too much of a problem, but as he grows longer and longer, he can't just keep going around in circles because he will bump inevitably into himself. This would again result in his demise:

For each apple eaten, we add an increasingly large amount to the score. Here is a sneak peek at what the game will look like after the basic implementation and before the enhancements:

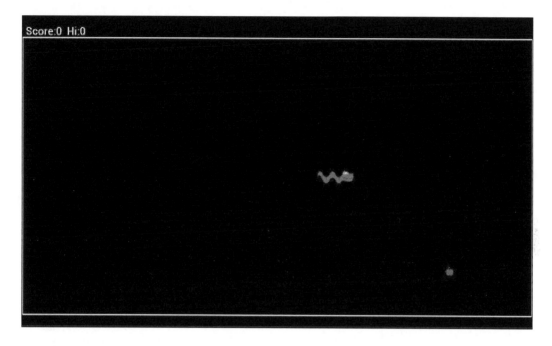

The player controls the snake by tapping on the left or the right side of the screen. The snake will respond by turning left or right. The turn directions are relative to the direction the snake is traveling, which adds to the challenge because the player needs to think like a snake—kind of!

At the end of the chapter, we will also take a brief look at enhancing the game, use that enhanced version in the next chapter to publish it to the Google Play Store, and add leaderboards and achievements.

The coordinate system

In the previous chapter, we drew all our game objects directly to points on the screen, and we used real screen coordinates to detect collisions, bounces, and so on. This time, we will be doing things slightly differently. This is partly out of necessity, but as we will see, collision detection and keeping track of our game objects will also get simpler. This might be surprising when we think about the potential of our snake to be many blocks long.

Keeping track of the snake segments

To keep track of all the snake segments, we will first define a block size to define a portion of a grid for the entire game area. Every game object will reside at an (x,y) coordinate, based not on the pixel resolution of the screen but on a position within our virtual grid. In the game, we define a grid that is 40 blocks wide, like this:

```
//Determine the size of each block/place on the game board
blockSize = screenWidth/40;
```

So we know that:

```
numBlocksWide = 40;
```

The height of the game screen in blocks will then simply be calculated by dividing the height of the screen in pixels by the previously determined value of `blockSize` minus a bit of space at the top for the score:

```
numBlocksHigh = ((screenHeight - topGap ))/blockSize;
```

This then allows us to keep track of our snake using two arrays for *x* and *y* coordinates, where element zero is the head and the last used element is the tail, a bit like this:

```
//An array for our snake
snakeX = new int[200];
snakeY = new int[200];
```

As long as we have a system for moving the head, perhaps something similar to the squash ball but based on our new game grid, we can do the following to make the body follow the head:

```
//move the body starting at the back
for(int i = snakeLength; i >0 ; i--){
  snakeX[i] = snakeX[i-1];
  snakeY[i] = snakeY[i-1];
}
```

The previous code simply starts at the back section of the snake and creates its location in the grid irrespective of what the section in front of it was. It proceeds up the body doing the same until everything has been moved to the location of the section that used to be just ahead of it.

This also makes collision detection (even for a very long snake) nice and easy.

Detecting collisions

Using our grid based on `blockSize`, we can detect a collision, for example, with the right side of the screen, like this:

```
if(snakeX[0] >= numBlocksWide)dead=true;
```

The previous code simply checks whether the first element of our array, which holds the *x* coordinate of the snake, is equal to or greater than the width of our game grid in blocks. Try to work out the code for collision with the left, top, and bottom before we see it during the implementation.

Detecting the event of the snake bumping into itself is quick too. We just need to check whether the first element of our array (the head) is in exactly the same position as any of the other sections, like this:

```
//Have we eaten ourselves?
for (int i = snakeLength-1; i > 0; i--) {
  if ((i > 4) && (snakeX[0] == snakeX[i]) && (snakeY[0] ==
    snakeY[i])) {
    dead = true;
    }
}
```

Drawing the snake

We simply draw every section of the snake relative to its grid location multiplied by the size in pixels of a block. The `blockSize` variable handles the entire challenge of making the game work on different screen sizes, like this:

```
//loop through every section of the snake and draw it
//a block at a time.
canvas.drawBitmap(bodyBitmap, snakeX[i]*blockSize,
    (snakeY[i]*blockSize)+topGap, paint);
```

Admittedly, there are probably more questions about how our implementation will work, but they are probably best answered by actually building the game.

Thus, we can easily follow along by either writing the code or just reading from the completed project. Let's take a look at the overall structure of our code.

The code structure

We will have two activities, one for the menu screen and one for the game screen. The menu screen activity will be called `MainActivity`, and the game screen activity will be called `GameActivity`. You can find all the completed code files as well as all the assets such as images, sprite sheets, and sound files in the `Chapter8/Snake` folder in the download bundle.

MainActivity

In contrast to our other projects, the menu screen will not have a UI designed in the Android Studio UI designer. It will consist of an animated snake head, a title, and a high score. The player will proceed to `GameActivity` by tapping anywhere on the screen. As we need to accomplish animations and user interactions, even the home screen will have a thread, a view object, and methods normally associated with our game screens, like this:

```
MainActivity.java file
    Imports
    MainActivity class
        Declare some variables and objects
        onCreate
        SnakeAnimView class
            Constructor
            Run method
            Update method
            Draw method
            controlFPS method
            pause method
            resume method
            onTouchEvent method
        onStop method
        onResume method
        onPause method
        onKeyDown method
```

We will not go deeper into the menu screen for now because at the end of this section, we will implement it line by line.

GameActivity

The game screen structure has many similarities to our Squash game and to the structure of the menu screen, although the internals of this structure vary a lot (as we have discussed and as we will see). There are some differences towards the end of the structure, most notably, a `loadSound` method and a `configureDisplay` method. Here is the structure (we will see afterwards why the two extra methods are there):

```
MainActivity.java file
    Imports
    GameActivity class
        Declare some variables and objects
        onCreate
        SnakeView class
            Constructor
            getSnake method
            getApple method
            Run method
            updateGame method
            drawGame method
            controlFPS method
            pause method
            resume method
            onTouchEvent method
        onStop method
        onResume method
        onPause method
        onKeyDown method
        loadSOund method
        configureDisplay method
```

Tidying up onCreate

One of the first things you might notice when you examine the code from the `GameActivity` class we will soon implement is just how short the `onCreate` method is:

```java
@Override
    protected void onCreate(Bundle savedInstanceState) {
        super.onCreate(savedInstanceState);

        loadSound();
        configureDisplay();
        snakeView = new SnakeView(this);
        setContentView(snakeView);

    }
```

We have written two methods, loadSound and configureDisplay. They do most of the initialization and setup present in our squash game. This makes our code less cluttered. All that is left in onCreate is the initialization of our SnakeView object and a call to setContentView.

We will look in detail at our loadSound and configureDisplay methods when we implement them.

As we have had advanced sight of the structure as well as previous experience of this type of implementation, we will just go through all of the implementation of our game activity in one phase.

Let's quickly implement the menu screen.

Animation, sprite sheets, and the Snake home screen

In the previous chapter, we used a bitmap to draw text, a circle, a line, and a single pixel on the blank bitmap we created in Java code. We then displayed the bitmap with all of its doodling using the Canvas class. Now we will look at a technique to draw two dimensional images, sometimes referred to as sprites. These are made from predrawn images. The images can be as simple as a plain pong ball or as complex as a glorious two-dimensional character with muscle definition, elaborate clothing, weapons, and hair.

So far, we have animated with unchanging objects, that is, we have moved a static unchanging image around the screen. In this section, we will see how to not only display a predrawn bitmap image on the screen but also continually alter it to create the illusion of on-the-spot animation.

Of course, the ultimate combination would be to animate the bitmap both by changing its image and moving it around at the same time. We will see that briefly when we look at an enhanced version of this chapter's *Snake* game, but will not be analyzing the code.

To do this on-the-spot bitmap animation, we need some bitmaps, as you might expect. For example, to draw a snake's tail swishing back and forth, we would need at least two frames of animation, showing the tail in different positions. In the following screenshot, the flower's head is towards the left:

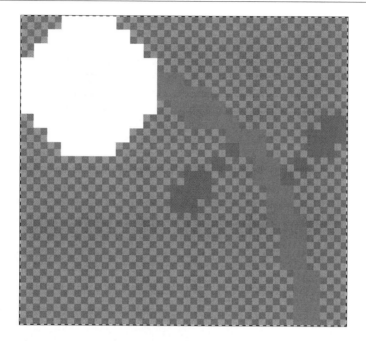

In this screenshot, the flower has been flipped:

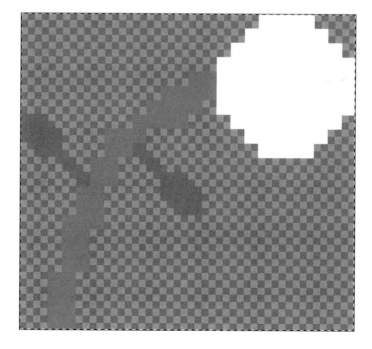

If the two bitmaps were shown one after the other, repeatedly, they would create the basic effect of a flower blowing in the wind. Of course, two frames of animation aren't going to contest for any animation awards, and there is another problem with these images as well, as we will learn, so we should add in more frames to make the animation as life-like as is practical.

We have just one more thing to discuss before we make an animated snake head for our game's home screen. How do we get Android to switch between these bitmaps?

Animating with sprite sheets

Firstly, we need to present the frames in a manner that is easy to manipulate in code. This is where sprite sheets come in. The following image shows some frames from a basic snake head animation that we will use on our game home screen. This time, they are presented in a strip of frames. All of them are parts of the same image, a bit like a series of images in a film. Also, notice in the following image that the frames are centered relative to each other and are exactly equal in size:

If we were to actually show the two previous flower images consecutively, they would not only would they sway but also jump around from one side to another on their stems, which is probably not the effect we were looking for.

Thus, with regard to the snake sprite sheet, as long as we show one frame after another, we will create a basic animation.

So how do we make our code jump from one part of the sprite sheet to the next? Each frame is exactly the same size, 64 x 64 pixels in this case, so we just need a way to display pixels from 0 to 63, then 64 to 127, then 128 to 192, and so on. As each frame of the sprite sheet image is subtly different, it allows us to use one image file with multiple frames to create our animation. Fortunately, we have a class to handle this, which is nothing quite as luxurious as a specific sprite sheet class but almost.

 Regarding sprite sheet classes, such a thing does exist, although not in the regular Android classes. An API specifically designed for two-dimensional games will usually contain classes for sprite sheets. We will look at examples of this in the next chapter.

The `Rect` class holds the coordinates of a rectangle. Here, we create a new object of the `Rect` type, and initialize it to start at 0, 0 and end at 63, 63:

```
Rect rectToBeDrawn = new Rect(0, 0, 63, 63);
```

The `Canvas` class can then actually use our `Rect` object to define a portion of a previously loaded bitmap:

```
canvas.drawBitmap(headAnimBitmap, rectToBeDrawn, destRect, paint);
```

The preceding code is much simpler than it looks. First, we see `canvas.drawBitmap`. We are using the `drawBitmap` method of the `Canvas` class just as we have before. Then we pass `headAnimBitmap`, which is our sprite sheet containing all the frames we want to animate, as an argument. Rect `rectToBeDrawn` represents the coordinates of the currently relevant frame within `headAnimationBitmap`. `destRect` simply represents the screen coordinates at which we want to draw the current frame, and of course, `paint` is our object of the `Paint` class.

All we have to do now is change the coordinates of `rectToBeDrawn` and control the frame rate with a thread and we are done! Let's do that and create an animated home screen for our *Snake* game.

Implementing the Snake home screen

With the background information we just covered and our detailed look at the structure of the code we are about to write, there shouldn't be any surprises in this code. We will break things up into chunks just to make sure we follow exactly what is going on:

1. Create a new project of API level 13. Call it `Snake`.

2. Make the activity full screen as we have done before, and put your graphics into the `drawable/mdpi` folder. Of course, you can use my graphics as usual. They are supplied in the code download in the `graphics` folder of the `Snake` project.

3. Here, you will find our `MainActivity` class declaration and member variables. Notice the variables for our `Canvas` and `Bitmap` class as well, we are declaring variables to hold frame size (width and height) as well as the number of frames. We also have a `Rect` object to hold the coordinates of the current frame of the sprite sheet. We will see these variables in action soon. Type the following code:

```
public class MainActivity extends Activity {

    Canvas canvas;
```

```
SnakeAnimView snakeAnimView;

//The snake head sprite sheet
Bitmap headAnimBitmap;
//The portion of the bitmap to be drawn in the current frame
Rect rectToBeDrawn;
//The dimensions of a single frame
int frameHeight = 64;
int frameWidth = 64;
int numFrames = 6;
int frameNumber;

int screenWidth;
int screenHeight;

//stats
long lastFrameTime;
int fps;
int hi;

//To start the game from onTouchEvent
Intent i;
```

4. The following is the implementation of the overridden `onCreate` method. We get the screen dimensions in the usual way. We load our sprite sheet into the `headAnimBitmap` Bitmap. Finally, we create a new `SnakeAnimView` and set it as the content view. Type the following code after the code from the previous step:

```
@Override
    protected void onCreate(Bundle savedInstanceState) {
        super.onCreate(savedInstanceState);

        //find out the width and height of the screen
        Display display =
            getWindowManager().getDefaultDisplay();
        Point size = new Point();
        display.getSize(size);
        screenWidth = size.x;
        screenHeight = size.y;

        headAnimBitmap =
            BitmapFactory.decodeResource(getResources(),
            R.drawable.head_sprite_sheet);


        snakeAnimView = new SnakeAnimView(this);
```

```
        setContentView(snakeAnimView);

        i = new Intent(this, GameActivity.class);

    }
```

5. Here is the declaration of our `SurfaceView` class, called `SnakeAnimView`, along with its member variables. Notice that it extends `SurfaceView` and implements `Runnable`. All its methods follow in the next steps. Type this code after the code from the preceding step:

```
class SnakeAnimView extends SurfaceView implements Runnable {
        Thread ourThread = null;
        SurfaceHolder ourHolder;
        volatile boolean playingSnake;
        Paint paint;
```

6. Here is the constructor that gets the `frameWidth` value by dividing the bitmap width by the number of frames, and the `frameHeight` value using the `getHeight` method. Type this code after the code from the previous step:

```
public SnakeAnimView(Context context) {
    super(context);
    ourHolder = getHolder();
    paint = new Paint();
    frameWidth = headAnimBitmap.getWidth()/numFrames;
    frameHeight = headAnimBitmap.getHeight();
}
```

7. Now we implement the short but crucial `run` method. It calls each of the key methods of this class one after the other. These three methods are implemented in the following three steps after this step. Type the following code after the code from the preceding step:

```
@Override
        public void run() {
            while (playingSnake) {
                update();
                draw();
                controlFPS();

            }

        }
```

8. Here is the `update` method. It tracks and chooses the frame number that needs to be displayed. Each time through the `update` method, we calculate the coordinates of the sprite sheet to be drawn using `frameWidth`, `frameHeight`, and `frameNumber`. If you are wondering why we subtract 1 from each horizontal coordinate, it is because like the screen coordinates, bitmaps start their coordinates at 0, 0:

```
public void update() {

  //which frame should we draw
  rectToBeDrawn = new Rect((frameNumber * frameWidth)-1,
    0,(frameNumber * frameWidth +frameWidth)-1,
    frameHeight);

  //now the next frame
  frameNumber++;

  //don't try and draw frames that don't exist
  if(frameNumber == numFrames){
    frameNumber = 0;//back to the first frame
  }
}
```

9. Next is the `draw` method, which does nothing new until the end, when it calculates the place on the screen to draw the bitmap by dividing the `screenHeight` and `screenWidth` variables by 2. These coordinates are then saved in `destRect`. Both `destRect` and `rectToDraw` are then passed to the `drawBitmap` method, which draws the frame required at the location required. Type this code after the code from the previous step:

```
public void draw() {

            if (ourHolder.getSurface().isValid()) {
                canvas = ourHolder.lockCanvas();
                //Paint paint = new Paint();
                canvas.drawColor(Color.BLACK);//the background
                paint.setColor(Color.argb(255, 255, 255, 255));
                paint.setTextSize(150);
                canvas.drawText("Snake", 10, 150, paint);
                paint.setTextSize(25);
                canvas.drawText("  Hi Score:" + hi, 10,
                    screenHeight-50, paint);

                //Draw the snake head
                //make this Rect whatever size and location you
                like
```

```
//(startX, startY, endX, endY)
Rect destRect = new Rect(screenWidth/2-100,
    screenHeight/2-100, screenWidth/2+100,
    screenHeight/2+100);

canvas.drawBitmap(headAnimBitmap,
    rectToBeDrawn, destRect, paint);

ourHolder.unlockCanvasAndPost(canvas);
}

}
```

10. Our trusty old `controlFPS` method ensures that our animation appears at a sensible rate. The only change in this code is that the initialization of `timeTosleep` is changed to create a 500-millisecond pause between each frame. Type the following code after the code from the preceding step:

```
public void controlFPS() {
        long timeThisFrame =
            (System.currentTimeMillis() -
            lastFrameTime);
        long timeToSleep = 500 - timeThisFrame;
        if (timeThisFrame > 0) {
            fps = (int) (1000 / timeThisFrame);
        }
        if (timeToSleep > 0) {

            try {
                ourThread.sleep(timeToSleep);
            } catch (InterruptedException e) {
            }

        }

        lastFrameTime = System.currentTimeMillis();
}
```

11. Next are our `pause` and `resume` methods, which work with the Android lifecycle methods to start and stop our thread. Type this code after the code from the previous step:

```
public void pause() {
        playingSnake = false;
        try {
            ourThread.join();
        } catch (InterruptedException e) {
```

```
                    }

            }

            public void resume() {
                playingSnake = true;
                ourThread = new Thread(this);
                ourThread.start();
            }
```

12. For our `SnakeAnimView` class and our `onTouchEvent` method, which simply starts the game when the screen is touched anywhere, we enter the following code. Obviously, we don't have a `GameActivity` yet:

```
@Override
        public boolean onTouchEvent(MotionEvent
            motionEvent) {


            startActivity(i);
            return true;

        }
}
```

13. Finally, back in the `MainActivity` class, we handle some Android lifecycle methods. We also handle what happens when the player presses the back button:

```
@Override
    protected void onStop() {
        super.onStop();

        while (true) {
            snakeAnimView.pause();
            break;
        }

        finish();
    }

    @Override
    protected void onResume() {
        super.onResume();
        snakeAnimView.resume();
    }

    @Override
```

```
protected void onPause() {
    super.onPause();
    snakeAnimView.pause();
}

public boolean onKeyDown(int keyCode, KeyEvent event) {
    if (keyCode == KeyEvent.KEYCODE_BACK) {
        snakeAnimView.pause();
        finish();
        return true;
    }
    return false;
}
```

14. Now you must temporarily comment out this line from step 4 to test the animation. The reason for this is that it causes an error until we implement the GameActivity class:

    ```
    //i = new Intent(this, GameActivity.class);
    ```

15. Test the app.

16. Uncomment the line from step 14 when we have implemented the GameActivity class. Here is our completed home screen:

In this exercise, we set up a class that extended `SurfaceView`, just like we did for our squash game. We had a `run` method, which controlled the thread, as well as an `update` method, which calculated the coordinates of the current animation within our sprite sheet. The `draw` method simply drew to the screen using the coordinates calculated by the `update` method.

As in the squash game, we had an `onTouchUpdate` method, but the code this time was very simple. As a touch of any type in any location was all we needed to detect, we added just one line of code to the method.

Implementing the Snake game activity

Not all of this code is new. In fact, we have either used most of it before or discussed it earlier in the chapter. However, I wanted to present every line to you in order and in context with at least a brief explanation, even when we have seen it before. Having said that, I haven't included the long list of imports as we will either be prompted to add them automatically or we can just press *Alt + Enter* when needed.

This way, we can remind ourselves how the whole thing comes together without any blanks in our understanding. As usual, I will summarize as we proceed through the implementation, and go into a few bits of extra depth at the end:

1. Add an activity called `GameActivity`. Select a blank activity when asked.

2. Make the activity full screen as we have done before.

3. As usual, create some sound effects or use mine. Create an `assets` directory in the `main` directory in the usual way. Copy and paste the sound files (`sample1.ogg`, `sample2.ogg`, `sample3.ogg`, and `sample4.ogg`) into it.

4. Create individual non-sprite-sheet versions of graphics or use mine. Copy and paste them in the `res/drawable-mdpi` folder.

5. Here is the `GameActivity` class declaration with the member variables. There is nothing new here until we declare our arrays for our snake (`snakeX` and `snakeY`). Also, notice our variables used to control our game grid (`blockSize`, `numBlocksHigh`, and `numBlocksWide`). Now type this code:

```
public class GameActivity extends Activity {

    Canvas canvas;
    SnakeView snakeView;

    Bitmap headBitmap;
    Bitmap bodyBitmap;
    Bitmap tailBitmap;
```

```
Bitmap appleBitmap;

//Sound
//initialize sound variables
private SoundPool soundPool;
int sample1 = -1;
int sample2 = -1;
int sample3 = -1;
int sample4 = -1;

//for snake movement
int directionOfTravel=0;
//0 = up, 1 = right, 2 = down, 3= left


int screenWidth;
int screenHeight;
int topGap;

//stats
long lastFrameTime;
int fps;
int score;
int hi;

//Game objects
int [] snakeX;
int [] snakeY;
int snakeLength;
int appleX;
int appleY;

//The size in pixels of a place on the game board
int blockSize;
int numBlocksWide;
int numBlocksHigh;
```

6. As explained previously, our new, small onCreate method has very little to do because much of the work is done in the loadSound and configureDisplay methods. Type this code after the code from the previous step:

```
@Override
    protected void onCreate(Bundle savedInstanceState) {
```

```
super.onCreate(savedInstanceState);

loadSound();
configureDisplay();
snakeView = new SnakeView(this);
setContentView(snakeView);

}
```

7. Here is the class declaration, member variables, and constructor for our
    SnakeView class. We allocate 200 int variables to the snakeX and snakeY
    arrays, and call the getSnake and getApple methods, which will place an
    apple and our snake on the screen. This is just what we want when the class
    is constructed:

```
class SnakeView extends SurfaceView implements Runnable {
    Thread ourThread = null;
    SurfaceHolder ourHolder;
    volatile boolean playingSnake;
    Paint paint;

    public SnakeView(Context context) {
        super(context);
        ourHolder = getHolder();
        paint = new Paint();

        //Even my 9 year old play tester couldn't
        //get a snake this long
        snakeX = new int[200];
        snakeY = new int[200];

        //our starting snake
        getSnake();
        //get an apple to munch
        getApple();
    }
```

8. Here is how we spawn a snake and an apple in our coordinate system. In the
`getSnake` method, we place the snake's head in the approximate center of
the screen by initializing `snakeX[0]` and `snakeY[0]` to the number of blocks
high and wide divided by 2. We then place a body segment and the tail
segment immediately behind. Notice that we don't need to make any special
arrangement for the different types of segments. As long as the drawing
code *knows* that the first segment is a head, the last segment is a tail, and
everything in between is a body, then that will do. In the `getApple` method,
the integer variables `appleX` and `appleY` are initialized to random locations
within our game grid. This method is called from the constructor, as we saw
in the previous step. It will also be called to place a new apple every time our
snake manages to eat an apple, as we will see. Type this code after the code
from the previous step:

```java
public void getSnake(){
        snakeLength = 3;
        //start snake head in the middle of screen
        snakeX[0] = numBlocksWide / 2;
        snakeY[0] = numBlocksHigh / 2;

        //Then the body
        snakeX[1] = snakeX[0]-1;
        snakeY[1] = snakeY[0];

        //And the tail
        snakeX[1] = snakeX[1]-1;
        snakeY[1] = snakeY[0];
}

public void getApple(){
    Random random = new Random();
    appleX = random.nextInt(numBlocksWide-1)+1;
    appleY = random.nextInt(numBlocksHigh-1)+1;
}
```

9. Next comes the `run` method, which controls the flow of the game. Type the
following code after the code from the previous step:

```java
@Override
public void run() {
    while (playingSnake) {
        updateGame();
        drawGame();
        controlFPS();

    }

}
```

10. Now we will look at `updateGame`, the most complex method of the entire app. Having said that, it is probably slightly less complex than the same method in our squash game. This is because of our coordinate system, which leads to simpler collision detection. Here is the code for `updateGame`. Study it carefully, and we will dissect it line by line at the end:

```
public void updateGame() {

    //Did the player get the apple
    if(snakeX[0] == appleX && snakeY[0] == appleY){
        //grow the snake
        snakeLength++;
        //replace the apple
        getApple();
        //add to the score
        score = score + snakeLength;
        soundPool.play(sample1, 1, 1, 0, 0, 1);
    }

    //move the body - starting at the back
    for(int i=snakeLength; i >0 ; i--){
        snakeX[i] = snakeX[i-1];
        snakeY[i] = snakeY[i-1];
    }

    //Move the head in the appropriate direction
    switch (directionOfTravel){
        case 0://up
        snakeY[0]  --;
        break;

        case 1://right
        snakeX[0]  ++;
        break;

        case 2://down
        snakeY[0]  ++;
        break;

        case 3://left
        snakeX[0]  --;
        break;
    }

    //Have we had an accident
```

```
boolean dead = false;
//with a wall
if(snakeX[0] == -1)dead=true;
if(snakeX[0] >= numBlocksWide) dead = true;
if(snakeY[0] == -1)dead=true;
if(snakeY[0] == numBlocksHigh) dead = true;
//or eaten ourselves?
for (int i = snakeLength-1; i > 0; i--) {
    if ((i > 4) && (snakeX[0] == snakeX[i]) &&
        (snakeY[0] == snakeY[i])) {
    dead = true;
    }
}
```

```
if(dead){
//start again
soundPool.play(sample4, 1, 1, 0, 0, 1);
score = 0;
getSnake();

}

}
```

11. We have worked out where our game objects are on the screen, so now we can draw them. This code is easy to understand as we have seen most of it before:

```
public void drawGame() {

    if (ourHolder.getSurface().isValid()) {
        canvas = ourHolder.lockCanvas();
        //Paint paint = new Paint();
        canvas.drawColor(Color.BLACK);//the background
        paint.setColor(Color.argb(255, 255, 255, 255));
        paint.setTextSize(topGap/2);
        canvas.drawText("Score:" + score + "  Hi:" + hi,
            10, topGap-6, paint);

        //draw a border - 4 lines, top right, bottom , left
        paint.setStrokeWidth(3);//3 pixel border
        canvas.drawLine(1,topGap,screenWidth-
            1,topGap,paint);
        canvas.drawLine(screenWidth-1,topGap,screenWidth-
            1,topGap+(numBlocksHigh*blockSize),paint);
```

```
                        //no such direction

                        if(directionOfTravel == 4)
                        //loop back to 0(up)
                        directionOfTravel = 0;
                    }
                } else {
                    //turn left
                    directionOfTravel--;
                    if(directionOfTravel == -1) {//no such direction
                    //loop back to 0(up)
                    directionOfTravel = 3;
                            }
                        }
                    }
                    return true;
                }
```

15. Back in the `GameActivity` class, we now handle the Android lifecycle methods and the "back" button functionality. Type this code after the code from the preceding step:

```
@Override
    protected void onStop() {
        super.onStop();

        while (true) {
            snakeView.pause();
            break;
        }

        finish();
    }


    @Override
    protected void onResume() {
        super.onResume();
        snakeView.resume();
    }

    @Override
    protected void onPause() {
        super.onPause();
        snakeView.pause();
```

```
        }

        public boolean onKeyDown(int keyCode, KeyEvent event) {
            if (keyCode == KeyEvent.KEYCODE_BACK) {

                snakeView.pause();



                Intent i = new Intent(this,
                    MainActivity.class);
                startActivity(i);
                finish();
                return true;
            }
            return false;
        }
```

16. Here is our `loadSound` method, which simply tidies up the `onCreate` method by moving all of the sound initialization to here. Type this code after the code from the previous step:

```
public void loadSound(){
    soundPool = new SoundPool(10,
        AudioManager.STREAM_MUSIC, 0);
    try {
        //Create objects of the 2 required classes
        AssetManager assetManager = getAssets();
        AssetFileDescriptor descriptor;

        //create our three fx in memory ready for use
        descriptor = assetManager.openFd("sample1.ogg");
        sample1 = soundPool.load(descriptor, 0);

        descriptor = assetManager.openFd("sample2.ogg");
        sample2 = soundPool.load(descriptor, 0);


        descriptor = assetManager.openFd("sample3.ogg");
        sample3 = soundPool.load(descriptor, 0);

        descriptor = assetManager.openFd("sample4.ogg");
```

```
sample4 = soundPool.load(descriptor, 0);


} catch (IOException e) {
//Print an error message to the console
Log.e("error", "failed to load sound files);
}
}
```

17. Then we have the `configureDisplay` method, which is called from `onCreate` and does the entire setup of bitmaps and screen size calculations. We will look at this in more detail later. Type the following code after the code from the previous step:

```
public void configureDisplay(){
        //find out the width and height of the screen
        Display display =
            getWindowManager().getDefaultDisplay();
        Point size = new Point();
        display.getSize(size);
        screenWidth = size.x;
        screenHeight = size.y;
        topGap = screenHeight/14;
        //Determine the size of each block/place on the game board
        blockSize = screenWidth/40;

        //Determine how many game blocks will fit into the
        //height and width
        //Leave one block for the score at the top
        numBlocksWide = 40;
        numBlocksHigh = ((screenHeight - topGap
            ))/blockSize;

        //Load and scale bitmaps
        headBitmap =
            BitmapFactory.decodeResource(getResources(),
            R.drawable.head);
        bodyBitmap =
            BitmapFactory.decodeResource(getResources(),
            R.drawable.body);
        tailBitmap =
            BitmapFactory.decodeResource(getResources(),
            R.drawable.tail);
```

```
appleBitmap =
    BitmapFactory.decodeResource(getResources(),
    R.drawable.apple);

//scale the bitmaps to match the block size
headBitmap = Bitmap.createScaledBitmap(headBitmap,
    blockSize, blockSize, false);
bodyBitmap = Bitmap.createScaledBitmap(bodyBitmap,
    blockSize, blockSize, false);
tailBitmap = Bitmap.createScaledBitmap(tailBitmap,
    blockSize, blockSize, false);
appleBitmap =
    Bitmap.createScaledBitmap(appleBitmap,
    blockSize, blockSize, false);

}
```

18. Now run the app. The game is much more playable on an actual device than it is on the emulator.

We covered the code as we progressed, but as usual, here is a piece-by-piece dissection of a few of the more complicated methods, starting with the `updateGame` method.

First, we check whether the player has eaten an apple. More specifically, is the snake's head in the same grid location as the apple? The `if` statement checks whether this has occurred, and then does the following:

- Increases the length of the snake

- Puts another apple on the screen by calling `getApple`

- Adds a value to the player's score, relative to the length of the snake, making each apple worth more than the previous one

- Plays a beep

Here is the code for the actions that we have just described:

```
public void updateGame() {

        //Did the player get the apple
        if(snakeX[0] == appleX && snakeY[0] == appleY){
            //grow the snake
            snakeLength++;
            //replace the apple
            getApple();
            //add to the score
            score = score + snakeLength;
            soundPool.play(sample1, 1, 1, 0, 0, 1);
        }
```

Now we simply move each segment of the snake, starting from the back, to the position of the segment in front of it. We do this with a `for` loop:

```
//move the body - starting at the back
for(int i = snakeLength; i >0 ; i--){
    snakeX[i] = snakeX[i-1];
    snakeY[i] = snakeY[i-1];
}
```

Of course, we better move the head too! We move the head last because the leading section of the body would move to the wrong place if we move the head earlier. As long as the entire move is made before any drawing is done, all will be well. Our `run` method ensures that this is always the case. Here is the code to move the head in the direction determined by `directionOfTravel`. As we saw, `directionOfTravel` is manipulated by the player in the `onTouchEvent` method:

```
//Move the head in the appropriate direction
switch (directionOfTravel){
    case 0://up
        snakeY[0]   --;
        break;

    case 1://right
        snakeX[0]   ++;
        break;

    case 2://down
        snakeY[0]   ++;
        break;

    case 3://left
        snakeX[0]   --;
        break;
}
```

Next, we check for a collision with a wall. We saw this code when we looked at collision detection earlier. Here is the complete solution, starting with the left wall, then right, then top, and then bottom:

```
//Have we had an accident
boolean dead = false;
//with a wall
if(snakeX[0] == -1)dead=true;
if(snakeX[0] >= numBlocksWide)dead=true;
if(snakeY[0] == -1)dead=true;
if(snakeY[0] == numBlocksHigh)dead=true;
```

Then we check whether the snake has collided with itself. Initially, this seemed awkward, but as we previously saw, we just loop through our snake array to check whether any of the segments are in the same place as the head, in both *x* and *y* coordinates:

```
//or eaten ourselves?
for (int i = snakeLength-1; i > 0; i--) {
    if ((i > 4) && (snakeX[0] == snakeX[i]) && (snakeY[0]
        == snakeY[i])) {
        dead = true;
    }
}
```

If any part of our collision detection code sets dead to true, we simply play a sound, set the score to 0, and get a new baby snake:

```
if (dead) {
    //start again
    soundPool.play(sample4, 1, 1, 0, 0, 1);
    score = 0;
    getSnake();

}

}
```

Now we take a closer look at the drawGame method. First, we get ready to draw by clearing the screen:

```
public void drawGame() {

    if (ourHolder.getSurface().isValid()) {
        canvas = ourHolder.lockCanvas();
        //Paint paint = new Paint();
        canvas.drawColor(Color.BLACK);//the background
        paint.setColor(Color.argb(255, 255, 255, 255));
        paint.setTextSize(topGap/2);
```

Now we draw the text for the player's score, just above topGap that we define in configureDisplay:

```
canvas.drawText("Score:" + score + "  Hi:" + hi, 10, topGap-6,
    paint);
```

Now, using `drawLine`, we draw a visible border around our game grid:

```
//draw a border - 4 lines, top right, bottom, left
                paint.setStrokeWidth(3);//4 pixel border
                canvas.drawLine(1,topGap,screenWidth-
                    1,topGap,paint);
                canvas.drawLine(screenWidth-1,topGap,screenWidth-
                    1,topGap+(numBlocksHigh*blockSize),paint);
                canvas.drawLine(screenWidth-
                    1,topGap+(numBlocksHigh*blockSize),1,topGap+
                    (numBlocksHigh*blockSize),paint);
                canvas.drawLine(1,topGap,
                    1,topGap+(numBlocksHigh*blockSize), paint);
```

Next, we draw the snake's head:

```
//Draw the snake
canvas.drawBitmap(headBitmap, snakeX[0]*blockSize,
    (snakeY[0]*blockSize)+topGap, paint);
```

The snake's head will be followed by all the body segments. Look at the condition of the `for` loop. This starts at `1`, which means it is not redrawing the head position, and ends at `snakeLength - 1`, which means it is not drawing the tail segment. Here is the code used to draw the body section:

```
//Draw the body
for(int i = 1; i < snakeLength-1; i++){
    canvas.drawBitmap(bodyBitmap, snakeX[i]*blockSize,
    (snakeY[i]*blockSize)+topGap, paint);
}
```

Here, we draw the tail of the snake:

```
//draw the tail
canvas.drawBitmap(tailBitmap, snakeX[snakeLength-
    1]*blockSize, (snakeY[snakeLength-1]*blockSize)+topGap, paint);
```

Finally, we draw the apple as follows:

```
                //draw the apple
                canvas.drawBitmap(appleBitmap, appleX*blockSize,
                    (appleY*blockSize)+topGap, paint);

                ourHolder.unlockCanvasAndPost(canvas);
            }

        }
```

Next, we will go through the `configureDisplay` method.

First, we get the screen resolution and store the results in `screenWidth` and `screenHeight` as normal:

```
public void configureDisplay(){
        //find out the width and height of the screen
        Display display = getWindowManager().getDefaultDisplay();
        Point size = new Point();
        display.getSize(size);
        screenWidth = size.x;
        screenHeight = size.y;
```

Here, we define a gap called `topGap`. It will be a space at the top of the screen and will not be a part of the game area. This gap is used for the score. We saw `topGap` used fairly extensively in the `drawGame` method. After this, we calculate the width and height of the remaining area in blocks:

```
        topGap = screenHeight/14;
        //Determine the size of each block/place on the game board
        blockSize = screenWidth/40;

        //Determine how many game blocks will fit into the height and
        width
        //Leave one block for the score at the top
        numBlocksWide = 40;
        numBlocksHigh = (screenHeight - topGap )/blockSize;
```

In the following part of the code, we load all our image files into `Bitmap` objects:

```
//Load and scale bitmaps
        headBitmap = BitmapFactory.decodeResource(getResources(),
            R.drawable.head);
        bodyBitmap = BitmapFactory.decodeResource(getResources(),
            R.drawable.body);
        tailBitmap = BitmapFactory.decodeResource(getResources(),
            R.drawable.tail);
        appleBitmap = BitmapFactory.decodeResource(getResources(),
            R.drawable.apple);
```

Finally, we scale each bitmap to be the same width and height as `blockSize`:

```
        //scale the bitmaps to match the block size
        headBitmap = Bitmap.createScaledBitmap(headBitmap, blockSize,
            blockSize, false);
        bodyBitmap = Bitmap.createScaledBitmap(bodyBitmap, blockSize,
            blockSize, false);
```

```
tailBitmap = Bitmap.createScaledBitmap(tailBitmap, blockSize,
    blockSize, false);
appleBitmap = Bitmap.createScaledBitmap(appleBitmap,
    blockSize, blockSize, false);

}
```

Now we can take a quick look at a few different ways we can improve the game.

Enhancing the game

Here is a series of questions and answers to lead us to an improved version of our *Snake* game. It doesn't matter if you can't answer some (or even all) of the questions. Just take a look at the questions and answers, after which you can take a look at the new game and the code.

Self-test questions

Q1) What can be used to provide a visual improvement for our game screen? Can we use a nice light green, grassy background instead of just black?

Q2) How about some nice flowers?

Q3) If you're feeling brave, make the flowers sway. Think about what we have learned about sprite sheets. The theory is exactly the same as that of the animated snake head. We just need a few lines of code to control the frame rate separately from the game frame rate.

Q4) We could set up another counter and use our snake head animation in `GameActivity`, but it wouldn't be that useful because the subtle tongue movements would be barely visible at the smaller size. But could we swish the tail segment?

Q5) Here is a slightly trickier enhancement. You can't help notice that when the snake sprites are headed in three out of the four possible directions, they don't look right. Can you fix this?

Summary

This is the end of yet another successful game project. You now know how to create and animate sprite sheets to add more realism to our games. Now we have an enhanced *Snake* game.

In the next chapter, we will see how simple it is to add leaderboards and achievements. This will make our game social and compelling by letting the player see the high scores and achievements of their friends and compare them with their own.

Making Your Game the Next Big Thing

The day has finally come when we can publish our first game. This chapter, despite being shorter than others, is probably the longest chapter to complete. It would be a good idea to scan through the different exercises to see what is involved before actually diving into them. Most of these tutorials are not suitable to do during the advertisements of your favorite TV program or when you get in from work and you are really tired.

Read the chapter and make a plan of when to perform each stage. The stages are arranged so you should be able to leave the project in between each of them. If you are really determined, have understood all the code until now, are confident with files and folders, and have no interruptions, you can probably get the work in this chapter completed in about a day.

As always, the completed code is in the relevant folder in the download bundle, in this case the Chapter9 folder.

Note that because I cannot share the login credentials for my developer account, had to mask some ID numbers within the code with a series of black lines. You will see these in the code in this chapter when talking about the ids.xml file which is NOT in the code bundle because of its confidential nature. However, as you will see in the *Setting up the Snake project ready for implementation* section, it is easy to get your own ID codes. Also note that a lot of the work in this chapter involves set up that takes place in your developer console. The leaderboards and achievements will not function until you have completed the necessary steps. However, you can review the entire code in the Chapter9 folder and download the enhanced version of the game from *Chapter 8, The Snake Game*, complete with working leaderboards and achievements from *Chapter 9, Making Your Game the Next Big Thing*, from https:// play.google.com/store/apps/details?id=com.packtpub. enhancedsnakegame.enhancedsnakegame.

If you want to implement everything yourself and also want to start with the enhanced version of the game, including all the improvements from the self-test questions from the previous chapter, then grab the `EnhancedSnakeGame` code from the `Chapter8` folder, and update your working project from `Chapter8`.

In this chapter, you will learn the following topics:

- How to publish your app

- Marketing your app, including making it social with leaderboards and public achievements

- Implementing leaderboards and achievements with the Google Play Game Services API

- Looking at what to do next depending on what you want to achieve

How to publish your app

Some of the steps in this guide involve writing descriptions and supplying screenshots, so you might like to read through the entire guide before implementing any of the steps:

1. Create an icon. Exactly how to design an icon is beyond the scope of this book, but simply put, you need to create a nice image for each of the Android screen density categories. This is easier than it sounds. Using a simple image, such as the snake head bitmap, you can customize and download a set from `http://romannurik.github.io/AndroidAssetStudio/icons-launcher.html`. There are many sites that offer a similar free service. Of course, you can just use the images in the enhanced snake project, and skip this step and the next.

2. Once you have downloaded your `.zip` file from the preceding link, you can simply copy the `res` folder from within the download to the `main` folder within the project explorer. All icons at all densities will now be updated.

3. Before we proceed further, optionally you will need to prepare some screenshots of the game. You will be prompted to upload a screenshot for several screen types, but since the game is nearly identical on all screen types, one image should do fine. You will also need an image of dimension 512 x 512 for a high-resolution icon and an image of dimension 1024 x 500 for a feature graphic. They don't need to be great, but you do need them to proceed. Create your own or grab a copy of my very simple graphics in the `Chapter9` folder.

4. Now, unfortunately, you will need to spend $ 25 to open a Google Play account. You can sign up at `https://play.google.com/apps/publish/`.

5. Once you have signed up, you can log in to your developer console at the same URL as mentioned in the previous step.

6. Once in your console, click on the **+ Add new application** button:

7. In the **Add New Application** dialog, type a name for your application, such as `Snake Game`. Now click on **Upload APK**.

8. We now need to make our app into the release version. Open the `AndroidManifest.xml` file and add the highlighted line of code in the location shown:

```
<application
        android:debuggable="false"
        android:allowBackup="true"
```

9. Rebuild your signed APK for the latest version of the *Snake* game, as discussed in *Chapter 2, Getting Started with Android*.

10. Now click on **Upload your first APK to production**.

11. Now go to your Snake game APK.

12. Wait for the APK to finish uploading. You can now see your game summary screen. Notice the highlighted progress indicator to the top-left corner of the next image. We have a green tick, indicating that the APK has been uploaded successfully:

13. The next thing we need to do is configure our Store Listing, so click on the **Store Listing** link, just below the APK link.

14. Write a short description and a long description. Also upload your screenshots, feature graphics, and high-resolution icon.

15. In the **Application Type** drop-down menu, select **Games**. In the **Category** drop-down menu, **Arcade** is probably most appropriate. For **Content Rating**, select **Everyone**, and for **Privacy Policy**, click on the checkbox for **Not submitting a privacy policy at this time**.

16. Add your website and email address to the relevant boxes.

17. Back at the top of the web page, click on the **Save** button.

18. Now we are at the final stage of this guide. Click on the **Pricing and distribution** link. It is just underneath the **Store Listing** link from step 13.

19. Click on the **Free** button at the top of the page.

20. Click on the checkbox of all the countries you want your game to be listed in.

21. Scroll down to the bottom of the page and click on the checkboxes for **Content guidelines** and **US Export laws**.

22. Click on **Save** at the top of the page.

23. Finally, from the **Ready to publish** drop-down menu at the top right corner of the page, click on **Publish this app** and you are done.

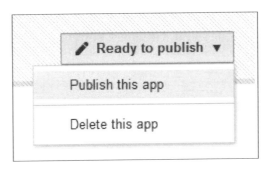

Congratulations! Your game will be live on Google Play somewhere between the next 5 minutes and 24 hours.

Marketing your app

The temptation at this stage is to sit back and wait for our game to hit the top position in the best-selling apps. This never happens.

To ensure that our app achieves its full potential, we need to do the following continuously:

Improve it

We have already made quite a few improvements to the *Snake* game but there are many more, such as difficulty settings, music, debugging (did you see the occasionally wonky body segments?), settings menu, and so on. You can pay a professional to design backgrounds and sprites, or add more sound effects. When you have improved your Android and Java skills further, you can rewrite the entire game using a smoother engine and call it Version 2.

Promote it

This could be the subject of another book but there are so many ways we can spread the word about our app. We can create a page/profile on all the social media sites—Facebook, Twitter, Flickr, and so on. Add regular updates, announcements, challenges (see compulsion). We can create a website to promote our app and promote it in all the ways we would promote any other website. We can add a message in the app itself asking players to rate it, perhaps pop up a message just after they have got a high score or achievement. We can ask everyone we know and everyone who visits our social media/website to give a rating and leave a review. There are many more ways to promote an app as well. The secret to all of them is this: keep doing it. For example, don't create a Facebook page and then expect it to grow in popularity on its own. Keep adding to all of your channels of promotion.

Keep the players' level of compulsion

Besides improving the game in the ways we have briefly mentioned, we need to give players a compelling reason to keep coming back to our game. One way might be to add new levels. For example, it won't be hard to implement levels in our *Snake* game. Each level could have walls in different places and the layouts could get progressively more challenging. All we would need to do is make an array of obstacles, draw them on the screen, and detect collisions. Then set a target for the snake length for each level and move on to the next level when it is achieved.

We could offer different snake designs to be be unlocked for certain challenges. How about the player saving all the apples they collect as a form of currency, and then strategically spending that currency to get a chance to continue after they have died?

How about offering time-limited challenges? For example, complete level 10 by the end of the month to receive a thousand bonus apples. Perhaps, we could come up with more things the apples could be spent on. Cool snake accessories or levels that can only be unlocked with apples. The point is that all of this compulsion can be added and updated at the same time as we upload our improvements. Nothing mentioned in this discussion about compulsion would be unachievable with the skills we have learned so far.

Probably, the most compelling aspect we can add to our game is online leaderboards and achievements so that players can compare themselves to their friends and the rest of the world. Google is aware of this and have done a lot of work to make it as easy as possible to add leaderboards and achievements to games. We will see how we can yet again take advantage of other people's hard work.

What's more, all the achievements that players of your game earn are fed into their overall Google Play profile. Here is a screenshot of my rather poor Google Play achievements profile:

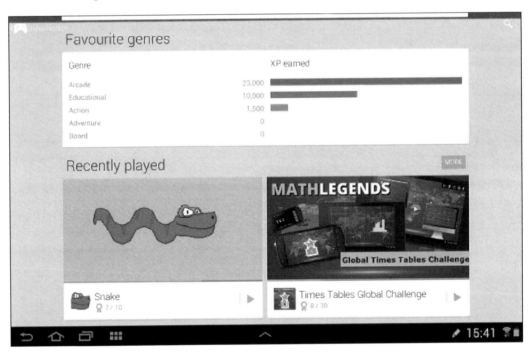

You might have noticed a few *Snake* achievements in that lot. This feature makes your game potentially even more compelling.

Let's do a quick reality check—I am not actually suggesting that you spend significant amounts of time trying to make a real business out of our humble Snake game. It just serves as a useful example for discussion. Also, if we can come up with so many ideas for a game this old and simple, then we can surely come up with some really amazing stuff for a game we are passionate about. When you have an idea you are passionate about, then that would be the time to go for it and expand the brief marketing plan we have discussed.

Adding leaderboards and achievements

So we know why leaderboards and achievements are a good thing. The first thing we need to do here is plan our achievements. A leaderboard is a high score table, and that's it! There isn't a great deal of things we can do to make them different. The achievements, however, deserve some discussion.

Planning the Snake achievements

At first, it might seem that a really simple implementation of a really simple game, like our *Snake* game, isn't deep enough to have many, or even any, achievements. So what follows is a quick brainstorming session of achievement ideas:

- **Score 10, 25, 50, 100, and so on**: Simply unlock achievements at different levels of high score.

- **Snake length**: Simply unlock achievements at different snake lengths.

- **Cannibal**: Unlock an achievement the first time the player collides with their own tail segment.

- **Collect x apples in total**: Keep a tally of all the apples ever collected, and unlock achievements at significant milestones.

- **Play 10, 25, 50, 100 games**: Reward the player for keeping on going. Whether they win or lose, achievements are unlocked for effort.

- **Treasure hunt**: What if there was a hidden spot in every game? It could give the player a reason to explore each level. They could be rewarded with points and apples. They could then unlock real achievements, perhaps for every 5, 10, or 20 hidden spots that they find.

Some of the achievements suggest that we would be required to keep a record of the player's progress. Surprisingly, Google Play Game Services can actually do this for us. These are known as incremental achievements. The number of apples collected in total is a good example of an incremental achievement. Others, such as snake length, are just dependent on the player's performance in any one game.

We will implement the total number of apples and the snake length achievements so that we can see how to implement both types.

We can have five achievements for reaching each of the following snake lengths: 5, 10, 20, 35, and 50. There can also be five incremental achievements for the total number of apples collected. Specifically, the player will get an achievement at 10, 25, 50, 100, 150, and 250 apples collected. Soon, we will see how to do it.

Finally, we need to decide how many points each achievement will be worth, out of the 1,000-point limit per game. As I might come back and add some more achievements later I am going to allocate 250 points to the apples' achievements, like this:

Number of eaten apples	Achievement points
10	10
20	30
50	40
100	70
250	100

I will also allocate 250 points to the snake length achievements, as shown in the following table:

Length of snake	Achievement points
5	10
10	30
25	40
35	70
50	100

Once you see how to implement these achievements in both the code and the developer console, it will be fairly simple to design and implement your own different achievements.

Step-by-step leaderboards and achievements

This is probably the longest part of the book to complete. However, once you have been through this process, it will be significantly easier the next time you do it.

Installing the Google Play Services API on your PC

First, we need to add the tools and the libraries needed to use the Game Services classes. This is nice and easy with Android Studio:

1. Click on the SDK Manager icon in the Android Studio toolbar:

2. The SDK manager will start. It looks a bit like this:

    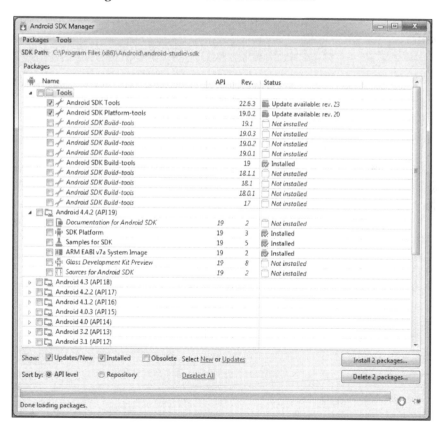

3. Scroll to the very bottom and underneath **Extras**, you will see **Google Play Services**. Check the box that is shown as highlighted in the following screenshot by clicking on it:

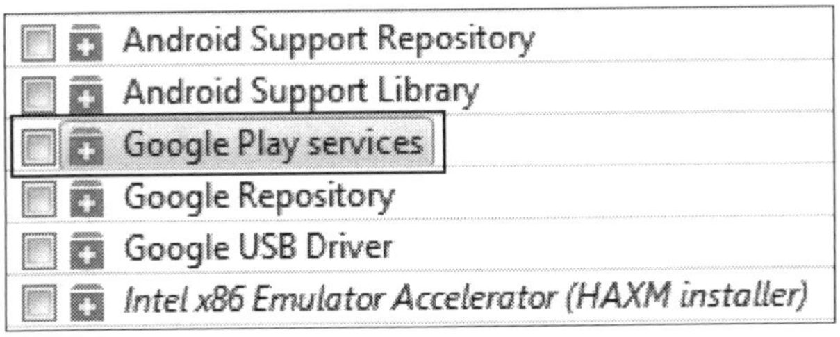

4. Now click on the checkbox for **Google Repository**, just below **Google Play Services**.

5. Click on **Install packages** and wait for the packages to download and install.

6. Save your project and restart Android Studio.

We now have the tools installed to start developing Google Play Game Services apps. Next, we need to set up our developer console to communicate with our app, ready for the features we will soon write code for.

Configuring the Google Play developer console

Here, we will prepare your developer console by creating a new Game Services application. This might sound a little counterintuitive; surely, Snake is our application, isn't it? Yes, but Google Play is structured in such a way that you create a Game Services application, and it is with this application that your actual games (Snake in this case) will communicate. It is the Game Services application that will have the achievements and leaderboards that we will award and display from our Snake Game:

1. Log in to your Google Play developer console at `https://play.google.com/apps/publish/`.

2. Click on the **Game services** tab on the left of the web page.

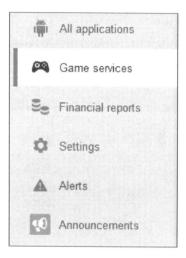

3. Now click on the **Add a new game** button.

4. Enter snake as the name of your game and choose **Arcade** from the **Category** drop-down menu. Now click on **Continue**. All of this is shown in the next screenshot:

5. Now we can configure our game. Type a game description in the **Description** field, and add the same high-resolution icon and feature graphic that we added when we uploaded the game.

6. Click on the **Save** button at the top of the screen.

7. Now we will link our Snake Game Services app with our actual *Snake* game. On the left of the web page, click on the **Linked apps** tab.

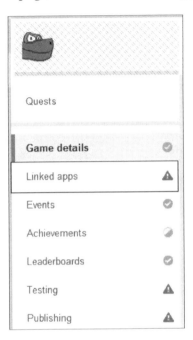

8. Google Play Game Services can be used with almost any platform, even Apple. We are using it for Android here, so click on the **Android** button.

9. All we need to do on this screen is click on the **Package Name** search box and click on our **Snake game** option.

10. Click on **Save and continue** at the top of the screen.

11. We're nearing the end of this phase. Click on **Authorize your app now** and review the information.

12. Finally, click on **Continue**.

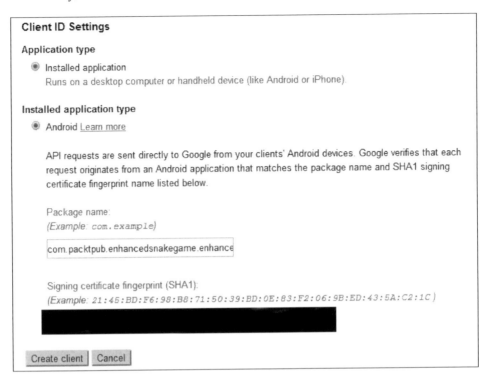

We now have a Google Game Services app set up, and linked to our *Snake* game.

Implementing the leaderboard in the Google Play developer console

Now we need to create our leaderboard in our developer console so that we can later interact with it in our Java code:

1. Log in to your developer console.

2. Click on **Game Services**, then on **Snake**, and then on **Leaderboards**.

3. Now click on **Add Leaderboard**. This is the **NEW LEADERBOARD** screen:

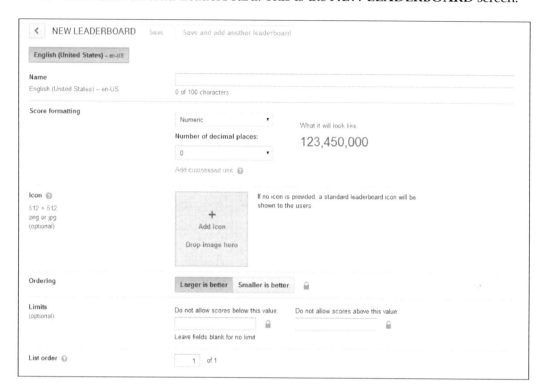

4. This might look like a bit of a marathon ahead, but all we need to do is enter a name (Snake will do) in the **Name** field, and we are done. It might seem strange entering a name for our leaderboard, but this is because it is possible to have multiple leaderboards for one game.

5. Read through all the options. You will see that they are just right for us and no further action is required. Click on **Save**.

Our leaderboard is now ready to communicate with our *Snake* app.

Implementing the achievements in the Google Play developer console

Here, we will set up in our developer console the achievements that we discussed previously.

You might like to prepare some graphics to represent each of these achievements. They need to be 512 x 512 pixels each. Alternatively, you can use an enlarged apple bitmap and perhaps a snake body segment for the apples and snake length achievements, respectively:

1. Log in to your developer console. Click on **Game Services**, then on **Snake**, and then on **Achievements**.

2. Click on **Add Achievement** and you will see the **New Achievement** screen:

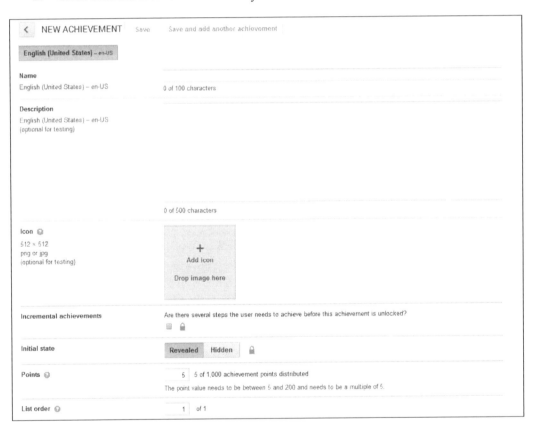

3. As we are implementing the incremental apple achievements, the first thing to do is to enter something in the **New Achievement** form. In the **Name** field, enter `Apple Muncher 1`.

4. In the **Description** field, enter `Munch 10 apples`.

5. Click on the **Add Icon** button and select your preferred 512 x 512 graphic.

6. Click on the **Incremental achievements** checkbox and enter 5 in the **How many steps are needed** field. This is because the first achievement is for eating 5 apples. This step is shown in the next screenshot:

7. Enter 10 for the number of achievement points in the **Points** field.

8. Click on **Save** and repeat steps 2 to 7 four more times for all the apple achievements, varying the **Name**, **Description**, **How many steps are needed?**, and **Points** fields as per our plans and tables of values for achievements.

9. Now we can move on to our snake length achievements. Click on **New Achievement**. In the **Name** field, enter `Super Snake 1`.

10. In the **Description** field, enter `Grow your snake to 5 segments`.

11. Click on the **Add Icon** button and browse to your preferred image.

12. Finally, enter 10 for the number of achievement points in the **Points** field.

13. Click on **Save** and repeat steps 9 to 13 four more times for each of the snake length achievements, varying the **Name**, **Description**, and **Points** fields as per our plans and tables of values for achievements.

We have now set up our achievements, ready to be implemented in code.

Setting up the Snake project ready for implementation

What we will do in this section is prepare our app to communicate with the Google Play servers:

1. Add this highlighted code to the `AndroidManifest.xml` file, just before the closing `</application>` tag:

```
<meta-data android:name="com.google.android.gms.games.APP_ID"
    android:value="@string/app_id" />
```

```
<meta-data android:name="com.google.android.gms.version"
    android:value="@integer/google_play_services_version"/>

</application>
```

2. Create the `ids.xml` file in the `values` folder in the Project Explorer. Now you need to get your unique code for your game to go to this file. Log in to your developer console, click on **Game Services**, and then click on **Snake**. Now click on **Achievements**.

3. Just below your list of achievements is a small **Get resources** link:

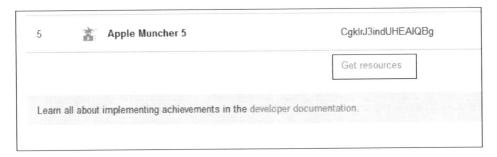

4. Click on the **Get resources** link.

5. Copy and paste the code into the `ids.xml` file. Then click on the **Finished** button in the developer console.

6. Now we need to get four code files from the Google Play Game Services GitHub repository. We will copy and paste the files directly into our project.

7. Create three new empty files in the `java` folder. Right-click on **GameActivity** in the project explorer and navigate to **New | Java class file**. Name the new file `BaseGameActivity`. Repeat this step and name the file `GameHelper`. Repeat this once more and name the file `GameHelperUtils`.

8. Now we will get the Java code to copy into the three files we just made. To get the code for `BaseGameActivity.java`, visit `https://github.com/playgameservices/android-basic-samples/tree/master/BasicSamples/libraries/BaseGameUtils/src/main/java/com/google/example/games/basegameutils`, where you can see further links to the code for the three files we created in step 7:

9. Click on **BaseGameActivity.java** as shown in the preceding screenshot. Select all of the code and copy and paste it into the identically named file that we created in Android Studio. Note that when we created the file, Android Studio created some basic template code. We need to delete all of this, except our package name at the top. When we paste in the copied code, we need to delete the Google package name.

10. Click on **GameHelper.java**, as shown in the previous screenshot, and repeat step 9.

11. Click on **GameHelperUtils.java**, as shown in the preceding screenshot, and repeat step 9.

12. There's one more file to create. Right-click on the **values** folder in the project explorer. Navigate to **New | File**. Name the file `gamehelper_strings.xml`.

13. Get the code that we need for this file in the same way as we did for the previous three Java files from but from this link: `https://github.com/playgameservices/android-basic-samples/blob/master/BasicSamples/libraries/BaseGameUtils/src/main/res/values/gamehelper_strings.xml`.

14. Paste the code in `gamehelper_strings.xml`, which we created in step 12.

15. Now change the `MainActivity` declaration in the `MainActivity.java` file.

    Consider this code:

    ```
    public class MainActivity extends Activity {
    ```

    Change it to the following code so that we can now extend the version of Activity that handles all the hard work of the Game Services API:

    ```
    public class MainActivity extends BaseGameActivity {
    ```

16. Now check out the code in the `GameActivity.java` file:

    ```
    public class GameActivity extends Activity {
    ```

    Change the preceding code to the following code so that we can now extend the version of Activity that handles all the hard work of the Game Services API:

    ```
    public class GameActivity extends BaseGameActivity {
    ```

17. Notice that for both Activities, we have an error in the class declaration we just typed. If you hover the mouse cursor over the code we typed in the previous step, you can see the reason. We need to implement some abstract methods of a class we are using. Recall from *Chapter 6*, OOP – *Using Other People's Hard Work*, that if a method in a class is declared abstract, then the class that extends it must implement it. That's us! Let's perform an empty implementation for now. Right-click on the line of code with the error and navigate to **Generate | Implement Methods**. Now click on **OK**. Perform this step for the `MainActivity.java` file and the `GameActivity.java` file. Our empty methods are now ready for our code. We will write the code in the next tutorial.

18. Next, using the project explorer, find the `build.gradle` file. Be careful; there are two files with the same name. The file that we need to find is a couple of lines below the `AndroidManifest.xml` file. It is highlighted in the next screenshot. Open it by double-clicking on the `build.gradle` file:

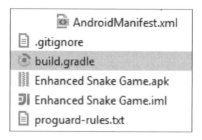

19. Find the section of code shown here and add the line that is highlighted. This makes all the classes we downloaded in the previous guide available for use in our *Snake* game:

```
dependencies {
    compile 'com.google.android.gms:play-services:+'
    compile 'com.android.support:appcompat-v7:+'
    compile fileTree(dir: 'libs', include: ['*.jar'])
}
```

Okay, I agree that was a fairly tough tutorial, but we are now ready to implement our code in three final steps:

1. Player sign-in and buttons.

2. Leaderboards.

3. Achievements.

We will then be able to upload our updated app and use our new leaderboards and achievements.

Implementing the player's sign-in, achievements, and leaderboard buttons

By the end of this section, players will be able to log in through the game to our empty leaderboards and achievements. The guides that follow this section will actually make the leaderboards and achievements work.

1. First, let's enable our Game Services. All of the work we have done so far in the developer console needs to be published before we can use it. Log in to your developer console. Navigate to **Game Services | Snake | Ready to publish | Publish game**. Then you will be shown a **Publish your game** button. Click on it. Finally, read the brief disclaimer and click on **Publish now**.

2. Now we need to build a UI that has **Sign in**, **Sign out**, **Leaderboards**, and **Achievements** buttons. Open the `layout_main.xml` file and edit it on the **Text** tab of the editor window by adding the following code. Obviously, there is a lot to type. You might like to copy and paste the code from the download package at `Chapter9\EnhancedSnakeGame\layout`. Here is the code. Type it in or copy and paste it:

```
<RelativeLayout xmlns:android="http://schemas.android.com/apk/res/
android"
    xmlns:tools="http://schemas.android.com/tools"
    android:layout_width="match_parent"
    android:layout_height="match_parent"
    android:paddingLeft="@dimen/activity_horizontal_margin"
    android:paddingRight="@dimen/activity_horizontal_margin"
    android:paddingTop="@dimen/activity_vertical_margin"
    android:paddingBottom="@dimen/activity_vertical_margin"
    tools:context="com.packtpub.enhancedsnakegame.
        enhancedsnakegame.MainActivity">

<Button

    android:id="@+id/llPlay"
    android:layout_width="140dp"
    android:layout_height="wrap_content"
    android:text="Leaderboards"
    android:layout_alignParentBottom="true"
    android:layout_alignParentRight="true"
```

```
            android:layout_alignParentEnd="true"
            android:visibility="gone"/>


        <Button
            android:id="@+id/awardsLink"
            android:layout_width="140dp"
            android:layout_height="wrap_content"
            android:text="Achievements"
            android:layout_gravity="center_vertical"
            android:layout_alignTop="@+id/llPlay"
            android:layout_toLeftOf="@+id/llPlay"
            android:visibility="gone"/>



        <!-- sign-in button -->
        <com.google.android.gms.common.SignInButton
            android:id="@+id/sign_in_button"
            android:layout_width="140dp"
            android:layout_gravity="center_horizontal"
            android:layout_height="wrap_content"
            android:layout_alignParentTop="true"
            android:layout_alignParentRight="true"
            android:layout_alignParentEnd="true"
             />


        <!-- sign-out button -->
        <Button
            android:id="@+id/sign_out_button"
            android:layout_width="140dp"
            android:layout_height="wrap_content"
            android:text="Sign Out"
            android:layout_alignParentTop="true"
            android:layout_alignParentRight="true"
            android:layout_alignParentEnd="true"
            android:layout_gravity="center_horizontal"
            android:visibility="gone"
             />


</RelativeLayout>
```

3. Explaining the code line by line is beyond the scope of the book, but this is not much different from the code we have been autogenerating when using the UI designer since *Chapter 2, Getting Started with Android*. Each block of the code in the last step defines a button and its position on the screen. You can switch to the design tab and move the buttons around to suit yourself. Note that the reason some of the buttons are not visible in the designer is that they are hidden until the player signs in. The reason we have done things this way is to make sure we implement the sign in button in just the right way. Note the `id` attribute for each of the buttons. We will be manipulating them in our Java code next. With some buttons set to `visibility = gone`, we see something like this:

4. With some buttons set to `visibility = visible`, we see something like what is shown in the following screenshot:

5. You might be wondering why we are designing a UI when `SnakeAnimView` is what the user sees. We could have implemented all our own buttons with bitmaps and used their screen coordinates to detect presses, but what we will do now is load our UI on top of `SnakeAnimView`, which will greatly simplify things. Switch to the **MainActivity** tab in the editor window.

6. First of all, we want to implement the `onClickListener` interface to handle our button clicks. To achieve this, change the class declaration to this:

```
public class MainActivity extends BaseGameActivity implements
View.OnClickListener{
```

7. Now we can get Android Studio to quickly implement the required `onClick` method by right-clicking on the class declaration, navigating to **Add | Implement methods**, and then clicking on **OK**.

8. Immediately after the previous line of code, we declare our four new buttons. Add this code after the code in the previous step:

```
//Our google play buttons
    Button llPlay;
    Button awardsLink;
    com.google.android.gms.common.SignInButton sign_in_button;
    Button sign_out_button;
```

9. In the `onCreate` method, just after the call to the `setContent` view, we use an object of the `LayoutInflater` class to load our UI on top of our `SnakeAnimView`. Add the highlighted code after the call to `setContentView`:

```
setContentView(snakeAnimView);

//Load our UI on top of our SnakeAnimView
LayoutInflater mInflater = LayoutInflater.from(this);
View overView = mInflater.inflate(R.layout.activity_main,
  null);
this.addContentView(overView, new
  ViewGroup.LayoutParams(ViewGroup.LayoutParams.MATCH_PARENT,
  ViewGroup.LayoutParams.MATCH_PARENT));
```

10. Immediately after the code in the previous step, we can get a reference to all our buttons and listen to clicks in the usual way:

```
//game services buttons
        sign_in_button =
            (com.google.android.gms.common.SignInButton)
            findViewById(R.id.sign_in_button);
        sign_in_button.setOnClickListener(this);
        sign_out_button =
            (Button)findViewById(R.id.sign_out_button);
        sign_out_button.setOnClickListener(this);
```

```
awardsLink = (Button)
    findViewById(R.id.awardsLink);
awardsLink.setOnClickListener(this);
llPlay = (Button)findViewById(R.id.llPlay);
llPlay.setOnClickListener(this);
```

11. Remember that in the previous guide, we overrode two abstract methods that we inherited when we extended the `BaseGameActivity` class. Now we will put some code into their implementation. The code is very straightforward. We hide the sign out button and show the sign in button when the sign-in fails, and we hide the sign in button and show all the other three buttons when the sign-in succeeds. Here are the two methods in their entirety. Type the highlighted code within the methods shown:

```
@Override
    public void onSignInFailed() {
        // Sign in failed. So show the sign-in button.
        sign_in_button.setVisibility(View.VISIBLE);
        sign_out_button.setVisibility(View.GONE);
    }

    @Override
    public void onSignInSucceeded() {
        // show sign-out button, hide the sign-in button
        sign_in_button.setVisibility(View.GONE);
        sign_out_button.setVisibility(View.VISIBLE);
        llPlay.setVisibility(View.VISIBLE);
        awardsLink.setVisibility(View.VISIBLE);
    }
```

12. Now we deal with the `onClick` method and what happens when the player clicks on any one of our four buttons. First, we type the code for our switch block. We will fill in the `case` statements in the next step:

```
switch (v.getId()) {

}
```

13. Here, we handle the sign in button. We simply call the `beginUserInitiatedSignIn` method. It is implemented for us in the `BaseGameActivity` class. Type this code in the `switch` block from the previous step:

```
case R.id.sign_in_button:
            // start the sign
            beginUserInitiatedSignIn();
            break;
```

14. Now we handle what happens when the player signs out. We just call `signOut`, which is implemented for us in the `BaseGameActivity` class. We then hide all our buttons and show the sign in button again. Type the following code after the code from the previous step:

```
case R.id.sign_out_button:
                // sign out.
                signOut();

                // show sign-in button, hide the sign-out button
                sign_in_button.setVisibility(View.VISIBLE);
                sign_out_button.setVisibility(View.GONE);
                llPlay.setVisibility(View.GONE);
                awardsLink.setVisibility(View.GONE);
                break;
```

15. Next, we handle what happens when the player clicks on the achievements button. One line of code gives us all of the achievement functionality. This is what OOP is all about—someone else's hard work doing everything for us. Type this code after the preceding code:

```
case R.id.awardsLink:

                startActivityForResult(Games.Achievements.getAchie
vementsIntent(getApiClient()), 0);

                break;
```

16. Finally, we handle what happens when the player clicks on the **Leaderboards** button. Again, one line of code gives us all of the leaderboard's functionality:

```
case R.id.llPlay:
                startActivityForResult(Games.Leaderboards.getLead
erboardIntent(getApiClient(), getResources().getString(R.string.
leaderboard_snake)),0);
                break;
```

We explained the code as we went, but let's summarize:

1. We designed a simple UI.
2. We loaded the UI on top of `SnakeAnimView`.
3. We got a reference to our four buttons and listened for clicks.
4. We handled what happens when people click on our buttons, which amounted to nothing more than hiding and showing buttons as appropriate, calling methods from `BaseGameActivity`, and using the `Intent` class to implement all our leaderboard and achievement functionalities.

You can actually run the *Snake* game and see the leaderboards and achievements screens. Of course, at this point, nobody will have any achievements or high scores yet. We will fix this now.

Implementing the leaderboards in code

Once more, we will witness the simplicity of using other people's well-designed code. Admittedly, there was some complexity to arrive at this point, but once you have set it all up, then your next game will take a fraction of the time you took setting up:

1. We want to submit a score to the `leaderboards` at the end of a game. Google Play will handle the process to check whether or not it is a high score. Google Play will even determine if it is a new high score for the week or month. Open the `GameActivity.java` file in the code editor window.

2. Find the `updateGame` method and add the highlighted code among all the other things we do when the game is over (when `dead` equals `true`). We wrap just one line of code within a check to ensure that the current player is signed in:

```java
if(dead){
    if (isSignedIn()) {
        Games.Leaderboards.submitScore(getApiClient(),
            getResources().getString(R.string.leaderboard_snake),
            score);
    }
```

3. That's it! Build the game and play it on a real Android device. You can now visit the leaderboards on Google Play and see your high score.

That was nice and easy. Here, we can see the login screen:

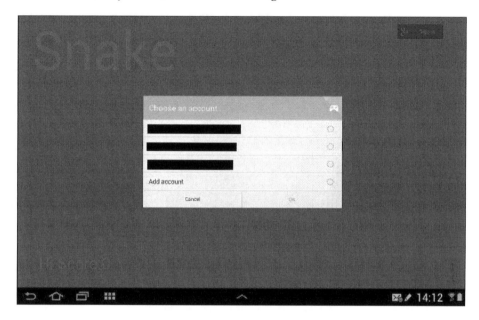

Then comes the welcome message and our **Achievements** and **Leaderboards** buttons as shown in the following screenshot:

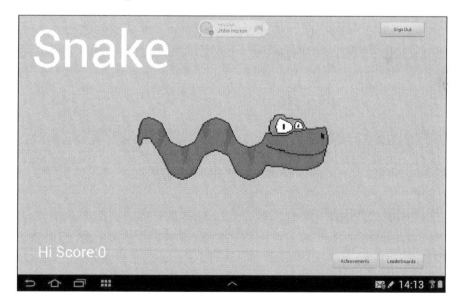

Finally, we can see our new leaderboards with just one player—me.

Just in case you're wondering, I can do a lot better than 39.

Implementing the achievements in code

This brief tutorial will first set up our game to post incremental updates to the progress of the apple achievements and the one-off achievement of the snake segment length:

1. In the `GameActivity.java` file, add an `applesMunchedThisTurn` variable just after the class declaration, as shown here:

    ```
    public class GameActivity extends BaseGameActivity {

        int applesMunchedThisTurn;
    ```

2. Find the `updateGame` method.

3. Add a line of code to increment `applesMunchedThisTurn` each time an apple is eaten by adding the highlighted line of code where it is shown:

    ```
    //Did the player get the apple
                if(snakeX[0] == appleX && snakeY[0] == appleY){
                    applesMunchedThisTurn++;
                    //grow the snake
                    snakeLength++;
                    //replace the apple
    ```

```
        getApple();
        //add to the score
        score = score + snakeLength;
        soundPool.play(sample1, 1, 1, 0, 0, 1);
    }
```

4. Notice that we place this highlighted line among the code that executes when the player dies (the `if(dead)` block). We could do it at the point the player eats an apple, but if we send five messages to the Google Play servers every time the player eats an apple, we might risk Google considering it as spam. We simply increment each achievement by the number of apples that have been eaten, and then reset the `applesMunchedThisTurn` variable to zero. We wrap our achievement method calls with a check that the player is signed in and that `applesMunchedThisTurn` is greater than zero. Now add the highlighted code:

```
if(dead){
//start again
if (isSignedIn())
if(applesMunchedTisTurn > 0){//can't increment zero
    Games.Achievements.increment(getApiClient(), getResources().
        getString(R.string.achievement_apple_muncher_1),
        applesMunchedThisTurn);
    Games.Achievements.increment(getApiClient(), getResources().
        getString(R.string.achievement_apple_muncher_2),
        applesMunchedThisTurn);
    Games.Achievements.increment(getApiClient(), getResources().
        getString(R.string.achievement_apple_muncher_3),
        applesMunchedThisTurn);
    Games.Achievements.increment(getApiClient(), getResources().
        getString(R.string.achievement_apple_muncher_4),
        applesMunchedThisTurn);
    Games.Achievements.increment(getApiClient(), getResources().
        getString(R.string.achievement_apple_muncher_5),
        applesMunchedThisTurn);
    applesMunchedThisTurn = 0;
}//end if(applesMunchedThisTurn > 0)


    Games.Leaderboards.submitScore(getApiClient(), getResources().
        getString(R.string.leaderboard_snake),score);


}//end if(isSignedIn)
```

```
soundPool.play(sample4, 1, 1, 0, 0, 1);
 score = 0;
 getSnake();

       }


   }
```

5. Now we will handle the segment length achievements. In the updateGame method, in the part of the code that executes when the player eats an apple, just after the line of code that increments snakeLength, we test for any of the lengths that warrant a Super Snake achievement. When the desired length is achieved (5, 10, 25, 35, or 50 segments), we ask Google Play to award it (if it hasn't been awarded yet). We wrap our achievement method calls with a check that the player is signed in and that at least one apple has been eaten. The highlighted code is the new code to add:

```
//grow the snake
snakeLength++;
if (isSignedIn()){
if(applesMunchedThisTurn > 0) {//can't increment by zero
                //Are we long enough for a new SuperSnake
                achievement?
                if(snakeLength == 5){
                    Games.Achievements.unlock(getApiClient(),
getResources().getString(R.string.achievement_super_snake_1));
                }
                if(snakeLength == 10){
                    Games.Achievements.unlock(getApiClient(),
getResources().getString(R.string.achievement_super_snake_2));
                }
                if(snakeLength == 25){
                    Games.Achievements.unlock(getApiClient(),
getResources().getString(R.string.achievement_super_snake_3));
                }
                if(snakeLength == 35){
                    Games.Achievements.unlock(getApiClient(),
getResources().getString(R.string.achievement_super_snake_4));
                }
                if(snakeLength == 50){
                    Games.Achievements.unlock(getApiClient(),
getResources().getString(R.string.achievement_super_snake_5));
                }
    }
```

6. That's it! You can now play the game and earn achievements:

Again, that was nice and easy. You can probably see how simple it would be to implement all other achievement ideas that we discussed earlier in the chapter. Let's move on and update our game on Google Play.

Uploading the updated Snake game to Google Play

This is nice and easy and is performed as follows:

1. First, we need to let Google Play know this is a new version. We do this by changing the version number. Open the `Build.gradle` file and find these lines of code:

```
versionCode 1
        versionName "1.0"
Change them to the following:
versionCode 2
        versionName "1.1"
```

2. Build your APK in the usual way.

3. Log in to your developer console.

4. Click on **Snake Game 1.0**, then on **APK**, and then on **Upload new APK to production**.

5. Go to your newly updated APK.

6. In the **What's new in this version** field, enter `Added leaderboards and achievements`.

7. Click on **Publish now to production**.

From now onwards, everyone who downloads your game will get the updated version. With our first game, complete with sprite sheet animations, leaderboards and achievements, it is time to take a break and do a little theory.

What next?

You should be proud of your creations to date, especially if this was your first attempt at programming. If some of the concepts, syntax, or projects are still not clear, then consider revisiting them after a break.

The one thing we haven't talked about is the even more new skills we need to progress further. The reason for this is that it very much depends on your initial motivation for reading this book.

Getting a programmer's job

If you want to be a Java employee, that is, working full time with a professional capacity for a medium or large company, then you will probably need a college degree, and this book hopefully has given you a glimpse into the world of programming and Java itself. If this describes you, then for further study, you could consider a more formal Java book, followed by a pure OOP book about object-oriented analysis and design. You could then move on to study design patterns.

Some of the best books that fit into these categories are *Head First Object-Oriented Analysis and Design: A Brain Friendly Guide to OOA&D, Brett McLaughlin and Gary Pollice*; *Head First Design Patterns*; *Eric Freeman and Elisabeth Robson, O'Reilly*; and *Design Patterns CD: Elements of Reusable Object-Oriented Software, Erich Gamma, Richard Helm, Ralph Johnson, and John Vlissides, Addison Wesley*. The first two are very beginner-friendly. The latter is highly regarded but a much more challenging read for a beginner.

My guess is that most likely, you didn't pick up a beginners' book on games and Java because you were headed in that direction, so let's consider our *piece de resistance* so far—our Snake game.

Building bigger and better games

If you compare our Snake game to a modern, professional title, even a two-dimensional game, never mind a modern big-budget First Person Shooter (FPS), then we still have a lot of learning to do. Let's consider some inadequacies of our *Snake* game compared to a professional game.

Think about our flower and tail animations. They worked because we set up a crude timing system within our `controlFPS` method. But what if we had a dozen or more game objects that needed to be animated?

Then what if they all had different frame counts and frame rates? We can further complicate things if some of the animations need to work on a loop and others need to reverse through each frame before restarting.

Now imagine a character that has to jump. How do we synchronize whatever frame happens to be displayed at the time the player jumps?

Actually, all of these problems and more are solvable with a quick web search and some study. The point is that things are starting to get fairly complicated, and we have only talked about animation.

What about physics? How will objects in our future games behave when they bounce? We were able to cheat with our Squash game because the environment and the objects were few and simple. What if the ball was round and there were lots of objects of different sizes and shapes, some moving fast and some stationary? How would we simulate this physics model?

Again, the answers are all out there but they add complexity. What about other environmental factors such as light and shadow? What happens when our screen needs to scroll to the left and right? What about up and down?

Now consider all of these problems and imagine implementing a solution in a virtual three-dimensional world. Once again, the solutions are out there, but it would take a determined beginner many months to implement their own solution using the raw mathematics involved in three-dimensional calculations.

Next, imagine that you want your new three-dimensional, physics-based, superbly animated game to be available on Android, Apple, and PC platforms.

If I have discouraged you from seeking some of these solutions but you are fascinated to find out the answer, then my advice would be to go and find it out anyway. It will definitely be a fascinating journey and make you a better game developer. Think twice, however, before implementing any of this stuff for any reason other than curiosity, self-improvement, or fun.

The reason for this is because we are not the first people to have these and many other problems—the solutions have already been implemented. And guess what? We can use those solutions, often at no cost to ourselves.

For example, there is a library called OpenGL that has one purpose—drawing in a three-dimensional coordinate system. It has classes and methods for everything you will ever need. There is even a version of OpenGL for mobile, called OpenGL ES, that you can program in Java. It is true that OpenGL has some complexities of its own, but they can be learned in a logical and straightforward manner from easy to hard.

If you got this far with this book, take a quick refresher on *Chapter 6, OOP – Using Other People's Hard Work*, and then grab a copy of *OpenGL ES2 for Android, K. Brothaler, Pragmatic Bookshelf*. The book explores the code library and some of the mathematics behind it, so it should satisfy both the curious and the purely practical reader. Alternatively, you can check out loads of free tutorials at `http://www.learnopengles.com/`.

If you just want to make more games and are not particularly fussed about the three-dimensional features, then the next logical step would be a Java-based game library. There are many, but one in particular uses pure Java to build games on Android, iPhone, PC, and the Web.

Indeed, you can build one Java game and it will run on almost any device in the world, even a web page. It also has classes that simplify the use of the aforementioned OpenGL ES. The library is called LibGDX, and I had loads of fun making a platform game following along with *Learning Libgdx Game development* (`https://www.packtpub.com/game-development/learning-libgdx-game-development`). LibGDX also solves all our animation, scrolling, and physics conundrums without any math, although it doesn't really address three-dimensional features.

 Note that both books have some quite in-depth OOP, but this is not out of reach if you understood *Chapter 6, OOP – Using Other People's Hard Work*, and are determined.

If you want to go 3D straightaway, then a really fun option is the Unreal Engine. Unreal Engine is used in lots of really big-budget games and can involve immense complexity in another programming language. However, for a way to make two-dimensional and three-dimensional games within a GUI development environment, it is probably unbeatable. Unreal Engine 4 uses a system called Blueprint, where you can drag and drop elements of flow chart-like elements, instead of coding. It still uses all the concepts of OOP as well as loops and branching, but you can do loads without a single line of *real* code. Take a look at the Unreal Engine version of Flappy Bird created without a single line of code, at `https://play.google.com/store/apps/details?id=com.epicgames.TappyChicken`.

Unreal Engine can also build games for multiple platforms, but unfortunately, there is a small monthly fee, and most restrictively of all, any commercial project you make will be subject to an agreement. Here, you pay 30 percent to Epic games, but for learning and having fun, it probably can't be beaten.

Alternatively, take a look at my blog (`www.gamecodeschool.com`), where I regularly add articles and fun game building guides aimed at beginner to intermediate game programmers. My blog discusses lots of different programming languages, target platforms, all the tools previously mentioned, and more.

Self-test questions

Q1) Try to implement local high scores on the device.

Q2) How many eminent computer scientists have made cameo appearances in the code throughout this book?

Q3) As a final challenge, try to beat my high score on the Snake leaderboards.

Summary

In this chapter, we covered a lot. We published our *Snake* game on Google Play. Then we added some online leaderboards and achievements. We also updated our publication. The process showed how very complicated tasks such as communication over the Internet can be made really simple using an API.

While putting the finishing touches to this book, I watched a YouTube video of a lecture from John Carmack, a software legend. He was a key engineer in the development of the *Doom* game, which was published in June 1995. I had to laugh, as did his audience, when he explained that while in school, he felt he was missing out on the technology revolution, and by the time he was old enough to work, it would all be over.

It is certainly true that lots of technology revolutions have come and many have gone. At least, many of the early adopters' opportunities have faded. John Carmack explained that there is always going to be another revolution just around the corner.

So you are probably going to develop your skills and watch out for the next big thing. Or perhaps, you just want a bit of fun programming anything in any language for any platform.

I hope you have enjoyed our journey through Android and Java, and that you will continue this journey as well. I sincerely wish you well, whichever path you choose for your future. Feel free to come and share your experiences and knowledge at `www.gamecodeschool.com`. The perfect sequel to this book will be published mid 2015 called *Android Game Programming by Example*.

Self-test Questions
and Answers

Here, we have included some questions you could ask yourself to see whether you have understood each chapter. Don't worry! The answers are also included.

Chapter 2

Q1) What should you do if all this talk of life cycles, classes, and methods is a bit confusing?

A) Don't worry about them. Understanding comes a bit at a time, and if they are not entirely clear at this stage, it will not hold you back from thoroughly learning Java, and all will become clearer as we progress.

Q2) What exactly is a Java class?

A) Classes are a fundamental building block of Java programs. They are like containers for our Java code, and we can even use other people's classes to simplify the programs we write, even without seeing or understanding the code contained within those classes.

Q3) What is the difference between a method and a class?

A) Methods are contained within classes and represent the specific functionality of the class, like another container within a container. As an example from a game, we might have a `Tank` class with `shoot`, `drive`, and `selfDestruct` methods. We can use a class and its methods by making our own class, as we will in *Chapter 6, OOP – Using Other People's Hard Work*, or by using the `@import` statement as we did earlier in this chapter.

Q4) Take a look at the Android developer site and its more technical explanation of the lifecycle phases, at `http://developer.android.com/reference/android/app/Activity.html`. Can you see the phase and its related method that we haven't discussed? When would it be triggered in an app? What is the precise pathway an activity takes from creation to destruction?

A) It's the restarting phase. Its corresponding method is `onRestart`. It is triggered when an app has been stopped and then restarted. We won't need the `onRestart` method in this book, but this exercise hopefully helped clarify the concept of life cycles. The precise pathway will vary; we just need to handle the phases that are relevant to our game. So far, we have just tinkered with `onCreate`.

Chapter 3

Q1) What does this code do?

```
// setContentView(R.layout.activity_main);
```

A) Nothing, because it is commented out with //.

Q2) Which of these lines causes an error?

```
String a = "Hello";
String b = " Vinton Cerf";
int c = 55;
a = a + b
c = c + c + 10;
a = a + c;
c = c + a;
```

A) The fourth line, `a = a + b`, has no semicolon, so it will cause an error. The last line, `c = c + a;`, will also cause an error because you cannot assign a string to an `int` value.

Q3) We talked a lot about operators and how different operators can be used together to build complicated expressions. Expressions, at a glance, can sometimes make code look complicated. However, when looked at closely, they are not as tough as they seem. Usually, it is just a case of splitting the expressions into smaller pieces to work out what is going on. Here is an expression that is more convoluted than anything else you will ever meet in this book. As a challenge, can you work out what x will be?

```
int x = 10;
int y = 9;
boolean isTrueOrFalse = false;
isTrueOrFalse = (((x <=y)||(x == 10))&&((!isTrueOrFalse) ||
(isTrueOrFalse)));
```

A) You can run the `SelfTestC3Q3` project in the `Chapter3` folder of the code bundle to check out the answer in the console, but `isTrueOrFalse` evaluates to true; here's why.

First, let's break down the nasty line into manageable sections defined by the brackets:

```
((x <=y)||(x == 10))
```

Previously, we were asking the question, "is x less than or equal to y or is x exactly equal to 10?". Clearly, x is not equal to or less than y but x is exactly equal to 10, so our use of the logical OR operator, ||, in the middle causes the entire part of the expression to evaluate to `true`.

&&

Both sides of an && operator must evaluate to `true` for the overall expression to be true. So let's look at the other side:

```
((!isTrueOrFalse) || (isTrueOrFalse)))
```

Well, `isTrueOrFalse` is a Boolean. It can only be true or false so this part of the expression must be true because we are essentially asking, "is `isTrueOrFalse` false or is `isTrueOrFalse` true?". It must be one or the other. So, regardless of how we initialized `isTrueOrFalse`, the last part of the expression will be true.

So the overall expression evaluates to `true`, and `true` is assigned to `isTrueOrFalse`.

Chapter 4

Q1) What is wrong with this method?

```
void doSomething(){
   return 4;
}
```

A) It returns a value but has a `void` return type.

Q2) What will x be equal to at the end of this code snippet?

```
int x=19;
do{
   x=11;
   x++;
}while(x<20)
```

A) Okay, this was a slightly tricky question. Regardless of the value of x, the do block always executes at least once. Then x is set to 11, and after that, it is incremented to 12. So when the `while` expression is evaluated, it is true and the do block executes again. Once more, x is set to 11 and then incremented to 12. The program is stuck in a never-ending (infinite) loop. This code is most likely a bug.

Chapter 5

Q1) Suppose we wanted to have a quiz where the question could be about naming the president, the capital city, and so on. How would we do this with multidimensional arrays?

A) We would just make the inner array hold three strings, perhaps like this:

```
String[][] countriesCitiesAndPresidents;
//now allocate like this
countriesAndCities = new String[5][3];
//and initialize like this
countriesCitiesAndPresidents [0][0] = "United Kingdom";
countriesCitiesAndPresidents [0][1] = "London";
countriesCitiesAndPresidents [0][3] = "Cameron";//at time of writing
```

Q2) In our persistence example, we saved a continually updating string to a file so that it persisted after the app had been shut down and restarted. This is like asking the user to click on a **Save** button. Summoning all your knowledge of *Chapter 2, Getting Started with Android*, can you think of a way to save the string without saving it by the button click but just when the user quits the app?

A) Override the `onPause` life cycle method and put the code to save the string in there, like this:

```
@Override
    protected void onPause() {
        editor.putString(stringName, currentString);
        editor.commit();
    }
```

Q3) Other than increasing the difficulty level, how could we make the memory game harder?

A) We could simply alter the pause in our thread execution to mention a lower number, giving the player less thinking time, like this:

```
myHandler.sendEmptyMessageDelayed(0, 450);
//This halves the players thinking time
```

Q4) Using the plain Android UI with the dull grey buttons isn't very exciting. Take a look at the UI elements in the visual designer. Can you work out how to use an image for our button background?

A) Simply add some `.png` graphics to the `drawable-mdpi` folder and then find the background property in the **Properties** window while your button is selected. Click to edit the property in the usual way and choose the graphic you added to the `drawable-mdpi` folder.

Chapter 6

Q1) What is encapsulation?

A) Encapsulation is the way we pack our variables, code, and methods in a manner that exposes just the parts and functionality we want to the parts of our app (or any app that uses our classes) that we want.

Q2) I don't get all this, and actually, I have more questions now than I had at the start of the chapter. What should I do?

A) You know enough about OOP to make significant progress with games and any other type of Java programming. If you are desperate to know more OOP right now, there are plenty of highly rated books that discuss nothing but OOP. However, practice and familiarity with the syntax will go a long way to achieving the same thing and will probably be more fun. The deciding factor in whether you rush off and learn the intricate details of OOP now will really depend on your personal goals and what you want to do with your programming skills in the future. Read the last few pages of *Chapter 9*, *Making Your Game the Next Big Thing*, for more discussion.

Chapter 7

Q1) The speed of the ball is calculated in pixels. Different devices have different numbers of pixels. Can you explain how to make the ball speed approximately the same on different screen resolutions?

A) A simple way to accommodate different screen resolutions would be to devise a system that that takes into account the number of pixels the screen has. We have already done this for the racket and ball sizes. We could declare a member variable like this:

```
int pixelsPerFrameX;
int pixelsPerFrameY;
```

We could then initialize these variables in onCreate after we have obtained the screen dimensions:

```
pixelsPerFrameX = screenWidth/50;
pixelsPerFrameY = screenHeight/50;
```

Then we can move our ball a bit, like this:

```
//moving in adjust our x any positions
        if (ballIsMovingDown) {
            ballPosition.y += pixelsPerFrameX;
        }

        //etc...
```

Chapter 8

Q1) What about a visual improvement for our game screen, perhaps a nice, light green grassy background instead of just black?

A) You can use most graphics programs such as Gimp or Photoshop to get the RGB value of a nice, light green grassy color. Alternatively, you can use an online color picker such as `http://www.colorpicker.com/`. Then look at this line in our `drawGame` method:

```
canvas.drawColor(Color.BLACK);//the background
```

Change it to the following line:

```
canvas.drawColor(Color.argb(255,186,230,177));//the background
```

Q2) How about adding some nice flowers to the background?

A) Here is the way to do this. Create a flower bitmap (or use mine), load it, and scale it in the usual way, in the `configureDisplay` method. Decide how many flowers to draw. Choose and store locations on the board in the `SnakeView` constructor (or write and call a special method, perhaps `plantFlowers`).

Draw them before the snake and the apple in the `drawGame` method. This will ensure that they can never hide an apple or a part of the snake. You can see my specific implementation in the methods mentioned and a copy of the flower bitmap in the `EnhancedSnakeGame` project in the `Chapter8` folder.

Q3) If you're feeling brave, make the flowers sway. Think of sprite sheets. The theory is exactly the same as that of the animated snake head. We just need a few lines of code to control the frame rate separately from the game frame rate.

A) Take a look at the new code in the `controlFPS` method. We simply set up a new counter for flower animations to switch flower frames once every six game frames. You can also copy the sprite sheet from the `EnhancedSnakeGame` project in the `Chapter8` folder.

Q4) We could set up another counter and use our snake head animation, but it wouldn't be that useful because the subtle tongue movements would be barely visible due to the smaller size. Nevertheless, we could quite easily swish the tail segment.

A) There is a two-frame tail bitmap in the `EnhancedSnakeGame` project in the `Chapter8` folder. As this is also two frames, we could use the same frame timer as that used for the flower. Take a look at the implementation in the `EnhancedSnakeGame` project in the `Chapter8` folder. The only required changes are in `configureDisplay` and `drawGame`.

Q5) Here is a slightly trickier enhancement. You can't help notice that when the snake sprites are headed in three out of the four possible directions, they don't look right. Can you fix this?

A) We need to rotate them depending upon the way they are heading. Android has a `Matrix` class, which allows us to easily rotate Bitmaps, and the `Bitmap` class has an overloaded version of the `createBitmap` method that takes a `Matrix` object as an argument.

So we can create a matrix for each angle we need to handle, like this:

```
Matrix matrix90 = new Matrix();
matrix90.postRotate(90);
```

Then we can rotate a bitmap using the following code:

```
rotatedBitmap = Bitmap.createBitmap(regularBitmap , 0, 0,
regularBitmap .getWidth(), regularBitmap .getHeight(), matrix90,
true);
```

Another problem is that as the snake twists and turns, how do we keep track of the individual orientation of each segment? We already have a direction finding scheme: 0 is up, 1 is right, and so on. So we can just create another array for the orientation of each segment that corresponds to a body segment in the `snakeX` and `snakeY` arrays. Then all we need to do is to ensure that the head has the correct direction, and update from the back on each frame just as we do for the snake's coordinates. You can see this implemented in the `EnhancedSnakeGame` project in the `Chapter8` folder.

The finished project with a few more enhancements is in the EnhancedSnakeGame project in the Chapter8 folder. This is the version we will be using as a starting point in the next and final chapter. You can also download the game from Google Play at https://play.google.com/store/apps/details?id=com.packtpub. enhancedsnakegame.enhancedsnakegame.

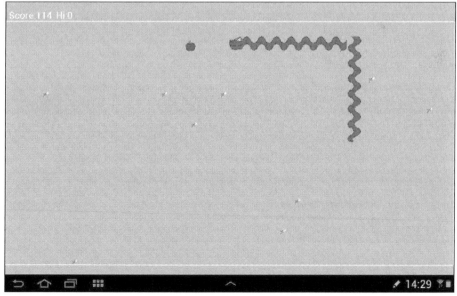

Chapter 9

Q1) Try to implement the local high scores on the device.

A) You already know how to do this. Just go back to *Chapter 5, Gaming and Java Essentials* in case you are unsure. The implementation is in the code for this chapter's project as well.

Q2) How many eminent computer scientists have made cameo appearances in the code throughout this book?

A) 9

Ada Lovelace

Charles Babbage

Alan Turing

Vinton Cerf

Jeff Minter

Corrine Yu

André LaMothe

Gabe Newell

Sid Meier

Why not search on the Web for some of these names? There are some interesting stories about each of them.

Index

A

abstract class **237, 238**
access modifiers
  classes use, controlling 215
  for methods 217, 218
  variables use, controlling 216, 217
AccessScopeThisAndStatic **225-229**
achievements, snake game
  adding 327
  implementing, in Google Play developer
    console 336, 337
  in code, implementing 350-353
  planning 327, 328
activities **40, 41**
addition operator (+) **66**
Android
  about 9
  benefits 11, 12
  code, structuring 38
  development environment 14
  life cycle phases 38, 39
  need for 10
  sounds, playing 167-172
  summary 13
  versions, URL 11
Android Canvas
  demo app 247-251
  drawing 244
Android coordinate system
  about 245
  pixels, animating 246
Android Run Time. *See* **ART**
Android Studio
  about 17, 18, 27, 28

  installing 18, 19
  preparing 22
  reference link, for keyboard shortcuts 26
  URL 18
Android Studio, key parts
  Editor 28
  important tool windows 28
  Menu bar 28
  Navigation bar 28
  Project Explorer 28
  Tool bar 28
Android Studio visual designer
  Android UI 31
  game menu, creating 35-37
  sample code, using 34, 35
  using 29-31
Android UI, on multiple devices
  URL 37
Android UI, types
  about 31
  ButtonView 34
  ImageView 33, 34
  RelativeLayout 33
  TextView 31-33
animation, snake game 292-294
array-out-of-bounds exception 158
arrays
  and objects 149
  array-out-of-bounds exception 158
  dynamic array, example 152, 153
  example 150, 151
  nth dimension, entering 154
ART 13
assignment operator (=) 66

B

boolean type 62
ButtonView 34
byte type 62

C

camel case 116
canvas 246
char type 62
class
  about 207
  access, in nutshell 216
  basic classes 210-212
  code 208, 209
  first class 213, 214
  use with access modifiers, controlling 215
comments 58
comparison operator 71
compiling 57
constructors
  objects, setting up with 222, 223
continue keyword 109
coordinate system, snake game
  about 287
  collisions, detecting 289
  snake, drawing 289
  snake segments, tracking 288

D

data
  storing 59, 60
  using, with variables 59, 60
deadlock 159
decisions
  in Java 89
declaration
  of variables 64
decrement operator (--) 66
development environment, Android
  setting up 14
division operator (/) 66
double type 62
do-while loop 110
dynamic
  with arrays 152

E

emulators
  creating 48
  game project, building 47
  game project, running 50
  running 48, 49
encapsulation
  about 206, 214, 215
  access modifiers, for methods 217, 218
  classes with access modifiers,
    controlling 215
  method access, in nutshell 218
  objects, setting up with constructors 222
  private variables, accessing with getter
    method 219-221
  private variables, accessing with
    setter method 219-221
  variable access, in nutshell 217
  variables with access modifiers,
    controlling 216, 217
eXtensible Markup Language (XML) 31

F

fields 208
float type 62
for loop
  about 110
  Change after each pass through loop 111
  Condition 111
  Declaration and initialization 111

G

GameActivity
  amending 129-132
GameActivity, snake game 291
game menu
  creating 35-37
  Java code 41-44
  Java code, deleting 44-46
game project
  about 22
  Android Studio, preparing 22
  building 46
  building, on emulators 47
  building, on real device 47-51

T

U

V

W

Thank you for buying
Learning Java by Building Android Games

About Packt Publishing

Packt, pronounced 'packed', published its first book, *Mastering phpMyAdmin for Effective MySQL Management*, in April 2004, and subsequently continued to specialize in publishing highly focused books on specific technologies and solutions.

Our books and publications share the experiences of your fellow IT professionals in adapting and customizing today's systems, applications, and frameworks. Our solution-based books give you the knowledge and power to customize the software and technologies you're using to get the job done. Packt books are more specific and less general than the IT books you have seen in the past. Our unique business model allows us to bring you more focused information, giving you more of what you need to know, and less of what you don't.

Packt is a modern yet unique publishing company that focuses on producing quality, cutting-edge books for communities of developers, administrators, and newbies alike. For more information, please visit our website at www.packtpub.com.

About Packt Open Source

In 2010, Packt launched two new brands, Packt Open Source and Packt Enterprise, in order to continue its focus on specialization. This book is part of the Packt Open Source brand, home to books published on software built around open source licenses, and offering information to anybody from advanced developers to budding web designers. The Open Source brand also runs Packt's Open Source Royalty Scheme, by which Packt gives a royalty to each open source project about whose software a book is sold.

Writing for Packt

We welcome all inquiries from people who are interested in authoring. Book proposals should be sent to author@packtpub.com. If your book idea is still at an early stage and you would like to discuss it first before writing a formal book proposal, then please contact us; one of our commissioning editors will get in touch with you.

We're not just looking for published authors; if you have strong technical skills but no writing experience, our experienced editors can help you develop a writing career, or simply get some additional reward for your expertise.

JavaScript Mobile Application Development

ISBN: 978-1-78355-417-1   Paperback: 332 pages

Create neat cross-platform mobile apps using Apache Cordova and jQuery Mobile

1. Configure your Android, iOS, and Window Phone 8 development environments.

2. Extend the power of Apache Cordova by creating your own Apache Cordova cross-platform mobile plugins.

3. Enhance the quality and the robustness of your Apache Cordova mobile application by unit testing its logic using Jasmine.

Testing and Securing Android Studio Applications

ISBN: 978-1-78398-880-8   Paperback: 162 pages

Debug and secure your Android applications with Android Studio

1. Explore the foundations of security and learn how to apply these measures to create secure applications using Android Studio.

2. Create effective test cases, unit tests, and functional tests to ensure your Android applications function correctly.

3. Optimize the performance of your app by debugging and using high-quality code.

Please check **www.PacktPub.com** for information on our titles

Android SQLite Essentials

ISBN: 978-1-78328-295-1   Paperback: 110 pages

Develop Android applications with one of the most widely used database engines, SQLite

1. Develop database-driven Android applications and stay ahead of the curve.

2. Explore the best techniques to use cursors and loaders to achieve optimum results.

3. A step-by-step approach to use SQLite for building Android applications.

Learning Android Intents

ISBN: 978-1-78328-963-9   Paperback: 318 pages

Explore and apply the power of intents in Android application development

1. Understand Android Intents to make application development quicker and easier.

2. Categorize and implement various kinds of Intents in your application.

3. Perform data manipulation within Android applications.

Please check **www.PacktPub.com** for information on our titles

38841792R00219